Monetary Union, Employment and Growth

Monetary Union, Employment and Growth

The Impact of the Euro as a Global Currency

Edited by

Pier Carlo Padoan

Professor of Economics, University of Rome 'La Sapienza', Italy and Director of Economic Studies, College of Europe, Bruges, Belgium

IN ASSOCIATION WITH CENTRO EUROPA RICERCHE SRL (CER), ITALY

Edward Elgar
Cheltenham, UK • Northampton, MA, USA

Published by
Edward Elgar Publishing Limited
Glensanda House
Montpellier Parade
Cheltenham
Glos GL50 1UA
UK

Edward Elgar Publishing, Inc.
136 West Street
Suite 202
Northampton
Massachusetts 01060
USA

Reprinted 2002

A catalogue record for this book
is available from the British Library

Library of Congress Cataloguing in Publication Data
Monetary union, employment and growth : the impact of the Euro as a global
    currency / edited by Pier Carlo Padoan.
        p. cm.
    Includes bibliographical references and index.
    1. Monetary unions—European Union countries. 2. Monetary
    policy—European Union countries. 3. Unemployment—European Union
    countries. I. Padoan, Pier Carlo, 1950–

HG925.M665   2000
332.4'94—dc21   00–029414

ISBN 1 84064 372 2

Printed and bound in Great Britain by Biddles Ltd, *www.biddles.co.uk*

Contents

Figures

Tables

Contributors

Claudio D'Auria, economist, Banking Analysis Department, Bank of Italy, Rome

Stefano Fantacone, economist, Centro Europa Ricerche, Rome

Stefano Manzocchi, Associate Professor of Economics, University of Perugia

Pier Carlo Padoan, Professor of Economics, University of Rome 'La Sapienza' and Director of Economic Studies, College of Europe, Bruges

Paola Parascandolo, economist, Centro Europa Ricerche, Rome

Marcello Pericoli, economist, Research Department, Bank of Italy, Rome

Giovanni B. Pittaluga, Professor of Monetary Economics, University of Genoa

Massimo Tozzi, economist, Centro Europa Ricerche, Rome

Claudio Vicarelli, economist, Centro Europa Ricerche, Rome

Introduction and overview

Pier Carlo Padoan

The relationship between the single currency and unemployment is twofold. On the one hand the working of the euro will be less than smooth if rigidities in labour markets persist. Hence unemployment may be a cause of poor performance of the single currency. On the other hand, the functioning of the euro will affect the evolution of European employment. This issue has just begun to be debated in the literature and this book will add to the debate. The perspective we adopt, however, offers a different approach, as we consider the linkages between the future of the euro as a global (not only regional) currency and European employment. In other words, we put the relationship between the euro and unemployment in a global, not only European, perspective. In what follows a detailed description of the chapters is presented.

Chapter 1 looks at the role of the euro as a global currency. It reviews the debate about the likely evolution of the single currency vis-à-vis the dollar in international markets and it considers exchange rate policy options for the euro against the background of the European Union's macroeconomic performance. Europe's macroeconomic problem is identified in the excess of internal savings with respect to investment. This problem is likely to become worse as fiscal adjustment and discipline decrease the financing requirements of European governments. The policy implication is that the macroeconomic policy stance of the EU should be targeted at low and stable interest rates and hence a stable external value of the euro. The chapter also considers the perspectives for co-operation between the EU and the US in a bipolar currency system.

As the EU's external policy will have to be implemented taking into account the policy behaviour of the USA, *chapter 2* looks at the likely conduct of the EU's monetary policy taking into account the past behaviour of the dollar/Dmark relationship. In particular Germany's monetary policy over the past decade is analysed both through a descriptive analysis and econometric estimation of policy reaction functions for Germany, the USA and an EU aggregate. The implicit assumption is that although the ECB's policy will develop according to largely new lines, Germany's monetary

1

policy may provide some insight into the characteristics of a stability oriented European monetary policy. The analysis points to a marginal role of the Dmark/dollar exchange rate in determining Germany's monetary policy and to the progressive decoupling of European interest rates from US rates. These results lend support to the idea that EMU will behave much like a closed economy and that its monetary policy will take into account this structural aspect. The emergence of the euro as a global currency to the degree that it will increase the inward looking features of EMU will influence the way in which monetary policy will be carried out, i.e. looking increasingly at domestic targets such as price stability and, possibly, growth.

The independence of European monetary policy will be increasingly strengthened by the process of integration of the euro's financial markets. As is discussed in *chapter 3*, the introduction of a single currency will favour the development of extensive and inter-related financial markets, even if the initial non-participation of the UK were to slow the process down. The expanded financial market will lead to greater diversification of financial instruments and greater competitive pressure on the banks from other intermediaries as well as within the banking system. This, in turn, will lead to greater efficiency of the banking system, lower cost of financing and greater effectiveness of the transmission of monetary policy, even though there will continue to be differences among the EMU's member countries owing to differences among the financial structures of their businesses.

The results of this chapter thus support the idea that introduction of the euro will enhance the EU's cohesiveness and efficiency because it will stimulate development of its internal market to a much greater extent than in the past. This emphasises the euro's medium and long-term implications for external policies. In the medium run there will be increasing benefits from an external policy focused on the euro's internal and external stability inasmuch as it will highlight the advantages in terms of lower financing costs while stable and contained interest rates may support investments, above all in the continental economies. In the long run the consolidation, deepening and broadening of the financial markets in euros will constitute the basic conditions that will allow the European currency to take on the role of an international currency.

This leads us to the relationship between the single currency and unemployment. Persistent and large unemployment in Europe has been scrutinised under several perspectives. *Chapter 4* reviews the different interpretations of European unemployment, as compared to the US case, starting from the now traditional distinction between macroeconomic and microeconomic approaches. The first stresses the role of restrictive policies associated with the disinflation process in Europe. The second highlights the role of labour market rigidities. We also consider the role of product market rigidities, sectoral aspects of unemployment and the role of spatial distribution of unemployment. The latter aspects are particularly relevant for the functioning of the euro as they point to the role of possible asymmetric shocks, both sectoral and regional, in affecting employment. One conclusion of the chapter is that European unemployment is a consequence of several interacting factors which cannot be considered in isolation.

The following chapters look at the employment issue in Europe in more detail. *Chapter 5* considers the macroeconomic aspects. It provides an analysis of the trend and cycle components of unemployment and links the aggregate evolution of employment to the stagflation crisis of the 1970s and its developments. It also considers the relationship between investment formation and unemployment looking at the issue of whether capital formation is a complement to or a substitute for labour. Significant differences are found among the performance of single European economies, and in particular the unsatisfactory performance of the three major continental economies, both in terms of investment and employment formation. The chapter thus provides a link with the analysis developed in chapter 1 where Europe's macroeconomic problem is identified as the scarcity of investment.

This point is developed in *chapter 6* where the role of the euro's exchange rate in supporting growth is explored. A number of issues are considered. First, whether different national economic structures in the euro would be affected differently by a given euro/dollar exchange rate behaviour. The exercise is carried out by building a virtual 'eurozone' and considering its export performance (i.e. extra-EU export behaviour). The result is that, contrary to a widespread idea, Mediterranean countries are not more dependent on the evolution of the exchange rate than northern EU countries. What matters most for the export performance of these countries is intra-EU trade, i.e. they benefit from the strengthening of EU integration. This point is explored by looking at the possible export-led nature of the major EU economies. Results do not point to the existence of an export-led mechanism for these economies. One relevant exception is Germany which, being the economy most dependent on export-led growth, would paradoxically benefit most from a weak euro.

The role of international trade and competitiveness in affecting Europe's performance and employment is further discussed in *chapter 7* where an analysis of specialisation structures is presented. Three main points are discussed. First, we consider whether employment creation is different across manufacturing sectors. The result is that technologically advanced sectors have been characterised by positive employment creation while traditional sectors have been associated with employment destruction. We then introduce and compute flexibility and mobility indicators of industrial specialisation as well as of sectoral allocation of employment. A flexible economy is one where comparative advantages have deepened over time and where relative employment has increased. A mobile economy is one where new sectors of comparative advantage and labour reallocation have been obtained. European countries differ greatly according to both indicators. We consider this a sign of the fact that flexibility, in a broader sense, is a problem affecting product as well as labour markets. Finally we consider the sectoral exposure of European labour markets to international trade. One important result is that domestic employment is less exposed to international competition (one of the most widely considered effects of globalisation) in sectors where the economy enjoys strong comparative advantages. In this case too European countries show relevant differences.

Chapter 8 looks at the geography of employment. Increasing regional specialisation has a number of implications for the functioning of EMU. Institutional differences among national labour markets become less important while regional policies appear to be an essential tool for the functioning of EMU. The chapter offers a description, based on cluster analysis, of different regional specialisation patterns and their relationship with unemployment The following results are obtained. There is a positive relationship between specialisation in advanced manufacturing sectors and employment. As far as services are concerned we find that regions with a relative intensity of advanced sectors, i.e. sectors closely integrated with industry, are associated with low unemployment; the opposite occurs in regions with a high intensity of traditional services and commerce. We consider the evolution of regional specialisation between 1981 and 1991, which covers most of the period of the ERM of the EMS. Over this period we find a deepening of regional specialisation in accordance with results found in the literature.

We also discuss the catching-up mechanism among European regions. Our estimates show that the convergence among regional incomes in Europe is almost trivial unless a variable is introduced that accounts for the structural differences between groups of homogeneous regions. More precisely, if each region is identified on the basis of product composition according to cluster analysis, convergence among the regions increases. In other words, we identify a case of conditional convergence in the sense that not all regions move towards the *same* income level, but rather towards *different levels* according to their structural characteristics. The relevance of this result lies, on the one hand, in highlighting the role of the production structure for medium-term macroeconomic performance and, on the other hand, in stressing the importance of cohesion policies to reduce regional disparities in the long run.

A further medium-term aspect of the euro's external policy is examined in *chapter 9*, that is, the utilisation of excess reserves that will be freed by the changeover to the euro. The chapter adopts a conservative hypothesis regarding the volume of excess reserves, which are estimated at around $100 billion. Four hypotheses are considered for the utilisation of the reserves: (a) their retention by the ECB for intervening in the exchange markets; (b) utilisation of the reserves for repurchasing part of the EMU member countries' public debt; (c) refinancing of the structural funds to be allocated to the Central and Eastern European countries that will be future candidates for membership in the EU; (d) paying off the latter's external debt. The chapter considers in more detail the latter two options and concludes that, in both cases, the Central and Eastern European countries could achieve substantial, permanent rates of growth increases with clear benefits for themselves and for the Union as a whole.

The purpose of the exercise presented in chapter 9 is to offer an example of the kind of concrete and operational ties that may be created between the introduction of the euro and the next great adjustment facing the EU, i.e., precisely its further enlargement.

Chapter 10 offers general conclusions. The basic idea can be stated as follows. Tackling Europe's unemployment requires the interaction of a growth supportive macroeconomic strategy and an increase in the degree of flexibility and adaptability of the European labour and product markets and specialisation structures. Both aspects should be assessed from the perspective of the euro as an international currency. The appropriate strategy for Europe implies a stable external value of the euro and stable and low interest rates so as to support and encourage aggregate investment. Higher investment would be possible thanks to the resources available from fiscal adjustment and from more integrated and efficient financial markets which would support growth and employment. Sustained growth would make the implementation of flexibility oriented reforms in labour and product markets faster and more effective. On the other hand, more flexible and adaptive markets would increase the growth component of macroeconomic policies in a context of monetary stability and would also increase the long-term attractiveness of the euro as an international currency. In sum, macroeconomic and micro (structural) policies would mutually reinforce each other in much the same way as would the external dimension of the eurozone (a strong and attractive global currency) and its internal dimension (an area of monetary stability and growth).

The chapter also discusses the evidence presented in the book from the point of view of 'endogenous currency areas', i.e the fact that conditions required for a monetary union to operate may partially be a consequence of monetary integration itself. The point is discussed by looking at both adjustment in labour and product markets and economic policy convergence. In this respect the chapter discusses other policy areas, fiscal policy in the context of the Stability Pact, competition policy, innovation policy and labour market policy, that would have to be implemented to complete the European economic model and make the euro work.

1. The euro's external value and Europe's macroeconomic problem

Pier Carlo Padoan

INTRODUCTION

This chapter discusses the issue of the euro's external value from a broad viewpoint. This implies that several analytical approaches have to be considered. The characteristics of the new European currency – the second most important world currency – suggest that dealing with this issue only on the basis of the standard theory of exchange rate determination might be misleading. More useful insights can derive from the theory of 'key currencies' and from the analysis of the role played by the economic and monetary policy that the economy concerned – i.e., that of the EU – will follow.

The problem then arises of discussing what are the guiding principles of such policies which must aim at maximising the benefits from the introduction of a single currency. This in itself obvious approach is discussed within the framework of the theory of optimal currency areas, extended to include the advantages to be derived by users of the currency outside the area. This leads us to assert that it is in the EU's interest to support the euro's use as a 'key currency'.

Such a conclusion, in turn, raises the issue of relations with the dollar. The outlook for co-operation or conflict with the USA in the macroeconomic and monetary fields is explored. Next, we relate the issue of the long-term value of the euro to the characteristics of the macroeconomic equilibrium of the EU in a context of fiscal equilibrium as guaranteed by the stability and growth pact. This leads to the complementarity between a policy aimed at maintaining a stable value for the euro in international markets and the support of investment and growth in the EU.

MULTIPLE EQUILIBRIA AND THE TRANSITION PHASE

The debate on the role of the euro as an international currency offers different points of view regarding the evolution of the euro–dollar exchange rate during the initial phase of the EMU, i.e. over 5–10 years from the its launching on January 1, 1999. In the aftermath of the launching of the single currency some analysts have argued[1] that the euro would have been weak vis-à-vis the dollar at the moment of its introduction, inasmuch as (a) markets will be unable to identify with sufficient accuracy the ECB's monetary policy strategy, especially if it is perceived that the new institution's independence may be challenged; (b) the group of economies belonging to the euro area will include countries that do not offer all the guarantees for respecting the criteria of a strict fiscal policy; and, lastly, (c) the highly heterogeneous economies belonging to EMU will, at least in the medium term, pressure the ECB for excessively accommodating monetary policies, in view of asymmetrical shocks that might hit individual countries or regions within EMU. Hence, the ECB must earn its own reputation in the field, while the markets may prefer, in the meantime, to stick to dollar denominated investments.

A different view[2] emphasises structural factors that suggest that the introduction of the euro will generate an excess demand for the new currency (and a resulting excess supply of dollars). Such an excess demand may be generated either by shifts in the composition of private portfolios, or as a result of changes in the demand for euros and dollars as official reserve currencies.[3] Some of those who share the appreciation hypothesis (Alogoskoufis and Portes, 1997) offer a more sophisticated argument, based on the portfolio approach to exchange rate determination, according to which one should expect an initial revaluation of the euro that will overshoot the long-term equilibrium value, thus leading to a rise of the euro interest rate incorporating devaluation expectations, which would occur to compensate the initial appreciation. Finally, other analyses (Benassy, Benoit and Pisani-Ferry, 1997) show that the elimination of a large number of EU national currencies will increase the volatility of the euro-dollar rate, leading to higher interest rates owing to the greater risk associated with such volatility.

The relative weakness of the euro vis-à-vis the dollar after the first few months of its life is generally ascribed to the growth differential between the US and Euroland.[4] While this is probably true it remains to be clarified what are the causes of such a difference in performance. It is not unrealistic to assume that much of the reason lies in 'structural' more than in 'macroeconomic' determinants, i.e. weak EU growth partly, or perhaps largely, reflects structural imbalances in the EU economy.

It is difficult to choose among the different alternatives inasmuch as the behaviour of the euro–dollar rate will be a function of both a combination of structural factors and of economic policy implementation. The nature and intensity of the changes in the international currency system is, to say the least, enormous considering that the introduction of the euro introduces four major structural and institutional changes in international monetary relations: (a) the elimination of a substantial portion of international trade (which becomes regional trade within EMU); (b) the disappearance of a number of national currencies and of their respective markets; (c) the introduction of a completely new currency; (d) the creation of an important new institution (the ECB). The first three changes, which are structural, will interact with the ECB's policy and the external value of the euro rate will reflect this (complex) interaction.

As mentioned above, only partial insight into the nature of this evolution can be obtained by looking at the standard theory of exchange rate determination. Additional indications can be obtained by applying the theory of 'key currencies' as the euro is a natural candidate for the role of international currency alongside the dollar. If the stipulations suggested in the literature[5] for a currency to take up the role of 'key currency' are considered, it can be seen that the euro (and EMU) satisfies – or will soon be able to satisfy – these requirement, which are: (a) a significant weight in world trade and product of the economy that supports the currency; (b) absence of a significant external constraint; (c) full freedom of capital movement; (d) depth and liquidity of financial markets; (e) strength and stability of the economy.

As regards the first criterion, Europe exceeds the USA with respect to share of both world trade and world product.[6] The second criterion, which may be defined as the economy's need to draw resources from the rest of the world, seems to have been easier to fulfil for the EU than for the US (Figures 1.1 and 1.2) considering that, in the last two decades, the EU has maintained a substantially balanced current account – which has recently turned into a surplus – while the US has shown a deficit. The third criterion does not offer any problems. The fourth, on the other hand, has to do, at least in part, with the euro's composition and, to some extent, with the UK government's decision not to participate in the first phase of EMU as the non-participation of the UK leaves the financial market in euros less developed than the US's. Lastly, the fifth criterion crucially depends upon the extent to which the EU succeeds in restoring a sustainable growth and employment scenario.

Beyond these latter aspects, in any case, it can reasonably be expected that the euro will – at least in the medium term – play the role of a second key currency alongside the dollar. It remains to be seen whether this will make

Figure 1.1 National account balances: European Union (% of GDP)

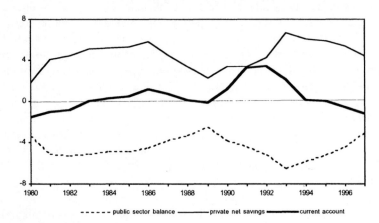

the euro substantially equivalent to the American currency or whether, instead, it will merely remain a 'regional' currency.

The theory of international transactions (e.g., Krugman, 1992 and Alogoskoufis, Portes and Rey, 1997) tells us that multiple equilibria in key currency positions can occur owing to the presence of externalities associated with the role of 'vehicle currency'. The equilibrium point of a currency in official international reserves and private portfolios – as well as its holding for transactions – may be 'low', as an indication of its 'regional' role, or it may be 'high', indicating that the currency has assumed a global role. The shift from one equilibrium to the other requires that the currency concerned surpass a minimum critical mass that would allow network externalities to operate. Until the introduction of the euro, while only the dollar has played and continues to play a global role, the D-mark – even though it is the second-place international currency – plays a role that may be defined as regional. It seems reasonable to believe that, the moment the euro is introduced, its role on international markets will be closer to the D-mark's than to the dollar's, even though some analyses of the possible private use of the euro (Hartmann, 1996) estimate that international trade invoicing at the new European money will amount to around 24% as against the D-mark's current 15%. Of course any such process will take time.

Multiple equilibria imply a different share for the euro as an international currency, as well as, ultimately, a different long-term equilibrium level of the E/$ rate, to the extent that the different levels of demand for euros ensuing from its role as key currency are related to different supply behaviours. Shifting from one equilibrium to another will be largely a function of the policies pursued by the EMU's economic policy-makers with respect to the

Figure 1.2 National account balances: United States (% of GDP)

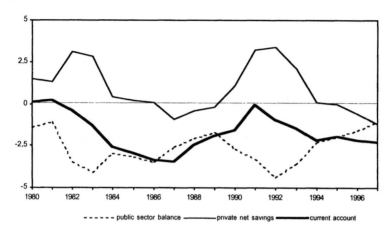

euro's external value.[7] A larger role for the euro and its evolution from 'low' to 'high' equilibrium as international currency will very probably be associated with the perception of the single currency's stability by the markets and monetary authorities of third countries. An EMU policy focused on stability would lead to growing international demand for euros as well as, perhaps, to a (temporary) revaluation. Conversely, EMU economic policies not conducive to stability would lessen the desirability of the European currency and thus, in the long run, its international role.

The euro's desirability would, moreover, be enhanced by the perception that, following its introduction, the EU economy would come out of its low-growth/high-unemployment stage and resume sustained development (the above-mentioned fifth requisite for a key currency). From this point of view, EU economic polices in support of growth could not fail to make a positive impact on the euro's role in international markets, just as the behaviour of the American economy underpins the dollar's desirability. An 'attractive' currency, in turn, make the EU economy 'attractive' for international capital, in a way similar to what happened to the American economy and to the dollar during recent decades. In other words, then, the introduction of the euro presents a unique opportunity for simultaneously achieving monetary stability and sustained growth.

Lastly, policies which enhance EU growth are advantageous for both the EU and the USA, *inter alia* because international co-operation is evidently strengthened by a solid and expanding economic environment, while conflicts – in both monetary and commercial relations – become more acute during periods of low growth (Padoan, 1995).

ECONOMIC POLICY OPTIONS FOR THE EUROZONE

If multiple equilibria are possible, then the management of economic and monetary policy during the transition is crucial not only for steering convergence towards a new equilibrium but for the actual position of that equilibrium. The direction that this path will take is – as was mentioned earlier – a function of the policies that will be followed during the EMU's initial phase. The question then arises of what would be a desirable policy for the external value of the euro. Before the introduction of the single currency the question was frequently asked in the form of an alternative between an exchange rate policy for the euro focused on stability of internal prices ('strong euro') and one supporting competitiveness ('weak euro'). This is largely a spurious problem. Let us start with an obvious consideration: the most appropriate policy is one taking greatest advantage of the characteristics of a common currency. This point may be clarified by considering the estimated cost and benefits for the EMU members from the introduction of the single currency through an extension of an approach suggested by Collignon (1997) based on the literature regarding monetary unions.

This approach (see Appendix 1, Costs and benefits of a monetary union) suggests that the benefits from a monetary union increase with the extension of the union, as expressed in terms of either the number of participating countries or of economic size. This relation arises from the fact that the larger the size of the union, the greater are the benefits accruing to each member from the elimination of transaction costs and exchange rate uncertainty, in addition to those stemming from lower variability of interest rates (Collignon, 1966).[8] These advantages, furthermore, increase with the degree of openness of the economies of the union's members. If these two elements are applied to the European case it follows that the EMU's benefits grow with the increase of (a) the number of member countries; (b) the EMU's GDP; and (c) the degree of integration and openness of the internal market.

Costs increase with the increased diversity of the preferences of the area's policy-makers regarding monetary stabilisation policies. In other words, the costs of membership of the union for a country with a high preference for containing inflation increase if other union members have a strong preference for active (stabilisation oriented) monetary policies. In general, the higher the convergence of the member countries' preference for low inflation and stability-oriented monetary policy, the lower the costs. From this point of view, EMU's composition becomes crucial, but it is equally evident that the process of convergence towards the Maastricht parameters as well as the application of the stability and growth pact suggest that the costs of the EMU will be moderate if even the least disciplined among the Union's members implement rigorous anti-inflationary and fiscal reform policies.

To sum up, the net benefit from the EMU will increase with the growth of the number of members, of the size of the EU's GDP, of the degree of internal market integration and of the completion of monetary and financial convergence. We can the apply the approach to the euro's external dimension, for which the concept of *currency region* (Cohen, 1997) may be useful. A currency region differs from a currency *area* in that the latter's size is determined by the countries that agree formally to a fixed exchange rate or to a monetary union, while the former's size is determined by the extension of the area within which a given currency is used without reference to that currency's legal status. In other words, the size of the currency region depends on the behaviour of the markets and not on formal agreements. Such a region is therefore measured by the extent to which a vehicle currency, such as the dollar and the D-mark, is used for international transactions; this, in turn, depends largely on the operation of network externalities that are associated with such a role (Krugman, 1992, Alogoskoufis; Portes and Rey, 1997).

The concept of currency region leads to the conclusion that the *external* benefits of EMU will increase with the size of the euro's currency region, i.e., with its use as international currency by countries and markets that do not belong to the EMU.

As to costs associated with the euro's external dimension, i.e., of using the euro as an international currency, these will increase with increasing EMU member country preference for 'activist' exchange rate policies for the euro vis-à-vis third-country currencies (primarily the dollar) in order to promote exports via real devaluation. In this case, too, net (external) benefits of the currency may thus depend on the EMU's composition. We shall return to this point, which suggests that the net benefits of the EMU would be maximised by a *stable* external value of the euro.

To sum up: given that an international reserve currency may have multiple equilibria in the international monetary system, and that the euro, at the moment of its introduction, should settle at a 'low' equilibrium value, the objective of the external policy for the euro should be to reach a 'high' equilibrium, i.e., to enlarge the extension of its currency area from that covered by the D-mark to one proportional to the economic size of the EU.

ONE OPEN QUESTION: RELATIONS WITH THE USA

The above reflections obviously lead to the issue of the euro's relations with the dollar and hence to the outlook for the EU's co-operation with the USA.

The latter issue, in turn, can be split into at least two aspects: one, connected to the transitional phase, concerns the impact of the EMU's debut on the E/$ exchange rate, and a longer-term aspect regarding the type of relations that may be established in a bipolar monetary context.[9] With respect to the former issue opinions differ. The uncertainty regarding post-euro monetary relations suggest that the main question is whether the introduction of the single currency may call for, and ultimately effect, more or less co-operation between the European and American authorities in controlling the fluctuations of the exchange rate to the extent that excessive volatility might damage transatlantic relations. In other words, we ask whether the introduction of the euro will increase or lower the incentives for macroeconomic co-operation between the two major economies.

The theory of international economic relations might be of help in trying to address the issue, especially in the aspects suggesting why international agreements are made and what conditions favour their success.[10] The theory suggests that, in the absence of a single dominant actor able and willing to play a hegemonic role in the international system, co-operation is favoured by (a) a small number of actors involved, inasmuch as this reduces the propensity towards free riding and enhances the possibility punishing such behaviour; (b) extending the time horizon of the actors, as this allows allocating a higher premium to future benefits from co-operation; and (c) the existence of institutions that favour the dissemination of information on the behaviour of the actors involved and thus the transparency and predictability of their behaviour.

In the post-euro era, the first condition is obviously being fulfilled, and so is the third if it is assumed that such institutions as the economic G-7 will continue to operate – and perhaps even more effectively[11] – and that international institutions such as the IMF will be strengthened.[12] The second condition deserves greater attention. To consider its importance let us recall the post-war evolution of monetary relations between Europe and the USA or, rather, the consequences of the behaviour of the USA for Europe's international monetary policy options. As Henning (1997b) shows, these relations may be summarised as follows: whenever the USA has behaved 'aggressively' in macroeconomic and monetary relations with Europe, the European countries increased the degree of monetary co-operation among themselves to stem such 'aggressiveness'. Vice versa, periods of a 'benign' attitude on the part of the American authorities slowed down monetary convergence in Europe.

Henning's framework – while quite persuasive – must be adapted to the post-euro phase, which represents the highest degree of monetary co-operation in Europe. It may be extended as follows: an 'aggressive' US attitude towards Europe would probably favour a European attitude of 'non-co-operation'», and perhaps even an attempt to unload abroad factors of instability that might arise inside the EU,[13] while a benign American attitude would favour adoption of a similar attitude by Europe.[14]

In the present phase, it is not easy to predict the future US attitude, given the cyclical behaviour of US foreign economic policy towards Europe. This point deserves more thorough treatment;[15] here we may observe merely that it offers a rather optimistic picture of the future of transatlantic monetary relations. We may add that the level of interdependence between the transatlantic economies is so high that the benefits from co-operation and from greater integration exceed the benefits from the opposite option, i.e., conflict or, better, absence of co-operation. It follows that both regions should have an interest in transatlantic monetary co-operation, at least to the extent of minimising exchange rate instability.

LONG-TERM MACROECONOMIC OBJECTIVES AND THE EURO'S EXCHANGE RATE

One conclusion of the previous paragraph is that, at least in the long run, the degree of integration of transatlantic relations will be such as to make desirable – and achievable – a scenario of co-operation between the USA and the EU with respect to exchange rate management. There remains open the question of whether a long-term stable level of the euro's external value is a possibility, or at least whether in the long run a devaluation or revaluation of the euro should be expected.

We stated earlier that traditional exchange rate theory is of limited use for addressing this question given the structural changes in international monetary relations entailed by the creation of the euro. We will look at the problem here using the concept of 'fundamental equilibrium exchange rate' (FEER),[16] i.e., the real rate at which internal equilibrium (where aggregate demand equals potential income under constant inflation) and external equilibrium (on current account) are simultaneously obtained. This concept is useful over the long run because it ignores the effects of fluctuations of the (real) exchange rate owing to financial capital flows.

To obtain an idea of the FEER level for the EU one must look at the characteristics of the EU's long-run macroeconomic equilibrium. As shown in Figure 1.1, since 1980 the EU has substantially maintained an external equilibrium and an excess of private savings over investment, which has largely financed the public sector deficit. Viewed from this perspective, the disequilibrium in public finances may be considered symmetrical to insufficient private sector demand.[17] By contrast, the United States has been characterised (Figure 1.2) by a (long-run) private sector equilibrium and public sector deficit, financed by capital inflow. Of course the recent and, in many respects, spectacular improvement in US public finance introduces a major change in the picture, but does not significantly change the perspectives for the Euro-area macroeconomic scenario.

The EU is completing the process of fiscal adjustment. The stability pact will ensure that the equilibrium will be maintained over time and the issue of achieving a new macroeconomic equilibrium compatible with fiscal equilibrium will represent the main macroeconomic issue in the eurozone. A number of different paths can be imagined, each with different implications for the euro's FEER. To the extent that the private sector demand gap is filled by boosting investment – the most desirable solution[18] – internal and external equilibria would be attained at a higher level of income without affecting the euro's long-term exchange rate. A different scenario entails that, in the face of an unchanged demand gap, i.e., without raising investment, a current account surplus is generated. In such a case the EU would transfer resources to the rest of the world by means of a capital account deficit which would be the counterpart of the surplus on current account. This alternative scenario would entail implications for the euro's FEER. In the long run, the accumulation of net foreign financial assets would appreciate the euro, causing a reabsorption of the current account surplus and attainment of an internal equilibrium at lower levels of income (see Appendix 2: Determination of the FEER and macroeconomic equilibrium). Finally, a third scenario may be considered where the EU could support a current account deficit and a corresponding capital inflow at a constant exchange rate – as in the US case – whenever the level of internal savings was lower than domestic investment. This scenario has not materialised for the EU in general, but it is worthy of note that in recent years Germany has been able to rely on the D-mark's status as international currency for supporting capital inflows to cover the needs that arose from Germany's unification (Deutsche Bundesbank, 1997b).

CONCLUSIONS

Several implications arise from the analysis of the macroeconomic policy options and for managing the euro's external value, as well as, more generally, for the outlook for the EU's economic policy. The first implication is that completion of the fiscal adjustment required by the Maastricht treaty creates macroeconomic manoeuvring space for the EU. This space should be used to raise the private investment rate tangibly, which, in turn, could absorb private sector resources that in recent years have been going largely into financing public sector needs. The second implication is that such a macroeconomic policy stance is not only congruent with the objectives of EMU monetary stability and of the euro's external value, but that it is the latter which allows an increase of investments to the extent that low and stable interest rates are associated with monetary and exchange rate stability. The third implication is that, in the medium run, such a policy underpins the euro's attributes as an international currency for private investment and as reserve or reference currency for third countries, inasmuch as bolstering the EU's economy reinforces the fifth condition for begetting an international currency.

The fulfilment of the above conditions calls for a number of explanations that will be explored in the following chapters. In the first place, it needs to be clarified to what extent it is not appropriate to rely on the euro's exchange rate for stimulating growth and investment. This aspect, which is discussed in chapters 5 and 6, is even more relevant as EMU turns the EU economy into more of a closed economy much less dependent on exports for its growth than each single EU economy. In the second place, EMU opens up the possibility of managing interest rates much more independently of the USA's monetary conditions (chapter 2). This increased independence will be strengthened by the consolidation of the euro's financial markets (chapter 3). Lastly, the introduction of the euro will constitute but a stage towards the definition of a 'new European model'.

NOTES

1. Certainly, the most criticism to the euro project come from Feldstein (1997).
2. See, for example, Bergsten (1997); Alogoskoufis and Portes (1997).
3. The different estimates in the literature reported by Bergsten (1997) indicate a range of portfolio diversification (and thus an excess demand for euros) of between $500 billion and $1,000 billion, while the estimate of excess dollar reserves ranges from 50 to 200 billion dollars. Evidence of the first euro denominated bond issues in the first six months of 1999 point to an equal amount of issues in dollar and euros in spite of the relative weakness of the European currency.
4. The euro started to regain strength in the second half of 1999, when the forecast of European growth had been revised upwards.
5. See, for example, Bergsten (1996).
6. In 1995 the world product shares of the USA and the EU were, respectively, 26% and 31%; for world trade (excluding infra-EU trade), they were, respectively, 18% and 20%.
7. In this regard, one must refer to 'EMU economic policy-makers' inasmuch as the Maastricht treaty, in addition to the monetary stability mandate it assigned to the ECB, provides for an important – but not yet precisely defined – role for the European Council, the ECOFIN and the so-called 'euro-X' in setting the external value of the euro, above all with respect to the establishment of exchange agreements with third-country currencies.
8. Costs and benefits of monetary unions are amply discussed in the literature, For an overall evaluation, see, for example, De Grauwe (1992).

9. For this purpose, the implications for the third international currency, the yen, are disregarded.
10. For a review see Padoan (1989, chs 1 and 2.)
11. Regarding these aspects, see Henning (1997a).
12. For the implications of the euro for international institutions, see Thygesen (1997).
13. Reference is to the scenario explored by Benassy, Benoit and Pisani-Ferry (1997) and D. Cohen (1997)
14. This would be 'tit-for-tat' behaviour; see Axelrod (1984).
15. For an analysis of transatlantic relations, see Padoan (1995).
16. This concept was popularised in the literature by Williamson (1994). 'Natural real exchange rate' is a similar concept (Crouhy Veyrac and Saint Marc, 1997). See also Gandolfo, Padoan and Paladino (1990).
17. In this respect, see the analyses of Allsop and Vines (1996). Muet (1997) and Fitoussi (1997) argue that the root of the problem of low European growth must be sought in the conspicuous slowing of investment owing in part to over restrictive monetary policies. Moreover, this slowing is supposedly responsible for the drop in potential equilibrium output and for the rise in the unemployment rate.
18. It might be recalled that in recent years the EU's investment/GDP ratio has been continuously declining, the opposite of what happened in the USA.

APPENDIX 1: COSTS AND BENEFITS OF A MONETARY UNION

Consider a very simple graphic presentation of costs and benefits of a monetary union, taken from Collignon (1997), which summarises the abundant literature on the subject (Figure.1.1A). Costs rise with the rise of A, which indicates the propensity of the Union's members to use monetary policy for income stabilisation. Increasing values of A fuel the Union's inflation and hence diminish monetary stability. The benefits rise as the size of S grows because of greater economies of scale from the use of a common currency. Line NB is the locus of the points where benefits and costs offset each other (net benefits equal zero). NB increases because greater monetary activism may be offset by an expansion of the Union's size. The slope of NB reflects the degree of openness of the Union's member economies. The points above NB indicate net negative benefits: there is no incentive to create a monetary union. The opposite occurs below the line. Rising propensity towards monetary activism for a given size of the Union clearly results in net negative benefits and must be offset by enlarging the Union and/or by a growing degree of openness (increasing slope of NB) in order to raise the scale benefits.

Next, we apply the reasoning to a specific *currency region* (B. Cohen, 1997) as an extension of the area of use of the currency and which therefore includes countries that are not members of the Union (see Figure 1.2A). The size of the currency region is clearly greater than that of the currency union only in the case of key currencies such as the dollar, the D-mark, and the euro. In this case

Figure 1A.1 Costs and benefits of a monetary union

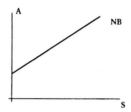

Figure 1A.2 Costs and benefits of a monetary region

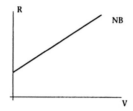

the costs R of the use of the money as key currency by internal and external operators (and thus not only public operators but also, and mainly, private operators) rise with growing use of the exchange rate to support the Union's exports, i.e., an 'activist' use of the exchange rate. This is so because such a policy not only depresses the value of the currency itself but it also increases its instability as it weakens its role as both a store of value and as a vehicle currency. Benefits V rise as the currency's use in international markets rises owing to network externalities. In this case, too, the points of zero net benefits are located along NB, and higher (lower) values reveal the net negative (positive) benefits. The diagram also shows why markets continue to use a given money as vehicle currency even if its exchange rate becomes unstable (owing to explicit or implicit policies for manipulating it). This happens if the use of the currency is already so extensive as to offset the costs of instability thanks to network externalities. The obvious reference is to the case of the dollar.

APPENDIX 2: DETERMINATION OF THE FEER AND MACROECONOMIC EQUILIBRIUM

This appendix offers a simple graphic presentation of the determination of the FEER (fundamental equilibrium exchange rate) by applying Williamson's (1994) definition. The FEER is the real exchange rate at which we obtain

Figure 1A.3 Determination of the FEER

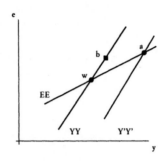

simultaneously a balance-of-payments equilibrium on current account and an internal equilibrium, i.e., where output equals aggregate demand at constant inflation. In the diagram (see Figure 1.3A), the *EE* schedule shows the combinations of exchange rate *e* and product *y* at which external equilibrium is obtained. *EE* slopes upward because, as output increases, increasing imports must be offset by exports and thus by a larger devaluation of the exchange rate. If we assume a zero inflation differential with the rest of the world, changes of *e* equal changes in the real exchange rate. The *YY* schedule indicates the locus of the points of internal equilibrium; it slopes upward because, if it is assumed (Gandolfo, 1986, ch 14) that the propensity to spend is less than one, rising income entails a smaller rise of demand which is, in turn, related to income. This requires, therefore, a devaluation of the exchange rate in order to sustain internal demand by squeezing imports and boosting exports. The points below (above) *YY* indicate aggregate demand deficit (surplus). The points below (above) *EE* indicate current account deficit (surplus).

The EU's case, characterised by external equilibrium and lack of aggregate demand, may be represented by point *a*. An increase of the autonomous component of aggregate demand – e.g., investments – shifts *YY* to *Y'Y'* and allows a full equilibrium to be reached which entails an unchanged exchange rate (FEER) at point *a*. If investment does not rise, the system will move towards point *b* owing to the deflationary effect of fiscal adjustment. Moreover, the current account surplus that would take place would shift the system towards point *w* which reflects a revalued FEER and a lower income level.

2. The external value of the euro and EMU's monetary policy

Marcello Pericoli *

INTRODUCTION

This chapter considers the external implications of the ECB's primary objective – monetary stability. We analyse how the evolution of the euro's exchange rate – vis-à-vis the dollar – may influence this strategy. As discussed in chapter 1, any market perception that the EU may pursue an activist exchange rate policy to support European exports 'aggressively' would entail both higher interest rates and greater inflationary pressure. At the same time, a 'strong' exchange rate policy would dampen European growth. What is desirable for EMU, then, is a stable exchange rate for the euro. However, such a strategy will be to large extent affected by the relation between the monetary policies of the EU and of the USA.

The chapter is organised as follows: after a description of the relationship between the exchange rate, interest rate and other macroeconomic variables in Europe and the USA, we offer an analysis of monetary policy in Germany and in the EU. The results lay the foundation for the – inevitably 'conjectural' – conclusions regarding the behavior of the EU's monetary policy in relation to the euro's external value.

INTEREST RATES AND EXCHANGE RATES

First hand evidence of the evolution of the dollar exchange rate points to some relatively marked cyclical behaviour.[1] The D-mark's nominal exchange rate against the dollar has undergone two phases of appreciation. The first, following the collapse of the Bretton Woods system, dragged the rate from

* Bank of Italy, Research Department. The article was written when the author was working at the San Paolo Bank, London. The views expressed in the article are those of the author and not of the Bank.

Figure 2.1 Exchange rate and short-term interest rate differential:
USA–Germany

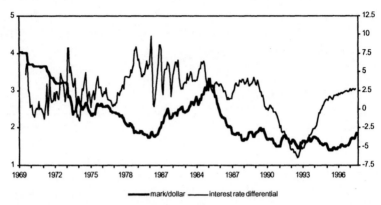

mark/dollar ——— interest rate differential

3.42 to 1.72 D-marks per dollar (January 1980). The reversal of the Fed's monetary policy in 1979 caused a dollar revaluation up to a peak of 3.3 in February 1985. Thereafter, the mark appreciated again against the dollar; the rate dropped steadily to 2.0 in January 1987. The mark/dollar rate then remained relatively stable in a band between 1.40 and 1.80. The short-term rates' differential fluctuated more or less widely around an average for long periods: aside from a few outliers in the early 1970s, the differential between short-term interest rates in the USA and in Germany remained positive from 1969 to 1990, with an average of 1.92% in 1969–76, and of 3.85% in 1977–90. German unification and the tight monetary policy followed by the German monetary authorities led to a negative differential of –1.17% between July 1990 and July 1994, with low of –6.43% in the summer of 1992. Figure 2.1 indicates that there is no clear relation between the nominal short-term interest rate differential and the nominal bilateral interest rate. This may perhaps be explained by the high differential between current and expected inflation rates over the period concerned.[2] It thus becomes necessary to analyse also the relation between the short-term interest rate and the exchange rate adjusted for the inflation differential. This relation is shown in Figure 2.2.

After adjusting for the inflation differential, we note a greater stability of the interest rate differential. In 1969–90 the average real short-term interest differential is 0.85%, diminishes to an average of –2.63% in 1990–95, and returns to 0.85% in 1995–97. The real bilateral exchange rate remains stable from 1971 to 1979, weakens in 1979–87 and returns to the earlier level in 1988–97. In this case, too, it is difficult to find a relation between the two variables.

Figure 2.2 Real exchange rate and real short-term interest rate differential:
USA–Germany

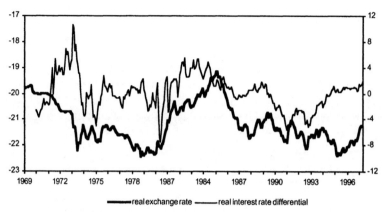

The descriptive analysis ends with the comparison of US, German and EU interest rates. The EU aggregate includes the eleven countries which joined EMU in January 1999. On that basis, it is possible to compare the short-term interest rates of the EU,[3] Germany and the USA (Figure 2.3).

The short-term EU interest rate shows a close relation with the US rate for 1983–87 and an even closer relation with the German rate beginning in 1987 – the year the 'hard EMS' phase began. Co-integration tests (see below) do not reject the hypotheses suggested by the initial graphic analysis, that US interest rates influence the European rate until 1987 in both the levels and the

Figure 2.3 Short-term interest rates in the United States, Germany
and the EU

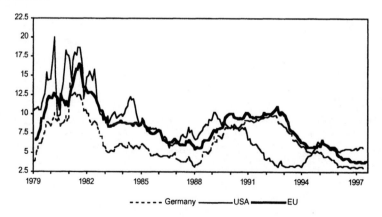

variations; after 1987 the German rate begins to govern the trend of the EU's short-term rate, and the linkage is strengthened following German reunification owing to the need of the EU countries to maintain parity with the D-mark.

The exchange rates of the mark against the dollar (Dm/$) and of the euro against the dollar (E/$) behaved similarly. The introduction of an exchange rate agreement in the EU area with virtually fixed rates entails an asymmetric trend for the E/$ rate against the Dm/$ rate, i.e., the European countries are obliged – by the ERM – to maintain their parity with the mark and, hence, a given short-term interest rate; conversely, the mark's effective exchange rate becomes an (intermediate) target for the German authorities. This asymmetric behaviour, as we will see, implies that the exchange rate becomes an argument of the reaction function of the German central bank while it does not significantly appear in that of the EU.

Beginning in 1979,[4] and until 1996, two separate sub-periods can be identified: the first, through December 1986 and the second from January 1987 to December 1996. The separation between the two periods is confirmed by a co-integration analysis between short-term interest rates (Table 2.1), respectively, in Germany and the EU against the US rates, in addition to visual data analysis (Figure 2.3). The co-integration hypothesis between the interest rates is accepted for the EU and Germany for 1979–86, while it is rejected for the subsequent period. The co-integration hypothesis between the EU and US rates for the entire sample period is accepted at 5% significance level.

We may now extend the analysis to include the business cycle and the rate of inflation in the three countries.

Table 2.1 Co-integration of short-term interest rates in Germany and the EU with US rates[a]

Period	EU L-max test	Germany L-max test
1979.3 – 1986.12	0.57	0.66
1987.1 – 1996.12	10.28	8.72
1979.3 – 1996.12	3.85	3.25

Note: [a] Johansen test; the hypothesis of cointegration is accepted at 10% if the value of test is less than 2.71 and at 5% if less than 3.84.

BUSINESS CYCLES, INTEREST RATES AND INFLATION

The joint analysis of the short-term interest rate and the business cycle points at a long-term relation between the two variables that is highly significant in the USA and weaker in Germany. Economic literature identifies the basis for such an empirical regularity as a reaction function of the central bank, known as *Taylor's Rule*;[5] monetary authorities fix the short-term interest rate to minimise a loss function whose arguments are the output gap and the divergence of the inflation rate from a desired value.[6] Figure 2.4 shows how the relation between the three months interest rate and the cycle is especially marked from 1979 onward in the USA. This relation is less obvious in Germany than in the USA.

Short-term interest rates, furthermore, exhibit a strong relation with the inflation rate in the USA as well as in Germany and, in part, in the EU. Figure 2.5 illustrates the relation between the two variables for the three countries.

The long-term relation among the three variables (cycle, short-term interest rate and inflation) is made clear by the shape of the cross-correlograms (the graphs in Figure 2.6 show the cross-correlograms for the USA, German and the EU). They indicate the cross-correlations among three pairs of variables for different lags; the *lag* with *n* periods indicates the correlation between the first and second variable lagged by *n* periods; conversely, the *lead* with *n* periods indicates the correlation between the first and the second variable forwarded by *n* periods. Inverting the order of the variables in the pair, the *leads* become *lags* and vice versa. Graphic analysis of the cross-correlograms indicates similar trends in the three countries – USA, Germany and EU – with the exception of the relation between cycle and inflation in the latter case.

Short-term interest rates and inflation are highly correlated, with maxima corresponding to simultaneous values of 0.75% for the USA and 0.50% for Germany and the EU. The *leads* between interest and inflation in the US are positive and significant for more than eight quarters, and they indicate that the short-term interest rate rises with the emergence of inflationary pressures and remains high for an extended period with positive correlations of around 0.50%. The size of the relation between short-term interest rates and rates of inflation differs between Germany and the EU, with a maximum correlation for the simultaneous period of 0.50%, and for length the short-term interest rate shows a positive correlation for up to four quarters forward. In terms of monetary policy, therefore, the graphic analysis of the cross-correlograms indicates the existence of an 'anticipated' policy for the three countries which, however, is much more marked for the USA than for Germany and the EU.

Figure 2.4 Business cycle and interest rates

USA

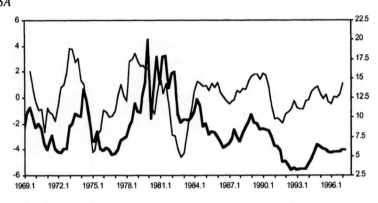

Germany

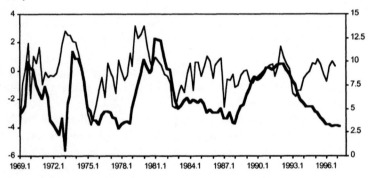

EU

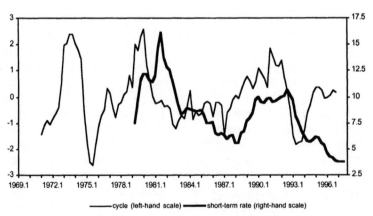

Figure 2.5 Inflation and interest rates

USA

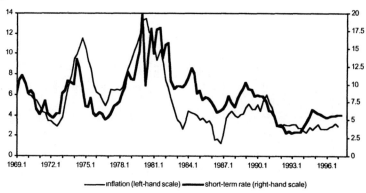

Germany

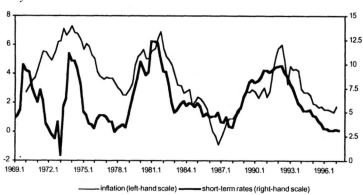

EU

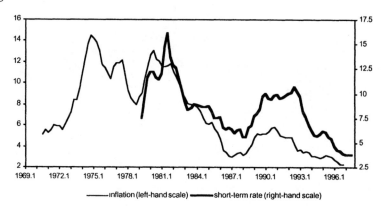

Figure 2.6 Cross-correlogram among cycles, inflation and interest rate

USA

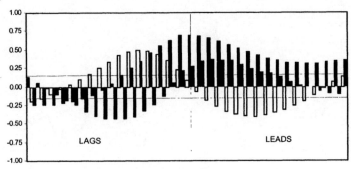

Germany

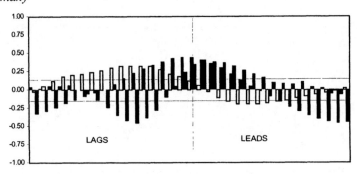

EU

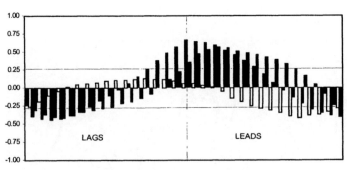

Note: Solid lines indicate a confidence interval of 5%.

The relation between short-term interest rates and cycle follows the same indication as those suggested by a rule of counter-cyclical monetary policy such as that observed for the relation between interest rate and inflation rate in all three countries. In the USA, an increase of the short-term interest rate anticipates an upswing of the business cycle by about three quarters, with a correlation that remains around 0.25% for about three to four quarters. In Germany and the EU, the correlation between short-term interest rate and business cycle is more marked than in the USA, with a *leads* correlation greater than, or equal to, that between interest and inflation. In any case, even in the case of these two countries a cyclical upswing is preceded by an increase in short-term interest rates.

On the other hand, the relation between cycle and rate of inflation is similar for the USA and Germany, while it is not found for the EU. The cross-correlogram between cycles and inflation indicates a zero correlation between business cycle and inflation for the same period; nevertheless, the cycle is positively correlated with inflation for previous periods. In other words, an overheating of inflationary dynamics precedes a cyclical upswing and, when the economy is cooling off, the inflation rate moves in the opposite direction; the relation is indicated by the negative figures in the *leads* between cycle and inflation. In the case of the EU, no statistically significant relation is found between the two variables.

The analysis of the cross-correlograms between business cycle, inflation rate and interest rate suggests the possible existence of counter-cyclical monetary policy – which in our analysis is represented by the movements of the short-term interest rate – designed to counteract emerging inflationary pressures as well as overheating of the economy. It is time, then, to move from graphic to structural analysis.

MONETARY POLICY IN EUROPE AND IN GERMANY: A STRUCTURAL ANALYSIS

The evidence presented above allows the formulation of a more precise hypothesis. A Taylor rule has never been explicitly followed by the European monetary policy-makers, who have preferred an eclectic approach. Monetary policies have been implemented in the context of exchange rate constraints imposed by the EMS which has acted as a co ordinating mechanism. Hence, in our exercise the behaviour of the EU aggregate reflects this structure of monetary relations. Germany represents the exception on the European scene. As indicated by Clarida and Gertler (1996) and by Juselius (1996), the Bundesbank has used the short-term interest rate to stabilise the rate of inflation and the real external value of the D-mark, and to stimulate growth. In other words, the Bundesbank has apparently followed a monetary policy design shaped on the Taylor rule.

We have tested this hypothesis by use of a VAR model. The model shows the simultaneous and lagged relations between policy and non-policy variables. For the model's construction, we follow the approach developed by Juselius (1996), Bernanke and Mihov (1996) and Clarida and Gertler (1996). We define a group of non-policy variables (NP) which include the rate of growth of the consumer price index, Δp, of industrial production, y, and of the short-term interest rate of the USA, r^*, and a group of policy variables (P) including the real bilateral exchange rate against the dollar, s, aggregate M3 in real terms, $m - p$, the short-term interest rate, r. All variables are expressed as logarithms. Let us assume that the NP variables respond with a lag of one period to the changes of the P variables, while the latter respond instantly to changes of the NP variables; let us also assume the following structural relations between the two groups of variables:

money demand – real monetary balances

$$m_t - p_t - y_t = \text{trend} - kr_r \tag{2.1}$$

modified Taylor rule

$$r_t = r_t^* + \beta\Delta p_t + (1 - B)(y_t - \text{trend}) + \gamma s_t \tag{2.2}$$

Phillips curve

$$(y_t - \text{trend}) = \alpha\Delta p_t \tag{2.3}$$

Equation (2.1) is the standard equation money demand; (2.2) is a modified Taylor rule that accounts for the dynamics of the real bilateral exchange rate; (2.3) is a positive relation between income and inflation described by the Phillips curve; in this way, the reaction function of monetary policy is solved endogenously without imposing a policy target *ex ante*.

In estimating the VAR, the three relations, (2.1), (2.2) and (2.3), are imposed as co-integration relations. Estimation of the impact matrix Π for Germany and the EU, shown in table 2.2, indicates the relations between the levels of variables and the variations of the single short-term variables; the boldface variables are significant.

Let us consider first of all the results for Germany (Table 2.2A). The impact matrix Π indicates the existence of a short-term relation between German short-term interest rates and the levels of all the lagged variables. The domestic interest rate exhibits an error-correcting mechanism (indicated by the negative coefficient of the lagged rate) and the standard relations

Table 2.2A Matrix Π: Germany, January 1983–December 1996 [a]

	r^*	Δp	y	s	$m-p$	r	du_{90}	trend
Δr^*	−0.003	−0.018	−2.739	0.020	2.745	0.004	0.212	−0.006
	(−0.421)	(−1.017)	(−2.416)	(0.421)	(2.487)	(0.240)	(2.962)	(−1.593)
$\Delta^2 p$	−0.111	−0.896	−2.702	0.746	7.368	0.242	0.465	−0.023
	(−2.736)	(−8.864)	(−0.407)	(2.736)	(1.140)	(2.564)	(1.108)	(−1.086)
Δy	0.000	0.000	−0.135	−0.001	0.170	−0.001	0.012	0.000
	(0.554)	(0.271)	(−2.987)	(−0.554)	(3.856)	(−0.793)	(4.322)	(−2.759)
Δs	0.000	0.001	0.149	−0.002	−0.113	−0.001	−0.010	0.000
	(0.609)	(0.754)	(1.797)	(−0.609)	(−1.406)	(−0.494)	(−1.829)	(0.727)
$\Delta (m-p)$	0.000	0.000	−0.026	0.001	−0.006	0.000	0.000	0.000
	(−1.649)	(1.373)	(−2.435)	(1.649)	(−0.623)	(1.633)	(0.343)	(1.638)
Δr	0.031	0.045	3.669	−0.212	2.174	−0.073	0.036	−0.012
	(6.578)	(3.742)	(4.675)	(−6.578)	(2.846)	(−6.538)	(0.735)	(−4.788)

Table 2.2B Matrix Π: EU, January 1983–December 1996 [a]

	r^*	Δp	y	s	$m-p$	r	du_{90}	trend
Δr^*	0.021	0.020	−2.546	0.192	1.323	−0.026	−0.005	−0.001
	(0.835)	(0.721)	(−1.462)	(0.585)	(0.941)	(−0.956)	(−0.063)	(−0.14)
$\Delta^2 p$	0.485	−0.753	−16.016	−2.032	18.307	0.068	0.875	−0.034
	(4.320)	(−5.874)	(−2.014)	(−1.355)	(2.850)	(0.549)	(2.206)	(−1.938)
Δy	0.002	0.000	−0.171	−0.019	0.214	−0.004	0.007	0.000
	(3.340)	(0.624)	(−4.314)	(−2.48)	(6.697)	(−6.237)	(3.526)	(−4.816)
Δs	−0.007	0.004	0.497	−0.076	−0.047	−0.003	0.007	−0.001
	(−3.871)	(1.883)	(4.159)	(−3.38)	(−0.483)	(−1.6)	(1.219)	(−2.065)
$\Delta (m-p)$	0.000	0.000	−0.011	0.013	−0.016	0.001	−0.004	0.000
	(1.923)	(−0.324)	(−0.63)	(3.878)	(−1.076)	(1.858)	(−4.65)	(1.604)
Δr	−0.028	0.026	4.330	−0.344	0.505	−0.034	−0.113	−0.007
	(−1.852)	(1.512)	(4.052)	(−1.706)	(0.584)	(−2.06)	(−2.121)	(−3.198)

Notes: [a] t statistic in brackets.

Table 2.3 Matrix Π: EU, January 1983–December 1996 [a]

	Δp	y	s	$m-p$	r	trend
Δr^*	0.066	–7.670	1.200	–25.313	0.140	0.096
	–0.566	(–1.053)	–1.145	(–1.075)	–0.481	–1.088
$\Delta^2 p$	–1.985	31.467	–9.275	287.689	3.039	–0.977
	(–4.944)	–1.316	(–2.698)	–3.724	–3.185	(–3.362)
Δy	0.007	–0.391	0.053	–1.481	–0.008	0.006
	–2.317	(–2.221)	–2.112	(–2.605)	(–1.102)	–2.579
Δs	0.001	–0.612	–0.005	–0.628	0.001	0.003
	–0.193	(–1.593)	(–0.093)	(–0.505)	–0.047	–0.703
$(m-p)$	0.000	–0.277	0.048	–0.733	0.008	0.003
	(–0.576)	(–7.996)	–9.674	(–6.549)	–5.844	–6.903
Δr	0.122	–1.055	–0.817	–2.958	–0.537	0.012
	–3.908	(–0.543)	(–2.923)	(–0.471)	(–6.919)	–0.491

Note: [a] t statistic in brackets.

assumed for the other variables. The results show a short-term monetary policy mechanism, based on the interest rate and targeted at the stabilisation of the business cycle, of the rate of inflation and of the exchange rate.

The sign of the coefficient associated with the exchange rate indicates that the German interest rate rises in the presence of a real dollar revaluation (lower s). In addition, there is a significantly positive relation with the US interest rate. We may interpret these results as a confirmation that German monetary policy has followed a 'modified' Taylor rule in order to account for the effects of US monetary policy and for changes in the dollar exchange rate.

The results of the equation for the EU in Table 2.2B are quite different. The short-term interest rate does not show any relation with the changes of the other variables with the exception of the rate of growth. The hypothesis that the Taylor rule can be applied to EU monetary policy is therefore rejected. On the other hand, the hypothesis that the US interest rate has no direct impact on the EU interest rate is confirmed but this effect is explained indirectly via the German interest rate. This conclusion can be further clarified by considering the results of the impact matrix estimates for the EU for January 1983–December 1996 (Table 2.3), i.e., the period preceding introduction of the 'hard EMS'. In this sub-period, in contrast with the preceding case, there was a significant impact of the US interest rate on that

Table 2.4 Co-integration vectors – January 1983 – December 1996

	Germany			EU			
	β_1	β_2	β_3	β_1	β_2	β_3	β_4
			Vectors [a]				
r^*	−0.607	0.000	0.000	0.000	0.000	0.000	0.868
	(0.171)						(0.091)
Δp	−2.155	−0.004	−0.016	0.095	−0.004	0.030	−1.829
	(0.248)	(0.002)	(0.003)	(0.018)	(0.003)	(0.002)	(0.118)
y	0.013	−1.000	1.000	0.000	1.000	−1.000	0.000
	(0.013)						
s	2.342	0.000	0.000	1.000	0.000	0.000	0.012
	(2.171)						(0.929)
$(m-p)$	0.000	1.000	0.000	0.000	0.000	1.000	0.000
r	1.000	0.004	0.000	−0.042	0.000	−0.030	1.000
		(0.002)		(0.013)		(0.002)	
$du90$	0.000	0.071	−0.026	−0.425	−0.056	0.005	0.000
		(0.019)	(0.014)	(0.059)	(0.014)	(0.015)	
trend	−0.013	−0.002	−0.001	0.000	−0.001	−0.002	0.000
	(0.013)	(0.000)	(0.000)		(0.000)	(0.000)	

Coefficients of adjustment [b]

Δr^*	0.011	2.336	−0.607	0.310	−1.015	−0.019	−0.010
	(0.711)	(1.870)	(−0.442)	(0.888)	(−0.582)	(−0.012)	(−0.316)
$\Delta^2 p$	0.297	8.859	13.742	−2.374	3.258	18.018	0.598
	(2.529)	(0.916)	(1.294)	(−1.520)	(0.418)	(2.526)	(4.258)
Δy	−0.001	0.236	0.070	−0.016	0.039	0.232	0.003
	(−1.601)	(4.145)	(1.121)	(−2.019)	(0.989)	(6.401)	(3.742)
Δs	0.000	−0.184	−0.022	−0.071	0.441	−0.100	−0.009
	(0.009)	(−2.083)	(−0.223)	(−3.118)	(3.898)	(−0.962)	(−4.217)
$\Delta (m-p)$	0.000	−0.019	−0.039	0.014	−0.027	−0.023	0.000
	(0.809)	(−1.327)	(−2.549)	(3.984)	(−1.538)	(−1.450)	(1.167)
Δr	−0.065	2.304	5.506	−0.319	4.581	0.734	−0.026
	(−6.367)	(2.758)	(5.999)	(−1.573)	(4.526)	(0.793)	(−1.435)

$x^2(5) = 10.02$ $x^2(4) = 3.09$
p–value = 0.07   p–value = 0.54

Notes:
[a] Standard error in brackets.
[b] t statistic in brackets.

of the EU; moreover, there appears a significant impact of the real bilateral E/$ exchange rate.

As had been indicated by the graphic analysis, these two results disappear in more recent years characterised by a greater degree of monetary integration in Europe.

The above results suggest two additional conclusions: (a) deeper European monetary integration, especially after 1987, shifts the management of the EU's external monetary policy relations – particularly vis-à-vis the dollar – increasingly on to German shoulders; (b) the Bundesbank discharged this responsibility by a partial delinking from the US interest rate and attempting to stabilise the bilateral D-mark/dollar exchange rate.

Finally, we may consider the long-term structural relations – co-integration vectors – that appear in Table 2.4. The most relevant results are that – both for Germany (vector $ß_1$) and the EU (vector $ß_4$) – no significant relation between the levels of interest rate and of bilateral real exchange rate is found. Moreover, in Germany as well as in the EU, a significant relation with the rate of inflation is observed.

CONCLUSIONS

A Taylor rule – modified to account for exchange rate changes – explains relatively well the behaviour of the short-term interest rate in Germany, but not in the EU. In the latter case, the growing monetary integration generated by the European exchange agreements leads, during the 'hard EMS' period, to greater independence of the short-term interest rate from that of the USA and to a lower relevance of the exchange rate vis-à-vis the dollar in the implementation of monetary policy. The EU's external monetary relations are thus 'mediated' by the conduct of German monetary policy.

Our results indicate that, in the short run, the German interest rate varied also in relation to *changes* in the D-mark/dollar exchange rate. In the long run, on the other hand, no significant relation is found between the levels of the German interest rate and the D-mark/dollar exchange rate, while there is one between interest rate and inflation. These results are consistent with Henning's (1997b) interpretation of the relation between European monetary integration and monetary relations between Europe and the USA discussed in chapter 1 in that they indicate that over time, as monetary integration has progressed in the EU, Europe, but especially Germany, has managed to decrease its dependence on US monetary policy.

These results may be projected into the future – perhaps a bit mechanically – if we accept the hypothesis that the ECB will not let its monetary conduct diverge significantly from the Bundesbank's and will enjoy the same reputation. Furthermore, the expansion of the euro market will reduce the influence of the extra-European currencies on those of the EU.[7] This does not necessarily lead to the assumption that the ECB will follow a Taylor rule,[8] but it does suggest the following conjecture.

In the medium run (5–10 years) the stabilisation of the exchange rate, particularly against the dollar will probably continue to be *one* objective of European monetary policy.[9] In the longer run, and on the other hand, EMU authorities could adopt an attitude of 'indifference' towards the level of the exchange rate on the grounds of the benefits of the greater size and closeness of the European economy and the relatively minor importance of the exchange rate as a support for growth. The indifference attitude could – and, in our opinion, should – leave room for greater transatlantic monetary co-operation, although this would, of course, also depend on the attitude of the USA. Lastly, in the long term, EMU's policy will have to consider the role of the euro as a 'global' currency alongside the dollar in order to bring the EU's monetary and financial weight into line with that of its real economy.

NOTES

1. It has been suggested that the evolution of the dollar exchange rate vis-à-vis other major currencies can be described through currency cycles (Engel and Hamilton, 1989).
2. We do not intend to consider the relation between nominal interest rate differentials and expected changes in the exchange rate, (i.e. the uncovered interest parity) but rather the effects of the differentials of short-term rates on the level of the exchange rate.
3. The short-term interest rate for the EU is the weighted average of the short-term interest rate of 11 out of 15 member countries of the ERM which entered into EMU from January 1999; the weights are the weights of the EMS currencies from March 1979 to December 1996, normalised in order to take in account the exclusion of the UK. For the years following 1994, when the third review was carried out, the weights of the previous five years were maintained.
4. Times series for short-term interest rates and E/$ exchange rates for the EU are not available for years prior to 1979.
5. In formal terms, Taylor's rule is defined as $r = \bar{r} + a \ (output \ gap) + (1 - a) \ (p - p^*)$, where r is the short-term interest rate and the hyphen indicates average value, the output gap can be calculated with various methods, p is the rate of inflation, p^* is the planned or desired rate of inflation, and a is a parameter that weights the two components of the loss function.
6. The former American treasury secretary, Rubin, has declared repeatedly that the Fed's monetary policy is designed to stabilise GDP growth around its trend value consistent with a programmed level of inflation, and referred explicitly to the Taylor's rule.
7. Similar hypotheses have been suggested by Masson and Turtelboom (1997) in their simulation analysis of the ECB's monetary policy.
8. Masson and Turtelboom (1997) suggest, and simulate, several hypotheses regarding the conduct of the ECB's monetary policy, including 'targeting' the exchange rate.
9. Over the first part of 1999, when the euro was depreciating against the dollar, members of the ECB board on the one hand denied any preoccupation with respect to what appeared to be a 'weak' euro, on the other hand they indicated a medium term 'equilibrium value' for the single currency of 1.07 dollar for euro.

APPENDIX: THE VAR MODEL

The VAR is defined by the following formula:

$$z_t = m + \sum_{j=1}^{p} C_j [z'_{t-j}, du_{90t}, \text{trend}] + Dd_t + \varepsilon_t$$

with

$$z' = [r^*, \Delta p, y, s, m - p, r],$$

where all variables are expressed as logarithms, du_{90} is a dummy variable whose value is equal to 1 from January 1990 and 0 in the preceding periods, d is the vector of the point and seasonal dummies, p equals 6, D is the matrix of the dummies coefficients e $\varepsilon \sim N(0,\Sigma)$.

The ECM (Error Correction Model) is

$$\Delta z_t = \mu + \Pi z_{t-1} \sum_{j=1}^{p} \Gamma_j \Delta z_{t-j} + Dd_t + \varepsilon_t$$

with $\Pi = -(I - C_1 - C_2 - \ldots - C_p) = -\alpha\beta'$, which are, respectively, the $(k \times r)$ matrix of the loadings and the matrix $(r \times k)$, with r equal to the rank of cointegration, $\Gamma_j = -(C_{j+1} + \ldots + C_p)$.

Monthly data were used (source: Datastream). The short-term EU interest rate was calculated as a weighted average of the short-term rates of the ERM member countries, where the weighting represents the current weight of each single currency, given the respective central parity with the ecu. The variables were defined as

> r^* = three month interest rate in the USA
> Δp = first logarithmic difference of the consumer price index
> y = logarithm of the index of industrial production
> s = logarithm of the real bilateral exchange rate vis-à-vis the dollar
> m-p = logarithm of M3 in real terms
> r = three month interest rate

The Johansen cointegration test indicates, at a 5% significance level, the existence of three vectors of cointegration for the German equation and of four vectors for the EU. For the EU, the fourth vector of cointegration is identified by a relation between the rate of inflation, the real bilateral exchange rate and the short-term interest rate. The estimates of the restricted cointegration vectors and the restrictions tests are shown in Table 2.4.

3. Financial markets and monetary integration

Claudio D'Auria and Giovanni B. Pittaluga

INTRODUCTION

The introduction of the euro could promote the development in Europe of the largest financial market in the world and thus support the global role of the common currency.

At the end of 1995 the market value of debt instruments, shares and bank assets issued in Europe amounted to about $27 billion (Table 3.1), which is about three times larger than the aggregate EU GDP. At that time the market value of assets circulating in North America was about $25 billion ($23 billion in the USA alone), against a population and GDP similar to those of the EU. Nevertheless, Table 3.1 indicates that – aside from total volume – the composition of the EU countries' financial assets was very different from that in North America, and especially in the USA. While private investment in Europe is financed mainly by bank loans, US firms preferentially issue direct liabilities, bonds and shares in the first place. The consequence is a pronounced segmentation of European financial markets. The majority of debt instruments circulating in the EU consists of government bonds and instruments issued by financial intermediaries. At the end of 1994, the proportion of corporate financial liabilities represented by debt instruments was 18.8% in the USA, 5.7% in France, and less than 1% in Germany. The limited share of market instruments in business financing is also related to their short maturity; whereas European firms resort heavily to short-term bank loans, American firms typically issue commercial paper.

Given the current context, the crucial issue is whether, how and how quickly the introduction of the euro will have a significant impact on the financial structure of the European countries. The following sections address these questions.

Changes in the financial structure have implications for the transmission of monetary policy. The development of broad and thick money markets in the EU can have a major impact not only on real interest rate levels but also on

Table 3.1 Capital markets indicators (1995)

	Population (mill.)	GDP	Reserve bonds less gold (US$ bil.)	Capitalisation of capital market (US$ bil.)	Debt instruments [b]			Bank assets (US$ bil.)[b]	Bonds, shares and bank assets (US$ bil.)[b]	Bonds, shares and bank assets in % of GDP [c]
					Public (US$ bil.)	Private (US$ bil.)	Total (US$ bil.)[a]			
EU 15 [d]	369	8.427	376	3.779	4.814	3.859	8.673	14.818	27.270	323.6
EU 11 [e]	286	6.804	285	2.119	3.910	3.084	6.993	11.972	21.084	309.9
EU 8 [f]	182	5.055	199	1.694	2.330	2.611	4.941	9.456	16.091	318.3
North America	388	8.066	107	7.315	7.332	4.412	11.744	5.652	24.711	306.4
Canada	30	566	15	366	589	93	682	516	1.565	276.6
Mexico	95	246	17	91	31	24	54	137	282	114.3
USA	263	7.254	75	6.858	6.712	4.295	11.008	5.000	22.865	315.2
Japan	125	5.114	183	3.667	3.450	1.876	5.326	7.382	16.375	320.2

Notes:

[a] Internal and external debt instruments based on nationality of issuer.

[b] The data include all banks except the following cases: commercial and savings banks for Denmark, commercial banks for Canada, Greece, Luxembourg and Mexico; authorised banks for Japan; commercial and savings banks and savings co-operatives for Sweden; commercial and savings bank, savings and loan associations for the USA.

[c] Sum of share market capitalisation, amount of debt instruments and bank assets.

[d] Austria, Belgium, Denkark, Finland, France, Germany, Greece, Luxembourg, Ireland, Italy, Netherlands, Portugal, Spain, Sweden, UK.

[e] Austria, Belgium, Finland, France, Germany, Ireland, Italy, Luxembourg, Netherlands, Portugal and Spain.

[f] Austria, Belgium, Finland, France, Germany, Ireland, Luxembourg and Netherlands.

Sources:

Bank for International Settlements; Bank of England, *Quarterly Bulletin* (November 1995); Bank of Japan, *Economic Statistics Monthly* (May 1996); Central Bank of Ireland, *Quarterly Bulletin* (Winter 1995); International Finance Corporation, *Emerging Stock Markets Factbook 1996*; Organization for Economic Cooperation and Development, *Bank Profitability: Financial Statements of Banks, 1985–1994*; and International Monetary Fund, *International Financial Statistics* and *World Economic Outlook Databases*.

the response of market and bank interest rates to monetary stimuli. Because changes in the financial structure may affect the individual EU countries with varying intensity and speed, marked asymmetries in the transmission of monetary policy measures taken by the ECB may occur. This aspect is also analysed below.

TRENDS IN THE EUROPEAN FINANCIAL SYSTEMS AND MARKET DEVELOPMENT

The differences between the financial systems of continental Europe and of the Anglo-Saxon countries are well-known. In the former, the banks continue to predominate on the market. This is illustrated by comparing the structures of corporate financial liabilities (Figure 3.1).

The structure of European financial systems will doubtless retain some of its special features in the short–medium run. Besides, these features cannot be understood separately from other aspects (mainly the labour market and labour relations) of continental European economies. It has been demonstrated [1] that it is easier in the bank-centred countries than in the market-centred ones to achieve an inter-temporal risk sharing between bank and company and between company and labour as banks smooth the impact of restrictive monetary policy on the loan rates to business and the latter smooth the impact of recessionary phases on the employment level.

The likely retention of a central role of the banks in the EMU's financial

Figure 3.1 Composition of corporate financial liabilities: 1994

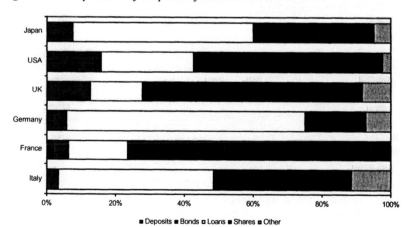

■ Deposits ■ Bonds □ Loans ■ Shares ■ Other

system should not hinder the development of a broad and thick European financial market. It is likely, in fact, that the banks, faced with a smaller share of traditional transactions, will develop new areas of activity, such as investment banking, asset management and the supply of insurance.

The introduction of the euro should support the development of a broad and efficient European financial market for at least five reasons.

In the first place, the elimination of exchange rate changes among the EMU member countries should promote a gradual integration of national financial markets.

In the second place, the role and weight of the public sector in the financial systems of many European countries will shrink. It is well known that in countries such as Italy and Germany many banks are publicly or semi-publicly owned. This feature, the result of choices made in past decades designed to guarantee bank stability,[2] was bound to have an impact on the allocation of funds.

A third way in which the EMU will exert a positive influence on the development of an efficient European financial market is linked to the impact of the new information technology on the relations between banks and business. The lower information cost on the credit-worthiness of the issuer should make it more advantageous for business firms to issue securities.

In the fourth place, the process of privatisation of the banks that is under way in some countries should lead to new forms of market control of the banks' performance. Banks will be compelled, over a relatively short period, to pay increasing attention to return over capital and should find it more costly to supply products and services carrying lower profit margins.

Lastly a stable monetary environment (such as the EMU should guarantee) by itself favours the development of financial markets. High inflation rates go along with high price volatility of prices[3] and of long-term interest rates (see Figure 3.2).

It follows that, in a stable price environment, the risk premium on long-term maturities will be smaller and the public's propensity to hold such maturities increase.[4]

In an efficient financial market, businesses should increase their propensity to borrow through direct instruments for two main reasons. On the one hand, given larger security markets, investors should expect a smaller liquidity premium for a given amount of securities. On the other hand, the possibility issuing securities with a wider range of characteristics will decrease the preference mismatch between supply and demand and should lead to a reduction of the cost of financing through direct instruments.

The development of an efficient European money market will increase the

Figure 3.2 Inflation and volatility of long-term interest rates

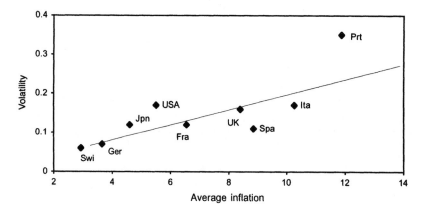

competitive pressure on the banks and especially on the conditions under which banks are prepared to finance business and collect funds.

How is the above-outlined scenario for development of the financial markets likely to develop in a relatively short time?

At present, stock market capitalisation is much higher in the USA than in Europe. In 1995, it amounted to $7 trillion in the USA (about 48% of financial assets in circulation), while in the EU it was less than $4 trillion (26% of financial assets in circulation) (see Table 3.2).

European figures, however, should be considered in greater detail. In 1995 the ratio of stock market capitalisation to GDP for UK firms was larger than in the USA,[5] while the continental European countries were present only marginally in the stock market. The London market represented only 40% of total EU stock market transactions in 1996, and was 12 percentage points larger than the Frankfurt market, four times that of Paris and ten times that of Milan (see Table 3.3).

The UK market's relevance is also demonstrated by the fact that. in 1993, the ratio of stock market capitalisation to GDP declined from 39% of the EU's total to 26% of the total of the member countries of the EMU. In fact, as the UK has not joined, the euro's ratio of market capitalisation to GDP will be three times less than that of Japan and the USA (see Table 3.4).

These data suggest that, to the extent that the UK will not join EMU, the development of a stock market of a size comparable to those of the USA and Japan could require a long time.

Leaving the role of the UK aside, the development of a sizeable European

Table 3.2 Capital markets indicators, EU, USA and Japan: 1995

| | Stock market capitalisation (US$ bil.) | Share % | Debt instruments [a] | | | | Bank assets (US$ bil.) | Share % | Total shares, debt instruments & bank assets (US$ bil.) | Share % |
			Public (US$ bil.)	Private (US$ bil.)	Total (US$ bil.)	Share %				
EU	3,778.5	26.4	4,814.4	3,858.6	8,673.0	34.7	14,818.0	54.5	27,269.5	41.0
UK	1,407.7	9.8	429.9	395.8	825.7	3.3	2,424.4	8.9	4,657.8	7.0
UE 11	2,119.4	14.8	3,909.7	3,083.5	6,993.2	28.0	11,971.6	44.0	21,084.2	31.7
Germany	577.4	4.0	893.6	1,286.0	2,179.6	8.7	3,752.4	13.8	6,509.4	9.8
France	522.1	3.7	681.9	803.6	1,485.5	5.9	2,923.0	10.7	4,930.6	7.4
Italy	209.5	1.5	1,222.0	396.2	1,618.2	6.5	1,513.5	5.6	3,341.2	5.0
USA	6,857.6	47.9	6,712.4	4,295.1	11,007.5	44.0	5,000.0	18.4	22,865.1	34.4
Japan	3,667.3	25.6	3,450.3	1,875.5	5,325.8	21.3	7,382.2	27.1	16,375.3	24.6
Total (UE+USA+JPN)	14,303.4	100.0	14,977.1	10,029.2	25,006.3	100.0	27,200.2	100.0	66,509.9	100.0

Note: [a] Debt instruments issued on domestic market and on the international market by nationality of issuer.

Source: Schinasi and Prati (1997).

Table 3.3 Stock markets in the EU, USA and Japan 1996

| | Firms quoted | | Capitalisation of domestic firms | | Annual transactions | | | | |
| | Domestic | Foreign | Million Ecu | % on GDP | Domestic | Foreign | Total | % of EU | % of GDP |
					Million ECU				
Total EU	3,997	2,972	3,590,614	52.83	1,669,560	614,006	2,283,566	100.0	24.6
London	557	833	1,368,000	153.61	335,644	580,777	916,421	40.1	37.7
Frankfurt	681	1,290	531,553	28.34	621,454	18,778	640,232	28.0	33.1
Paris	686	187	472,426	38.48	220,608	4,828	225,436	9.9	18.0
Milan	244	4	206,997	21.79	82,532	18	82,550	3.6	8.7
New York	2,617	290	5,395,889	90.23	3,014,383	190,392	3,204,775	140.3	50.4
Tokyo	1,766	67	2,374,733	64.88	738,711	1,214	739,925	32.4	20.2
Total (UE+USA+JPN)	8,380	3,329	11,361,236		5,422,654	805,612	6,228,266		

Sources: Federation of European Stock Exchanges; Federation of International Stock Exchanges; Nasdaq; New York Stock Exchange; Tokyo Stock Exchange.

Table 3.4 Stock market capitalisation in the EU, USA and Japan (1993)

	No.of domestic firms	Market capitalisation (US$ mill.) (a)	Share %	GDP (US$ mill.) (b)	Ratio in % (a)/(b)*100
EU	4,458	2,831,826	20.3	7,223,269	39.20
UK	1,646	1,151,646	8.2	1,042,700	110.45
UE 11	2,307	1,518,700	10.9	5,749,967	26.41
Germany	426	463,476	3.3	1,902,995	24.36
France	472	456,111	3.3	1,289,235	35.38
Italy	210	136,153	1.0	1,134,980	12.00
USA	7,246	5,136,199	36.8	6,387,686	80.41
Japan	2,155	2,999,756	21.5	3,926,668	76.39
World total	28,768	13,963,831	100.0	23,050,405	60.58

Source: International Finance Corporation (1996)

financial market may well be inhibited by legislative, regulatory and fiscal hurdles for cross-border investments. These hurdles have a special impact on the homogeneity of the financial instruments issued in the different countries, leading to persistent capital market segmentation.

We have already mentioned that, unlike their American counterparts, EU firms scarcely resort to financing through commercial paper or other money market instruments. This is largely due to the inadequate development of the EU's money market.

Two measures can contribute to broaden and thicken this type of market: (a) changes in the management of monetary policy; specifically, a decision by the ECB to use swaps as the main tool of monetary policy should provide an incentive for the development of a repo market; (b) full implementation of the Target project and, hence, of the development of a single European banking market.

The development of an efficient money market has a double impact on business financing. On the one hand, it facilitates the issue of direct short-term securities, such as commercial paper. On the other hand, as it increases elasticity of supply of liquid assets it makes it easier to hold longer-term securities.[6]

THE IMPACT ON EUROPEAN BANKING SYSTEMS

In addition to its impact on specific aspects of bank management (e.g., earnings from exchange transactions, changes in data processing and accounting), EMU is bound to have a weighty impact on the structure of the European banking sector. Specifically, given the likely increase of the range of financial and savings instruments a simultaneous structural decrease of demand for bank loans and deposits is to be expected. This will press banks to lower the interest rate on loans and raise the deposit rate.

Banks will face greater 'internal' competition, in addition to sharper 'external' competition following the development of money and financial markets, which will increase the homogeneity of the products offered. One of the main effects of the increasing 'external' and 'internal' competition should be a gradual lowering of margins, particularly of the interest margin, which will prompt the banks to seek improvements in their internal efficiency.

The banks of the main continental European countries display higher operating costs than banks in the UK and the USA. Specifically, there is a higher incidence of such costs on intermediation margins (Table 3.5). Efficiency gains for European banks can occur essentially on two levels which are to some extent linked: at the level of the single firm and at multi-firm level.

At the level of the single firm, the pressure of competition and the resulting narrowing of bank margins give rise to three types of response. In the first place, European banks will likely raise labour productivity and reduce operating costs. These attempts could well be frustrated in many European countries by rigidities in labour contracts legislation and, in some cases, in labour reallocation. A second response might see banks increasing their profit margins by raising the degree of risk of their transactions. Such a strategy would produce negative repercussions on the solidity of the European banking system and supervisory authorities will probably discourage this type of response.

A third possibility of recouping profit margins is linked to the introduction of new products. German banks have pursued this strategy type in recent years, at least those among them that acquired English merchant banks and thus have entered the investment banking sector. Asset management represents another area for broadening European banks' activities, also in view of the smaller degree of coverage of public social insurance schemes and of demographic trends.

This latter response strategy is, to some extent, connected with the first one. The introduction of new products and entry into new activity markets requires huge investments in technological innovation. These imply

Table 3.5 Labour force and total personnel costs in the banking sector

	Employees[a]						Personnel costs[b]		
	1980 c	1990	1994 d	Peak			1980/82 e	1986/88	1992/94 f
	(numbers 000)			numbers (000)	year	var. (%) g	as percentage of intermediate margin		
Belgium	68	79	76	79	1990	-5	41	33	39
France	399	399	382	401	1988	-5	47	44	44
Germany [h]	532	621	658	658	1994	-	48	44	39
Italy	277	324	332	333	1993	-	46	48	44
Netherlands	113	118	112	119	1991	-6	42	41	38
Spain	252	252	245	256	1991	-4	47	43	37
UK	324	425	368	430	1989	-15	47	38	36
Japan [i]	612	597	618	622	1993	-0	44	33	39
USA	1900	1979	1891	2156	1987	-12	36	31	27

Notes:
[a] Deposit banks; for Japan credit cooperatives are excluded.
[b] For Belgium and Netherlands, all banks; for other countries, commercial banks by OECD definition.
[c] For France 1985; for Netherlands, 1984; for Spain 1981.
[d] For Italy and Spain, 1993.
[e] For France and Belgium, 1981–82.
[f] For Belgium 1992.
[g] From peak level to most recent data.
[h] For employment, only West Germany.
[i] The data for employees do not include Credit Unions.

Sources: For personnel costs, OECD; for employees, British Bankers Association, Building Societies Association and national data.

substituting capital for labour and are based on the possibility of squeezing labour costs and lowering the age average of personnel.

EMU not only increases competitive pressure on the banks, but also entails a significant broadening of the size and range of markets. This will make it possible to exploit economies of scale and scope. Exploitation of scale economies – spurred by market globalisation even before the advent of EMU – has led to a world-wide process of growth of the average size of banking firms. This is shown by the decline in the number of banks in recent years in nearly all industrialised countries. Table 3.6 shows that, in 1995, the number of banks was smaller than the peak reached during the 15 preceding years, especially in the main European countries where it declined between 15% (Italy) and 43% (France).

Table 3.6 Number of banks and concentration of the banking sector

	Number of banks [a]						First five concentrations [b]		
	1980 [b]	1990	1995 [c]	Peak			1980 [d]	1990	1995 [e]
	number			number	year	var. (%) [f]	% share of total assets		
Belgium	148	129	159	163	1992	−8	64 (76)	58 (74)	59 (73)
France	1033	786	593	1033	1984	−43	57 (69)	52 (66)	47 (63)
Germany [g]	5355	4180	3487	5355	1980	−35	n.d.	n.d.	17 (28)
Italy	1071	1067	941	1109	1987	−15	26 (42)	24 (39)	29 (45)
Netherlands	200	180	174	200	1980	−13	73 (81)	77 (86)	81 (89)
Spain [h]	357	327	318	378	1982	−16	38 (58)	38 (58)	49 (62)
UK	796	665	560	796	1983	−30	63 (80)	58 (70)	57 (78)
Japan [i]	618	605	571	618	1980	−8	25 (40)	30 (45)	27 (43)
USA	95875	27864	23854	35875	1980	−34	9 (14)	9 (15)	15 (21)

Notes:
[a] Deposit banks; for Japan, the different types of co-operatives credit are excluded.
[b] Data between parentheses refer to the first ten banks.
[c] For Italy, 1983.
[d] For France, 1984; for Italy, 1983; for Netherlands, 1985.
[e] For Japan, UK and Belgium, 1994.
[f] Between peak and most recent data.
[g] For number of banks, only West Germany.
[h] Concentration data cover only commercial and savings banks.
[i] Excluding Credit Unions.

Sources: For personnel costs, OECD; for employees, British Bankers Association, Building Societies Association and national data.

The decline of the number of banks has entailed a gradual increase of the banking market concentration. This is largely attributable to the large number of mergers and acquisitions in recent years, as shown in Table 3.7. The ongoing restructuring of the banking sector is clearly a world-wide phenomenon. In Europe, this process will be speeded up by EMU and by the integration of the European banking markets.

At the multi-bank level higher profit margins may be secured by cross-border alliances, in addition to mergers and acquisitions. which will allow products and services to be offered over a much larger area.

THE IMPACT ON THE TRANSMISSION OF MONETARY POLICY

The likely structural changes of the European financial system described above will produce repercussions on the transmission of monetary policy. The

Table 3.7 Mergers and acquisition in the banking sector [a]

| | Number | | | | Value | | | | | | | |
| | | | | | Billion dollars | | | | per cent [b] | | | |
	1989-90	1991-92	1993-94	1995-96 [c]	1989-90	1991-92	1993-94	1995-96 [c]	1989-90	1991-92	1993-94	1995-96 [c]
Belgium	11	22	18	12	0.0	1.0	0.6	0.4	0.2	14.1	7.0	7.9
France	52	133	71	43	2.7	2.4	0.5	3.2	5.1	4.3	1.0	10.4
Germany	19	71	83	27	1.1	3.5	1.9	0.7	4.5	6.5	7.6	3.5
Italy	41	122	105	65	8.2	5.3	6.1	3.0	22.7	15.6	17.7	19.7
Netherlands	12	20	13	7	10.9	0.1	0.1	0.8	56.3	0.2	0.5	9.5
Spain	30	76	44	26	4.0	4.3	4.5	2.1	18.5	13.5	21.5	34.1
UK	86	71	40	28	6.4	7.5	3.3	21.7	2.6	6.5	3.4	12.4
Japan	8	22	8	17	31.2	0.0	2.2	33.8	71.8	0.3	18.8	77.0
USA	1,500	1,350	1,470	1,170	27.8	56.8	55.3	82.5	7.3	18.7	9.0	13.5

Notes:
[a] Contracts signed or being signed.
[b] Out of total mergers and acquisitions in the entire sector.
[c] As of April 1996.

Source: Security Data Company.

Figure 3.3 Inflation and volatility of real short-term interest rates

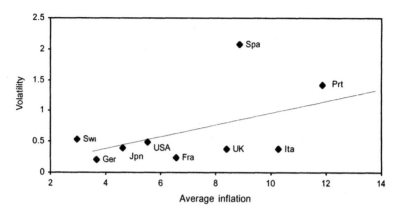

first affects the effectiveness of the monetary stimuli. Presumably, in order to attain a given target in the EMU, changes of real interest rates will be milder than those required to obtain the same effect in the single countries. There are three main reasons for this: (a) stable prices enhance the anti-inflationary credibility of the monetary authorities; the high correlation between the average rate of inflation and volatility of real short-term interest rates is an indication of this (Figure 3.3); (b) for a wider range of highly substitutable financial instruments any given change of money market rates is reflected more directly on the whole range of maturities;[7] (c) a higher degree of inter-bank competition leads to a higher response of bank interest rates to changes in monetary policy.[8]

While it is true that the development of financial and money markets should make the EU's monetary policy more effective, it is equally true that changes in the financial system can affect the different EMU member countries with varying degrees of swiftness and intensity. The problem arises, therefore, of whether the persistence of significant differences in the structure of the national financial systems could generate asymmetries in the effectiveness of the monetary stimuli.

The stimuli of monetary policy are reflected on the real economy not only through changes in the cost of financing but also through the credit channel. This channel is important because an imperfect distribution of information raises the cost of external financing above the cost of internal financing.

Theory has identified two main ways in which the cost differential between external and internal financing may be corrected: (a) the emergence of liquidity constraints for the firms; (b) the existence of firms that depend on bank credit. Different types of firms exhibit different degrees of substitutability of the

Table 3.8 Distribution of employees by size class of firm, 1990

	Percent of firms with less than 10 employees	Percent of firms with 10–499 employees	Percent of firms with 500 or more employees
EU 12	30.3	39.4	30.3
Belgium	17.0	47.7	35.3
France	28.0	41.0	31.0
Fermany	18.3	45.6	36.1
Greece	n.d.	82.7	17.3
Italy	42.5	37.8	19.7
Netherlands	30.1	45.4	24.5
Portugal	24.3	54.7	21.0
Spain	45.8	38.9	15.3
UK	27.1	39.1	33.8
USA	12.0	41.4	46.6

Source: European Commission, *Enterprises in Europe*, Third Report, Brussels (1994).

alternative forms of financing. It follows that the credit channel should play a more important role in the presence of large numbers of firms – above all small-size firms – for which it is more costly to obtain non-bank external financing.

As shown in Table 3.8, in industrialized countries, small and medium enterprises (with fewer than 500 employees) are more prominent in Europe than in the USA. Nevertheless, significant differences can be noted even among European countries; in Spain, Italy, Portugal and Greece, more than 80% of the labour force is employed by small and medium enterprises. The proportion is much smaller in Belgium, Germany and Luxembourg.

The share of small enterprises constrains the financial structure of the economy. In countries where this share is relevant the development of market financing instruments is limited. Table 3.9 shows that in these countries (especially Italy, Portugal and Greece), development of the stock market is limited when compared not only with the USA and UK but with the other European countries as well. Small and medium enterprises not only find it difficult to finance themselves through market instruments but they establish privileged – generally long-term – relations with local banks as this type of bank has lower costs for obtaining information on local enterprises and for monitoring them.

Table 3.9 Development of capital markets, 1995

	Number of firms	Stockmarket capitalisation (US$ bil.)	GDP (US$ bil.)	Capitalisation as % of GDP
Belgium	143	105.0	269.2	39.0
France	450	522.1	1549.2	33.7
Germany	678	577.4	2420.5	23.9
Greece	99	10.2	111.8	9.1
Italy	250	209.5	1091.1	19.2
Netherlands	387	356.5	396.9	89.8
Portugal	169	18.4	103.2	17.8
Spain	362	197.8	557.4	35.5
UK	2078	1407.7	1099.7	128.0
USA	7671	6857.6	7254.0	94.5
Japan	2263	3667.3	5114.0	71.7

Sources: International Finance Corporation, *Emerging Stock Markets Factbook*, 1996; OECD, *OECD Financial Statistics*, part 1; *Financial Statistics Monthly*, various numbers; and OECD, *Non-financial Enterprises Financial Statements*, 1995.

It should not be surprising, then, that in countries where small and medium enterprises prevail, we also find a great number of small-size banks and a low degree of concentration of the banking system (Table 3.10).

It has been pointed out[9] that where small and medium enterprises, and thus also small banks, predominate, the credit channel is more important and thus, *ceteris paribus*, monetary policy stimuli should be transmitted more effectively. According to this point of view, in the event of a monetary squeeze it is the small banks, not the bigger ones, that would find it exceedingly difficult to obtain liquid assets on the money market (e.g., by issuing high-denomination CDs). Inasmuch as they are affected by restrictive measures, small banks would thus be forced to raise the interest rate on loans and resort to credit rationing more than the large banks. With this perspective we are led to conclude that, in economies with greater incidence of small and medium enterprise and small banks, monetary stimuli are more effective. It follows that in EMU the countries that are more heavily affected by centralised monetary policy will be the Mediterranean ones, above all Italy, which we will take as a case study to clarify the point.

Table 3.10 Distribution of banks by size, 1995

	Sample of banks covered by OECD data	Total assets [a] (billion of dollars)	Share of total assets of banks amalgamated into the first three institutions [b] %	Share of total assets of credit institutions amalgamated into the first three commercial banks [b] %
Belgium	All banks	843	44	44
France	»	3798	64	33
Germany	»	4151	89	24
Greece	Commercial banks	70	98	73
Italy	All banks	1520	36	28
Netherlands	»	917	59	59
Portugal	»	201	38	n.a.
Spain	»	951	50	34
UK	Commercial banks	1184	29	n.a.
USA	»	4149	13	10
Japan	»	6734	28	n.a.

Notes:
[a] Exchange rates are from *IMF Financial Statistics Yearbook*, 1996.
[b] Cf. Barth, Nolle and Rice, 1997, Table 3.

This point of view is open to several objections. In the first place, at least in Italy, small-size banks carry sizeable reserves of secondary liquidity. These reserves are held in the form of positive net interbank balances and the high ratio of public (i.e., extremely liquid) securities to assets. Table 3.11 shows that the small and minor Italian banks are carried on the interbank market nearly always as net creditors. Table 3.11 also shows that, at the end of 1996, the securities/deposit ratio was 61.7% for small banks and 49.5% for minor banks, both figures far higher than the system's average. The availability of a large amount of liquid means of payment favours small banks over big ones in case of a liquidity squeeze. It is thus difficult to assert that in Italy small banks, more than any other class of bank, tend to tighten their loan terms in case of a restrictive monetary policy stance. If anything, the opposite is true, that is small banks smooth the impact of monetary policy on the real economy. This is confirmed indirectly by looking at the rigidity of loan interest rates by size of loan. Figure 3.4 reveals that bank loan rates are less volatile for smaller loan amounts, i.e., those typical for the local banks' clients. As shown by some

Table 3.11 Italy: interbank ratios and securities/deposits ratios

	Interbank ratios (billion lire)			Securities/deposits lire
	Assets	Liabilities	Balance	
	Major banks			
1992	59,059	59,577	−518	37.36
1993	64,781	59,384	5,397	29.25
1994	65,867	57,608	8,259	32.68
1995	41,756	47,064	−5,308	29.83
1996	52,412	60,282	−7,870	30.42
	Large banks			
1992	24,782	23,767	1,015	32.2
1993	26,836	31,621	−4,785	39.5
1994	24,632	30,584	−5,952	42.9
1995	28,386	25,758	2,628	35.8
1996	35,065	32,968	2,097	36.2
	Medium banks			
1992	32,659	35,707	−3,048	34.9
1993	30,257	39,663	−9,406	40.3
1994	28,385	40,331	−11,946	42.0
1995	33,598	44,928	−11,330	38.3
1996	37,552	48,576	−11,024	42.6
	Small banks			
1992	29,908	29,768	140	47.8
1993	36,053	35,634	419	46.6
1994	34,453	28,767	5,686	56.0
1995	35,724	36,372	−648	56.0
1996	41,041	40,153	888	61.7
	Minor banks			
1992	11,441	10,502	939	56.3
1993	13,178	12,784	394	56.0
1994	12,099	9,381	2,718	56.2
1995	12,515	11,948	567	44.4
1996	15,340	12,482	2,858	49.5

Figure 3.4 Interest rates by size of loans

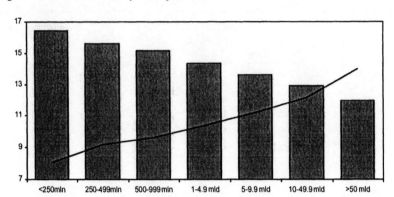

authors,[10] local banks, thanks to their long-term relations with small enterprises, insure the latter against the risk of high loan rate volatility by applying interest rates higher than the equilibrium rates during monetary expansion, and lower-than-equilibrium rates during monetary restrictions.

As a consequence it can be argued that the credit channel could lower the effectiveness of European monetary policy in Italy as compared to other countries. On the other hand the effectiveness of European monetary policy in Italy will be raised as a result of the peculiar financial structure of Italian firms as the latter resort to external financing (short-term bank loans or long-term loans with rates indexed to short-term financial parameters) to a greater extent than other European countries. It follows that, in a monetary restriction the average cost of financing of Italian firms, will rise more markedly than elsewhere. Hence, in Italy monetary policy may turn out to be being more effective than in other countries, not so much through the credit channel as through the traditional channel of the cost of credit.

This distinction, however, is bound to shrink in the future. In a medium-term perspective the structure of external financing of firms may change, while it is unlikely that there will be significant changes in the relations between bank and firm, and above all between small banks and small firms. At present most of bank loans owed by Italian firms are short-term and at indexed rates. As inflationary expectations in Italy are significantly lowered with EMU membership, it is plausible that the share of fixed-rate long-term bank loans will increase tangibly. As soon as these conditions apply, the effectiveness of European monetary policy in Italy will converge towards average figures via the cost-of-credit channel.

CONCLUSIONS

The introduction of the euro will favour the development of broad and thick financial markets in Europe. However, the intensity and pace of this development could be negatively influenced by the persistence of normative, fiscal and regulatory hurdles to cross-border investments. Negative influences can also arise from the UK failing to join EMU in a reasonable time span.

Regardless of the intensity and pace of the structural changes of Europe's financial systems these changes will inevitably generate a wider range of financial market instruments. As a result, the banks will be exposed to growing 'external' competition; specifically, the greater possibilities for firms to finance themselves in ways other than through banks will favour a reduction of the cost of external financing, particularly of bank loans. A single currency and the growing homogeneity of the products offered in money markets will also increase 'internal' competition among banks.

Both forms of competition will shrink bank margins. This will force the banks to improve their internal efficiency and reduce costs of production. Tangible benefits will arise from exploitation of economies of scale and scope, both of which will be made possible by larger markets as well as by technological innovations.

In market-oriented financial systems (USA and UK) a significant bank restructuring has taken place, the tangible shrinking of payrolls has followed the introduction of advanced technology and a great number of mergers and acquisitions. The extent of this has increased significantly.

The restructuring of the banking sector has been slower in continental Europe but it is being accelerated by EMU and by the changes in the structure of the financial systems. These changes are unlikely to affect European countries in the same way and to the same extent. For instance, in the case of Italy it may be that the development of financial markets will be inhibited by the structure of manufacturing industry given the large share of SMEs which, *ceteris paribus*, are less interested in direct financing instruments.

Inasmuch as changes in the financial systems will affect the various countries in different ways, homogenisation of financial structures within EMU will be only partial. This is bound to have inevitable repercussions on the transmission of monetary policy. In the first place, there should be a more pronounced response of short-term interest rates – and hence of the cost of financing – to monetary stimuli. Countries (such as Italy) in which a large part of firms' external financing is short-term debt or short-term indexed loans should experience this more intensely.

In the second place, the credit channel should maintain greater importance where firms with a high degree of bank dependency, such as the SMEs, prevail. In some cases, however, small banks soften, rather than accentuate, the impact of the monetary cycle on loan terms. In this way, they mitigate the effectiveness of monetary stimuli.

NOTES

1. Cf. Allen and Gale (1994); Ferri, Morelli and Pittaluga (1997).
2. As is well known, following the great crash of 1929 there was a widespread need to assure stability of the banking system. This was assured in the USA by introducing deposit insurance and in Europe by turning ownership of a large part of the banking system from private to public.
3. On this point, Okun (1971), Logue and Willett (1976) and Foster (1978).
4. Lower risk lowers the degree of risk aversion.
5. In 1996 the capitalisation of the 550 domestic firms quoted in London amounted to 154% of GDP while the 2,600 firms quoted in New York represented only 90%.
6. It is possible to view the exponential growth of the derivatives market in a somewhat different light. At the end of 1995, capital supporting swap operations amounted to over $15 trillion, of which 80% represented interest-rate swaps, and the rest currency swaps. With the launching of the EMU, the amount of exchange derivative operations should decrease, at least for the share that covers transactions between currencies joining the euro. On the other hand, operations on interest rates will not converge completely at the beginning of Phase 3. The differential among the European interest rates should reflect the risk premium associated with each member country, which should converge only in the medium run if at all.
7. Cf. Tobin (1969).
8. Cf. Cottarelli and Kourelis (1994).
9. Cf. Kashyap and Stein (1997).
10. Cf., among others, Ferri and Pittaluga (1996).

4. Europe's unemployment: a review of the debate

Pier Carlo Padoan

INTRODUCTION

European unemployment – its causes and remedies – is, with the exception of the EMU, the subject that has most intrigued economists and policy-makers in recent years.[1] There is a two-way relation between single currency and employment. On the one hand, as shown by the theory of optimal currency areas,[2] a monetary union cannot function satisfactorily if the labour market displays excessive rigidity and too little mobility. Thus, from this point of view, to the extent to which it is partly a result of such rigidities, European unemployment represents a major barrier to the euro's success. At the same time, the way in which the single currency is managed will affect the possibilities for reducing European unemployment. An evaluation of this two-way relation between single currency and employment, however, requires at least a quick analysis of the causes of this unemployment.

There is no simple and, above all, single-cause analysis of unemployment from which equally clear and straightforward remedies can be derived. On the contrary, present European unemployment is a result of interconnected mechanisms in different markets – i.e., not only in the labour market.

STYLISED FACTS

It has become a widespread habit to discuss the unemployment problem in Europe by contrasting it with the US case. We do not intend to dodge this ritual but we will also highlight the different national situations within the EU, as both approaches are relevant for an understanding of the phenomenon.

The first approach implies that the common characteristics of European unemployment are of primary importance, while the second approach, by emphasising national differences, allows us to identify some of the causes of this unemployment, and to consider some possible implications for EMU. In

Table 4.1 Unemployment rates (% of total labour force)

	Levels				Absolute variations			
	1970	1980	1990	1997	1970–80	1980–90	1990–97	1970–97
USA	4.8	7.0	5.5	4.9	2.2	-1.5	-0.6	0.1
Austria	1.5	1.9	3.2	4.2	0.4	1.3	1.0	2.7
Belgium	1.9	7.9	8.7	12.4	6.0	0.8	3.7	10.5
Finland	1.9	4.6	3.4	14.7	2.7	-1.2	11.3	12.8
France	2.5	6.3	8.9	12.3	3.8	2.6	3.4	9.8
Germany	0.6	3.2	6.2	9.8	2.6	3.0	3.6	9.2
Ireland	5.8	7.3	13.7	10.5	1.5	6.4	-3.2	4.7
Italy	5.3	7.5	11.2	12.2	2.2	3.7	1.0	6.9
Luxembourg	n.a.	0.6	1.0	2.9	0.4	1.9		
Netherlands	1.0	6.0	7.5	5.4	5.0	1.5	-2.1	4.4
Portugal	2.5	7.7	4.5	7.0	5.2	-3.2	2.5	4.5
Spain	2.5	11.1	15.9	20.6	8.6	4.8	4.7	18.1
EU 11	2.6	5.8	7.7	10.0	3.3	1.8	2.3	7.4
Denmark	0.7	6.9	8.3	6.1	6.2	1.4	-2.2	5.4
Greece	4.2	2.8	7.0	10.4	-1.4	4.2	3.4	6.2
UK	2.2	5.6	5.5	7.1	3.4	-0.0	1.6	4.9
Sweden	1.5	2.0	1.7	8.3	0.5	-0.3	6.6	6.8
EU 15	2.4	5.4	7.1	9.6	3.0	1.7	2.5	7.2

Source: OECD, *Labour Force Statistics*, 1997.

fact, one of the problems that single currency management must face is that
of asymmetric shocks. In this context, it is the differences within EMU that
will be relevant.

Table 4.1 shows the trend of unemployment rates in the USA, the EMU
group of 11 and the EU of 15, in addition to the trends in the individual
countries. The first aspect to be considered is the difference between the
European and US trends. In the latter, unemployment has fluctuated around a
constant value and has been clearly declining over the recent past. In Europe,
unemployment has been rising – although with some fluctuations – and has
settled at a double-digit level, without significant differences between the

Table 4.2 Long-term unemployment (% of total unemployment)

	1983	1990	1995	1996	1997
USA	13.30	5.60	9.70	9.50	8.70
Austria	n.a.	n.a.	27.50	25.60	28.70
Belgium	64.80	68.70	62.40	61.30	60.50
Finland	19.20	n.a.	37.00	39.30	31.10
France	42.20	38.00	42.30	39.50	41.20
Germany	41.60	46.80	48.70	47.80	n.d.
Ireland	36.70	66.00	61.40	59.50	57.00
Italy	58.20	69.80	63.60	65.60	66.30
Netherlands	48.80	49.30	46.80	50.00	49.10
Portugal	n.a.	44.80	50.90	53.10	55.60
Spain	52.40	54.00	56.90	55.70	55.50
EU 11	45.49	54.68	49.75	49.74	49.44
Greece	33.20	49.80	51.40	56.70	55.70
Sweden	10.30	4.70	15.80	17.10	29.60
UK	45.60	34.40	43.60	39.80	38.60
Denmark	44.30	30.00	27.90	26.50	27.20
EU 15	41.44	46.36	45.54	45.85	45.85

Source: OECD, *Employment Outlook*, 1995, 1998.

Union of 11 and that of 15. The individual countries display significant differences in terms of both levels and trends. In the three large continental countries – France, Germany and Italy – the unemployment level follows the average closely but, above all, it has been rising over the recent past. Spain shows the highest level of unemployment, although it has been recently dipping. UK data are slightly below the average. Ireland displays a similar trend although at markedly higher levels. Finally, the unemployment figures for Austria, Portugal and the Netherlands are below the average.

Table 4.2 confirms the contrast between the USA and Europe as regards long-term unemployment (which includes workers unemployed for more than one year). All European countries display very high percentages of this component which, in some cases, exceeds 50% of total unemployment. The debate regarding the difference between the economies of the two regions

Table 4.3 Youth unemployment rates (young persons 15–24 years old) [a]

	Levels				Absolute variations			
	1970	1980	1990	1997	1970–80	1980–90	1990–97	1970–97
USA	9.90	13.80	11.20	11.30	3.90	−2.60	0.10	1.40
Austria	n.a.	n.a.	n.a.	7.60				
Belgium	n.a.	n.a.	14.50	21.30			6.80	
Finland	2.90	8.20	6.40	24.80	5.30	−1.80	18.40	21.90
France	3.20	15.10	19.10	28.10	11.90	4.00	9.00	24.90
Germany	0.40	4.10	5.60	8.89	3.70	1.50	3.29	8.49
Ireland	9.30	14.70	17.60	16.10	5.40	2.90	−1.50	6.80
Italy	10.20	25.20	31.50	32.78	15.00	6.30	1.28	22.58
Luxembourg	n.a.	n.a.	3.70	9.20			5.50	
Netherlands	1.50	9.30	11.10	10.30	7.80	1.80	−0.80	8.80
Portugal	n.a.	16.30	10.00	13.85	−6.30	3.85		
Spain	3.90	25.40	32.30	39.00	21.50	6.90	6.70	35.10
EU 11	4.49	14.80	15.18	20.27	10.31	0.38	5.09	15.79
Denmark	n.a.	n.a.	11.50	8.10			−3.40	
Greece	n.a.	n.a.	23.30	31.00			7.70	
Sweden	2.90	5.00	3.70	15.40	2.10	−1.30	11.70	12.50
UK	n.a.	n.a.	10.10	13.50			3.40	
EU 15	4.29	13.70	14.31	18.66	9.41	0.61	4.35	14.37

Note: [a] The 1970 data for Ireland and Netherlands refer to 1971, and for Spain to 1972. For Luxembourg, the 1997 data refer to 1996.

Source: OECD, *Labour Force Statistics*, 1997.

often centres on this figure which is asserted to be a clear indicator of the greater role played by labour market rigidities in Europe.

In the case of youth unemployment, the differences between Europe and the USA are less marked (Table 4.3) and are greater among the European countries. The number of young unemployed is quite high in Italy, France and Spain but more moderate in the UK and Germany. Attention has concentrated on this phenomenon as well since it is a clear indicator of the economic systems' capacity for absorbing new entrants to the labour force.

This summary analysis of the data confirms the main characteristics of European unemployment, which are, of course, widely known: its constant deterioration in recent years, especially in comparison with the USA, the heavy burden of long-term unemployment, and the substantial differences among the national situations. However, the undisputed evidence has not led to an equally shared analysis. In the following paragraphs we review the main interpretation of this phenomenon.

THE DEBATE OVER THE CAUSES OF UNEMPLOYMENT

In the discussion of the analysis, and on the cures, of European unemployment a distinction is usually made between 'macroeconomic' and 'microeconomic' interpretations.[3]

The macroeconomic[4] interpretations detect the main cause of European unemployment in the application of excessively restrictive macroeconomic, especially monetary, policies implemented to combat rising European inflation in the 1970s. The institutional framework within which these policies were applied was the exchange rate agreements of the EMS which operated like a 'discipline' mechanism. The evolution of the EMS into EMU is supposed to have accentuated the restrictive stance of macroeconomic policy by extending it to fiscal policies compelled to respect the Maastricht Treaty's criteria and, subsequently, the stability and growth pact.

A further distinction can be drawn between cyclical and persistent macroeconomic unemployment. The significance of the former is evident, as well as scarcely relevant: macroeconomic policy is held responsible for the fluctuation of unemployment around an equilibrium level, i.e. the natural rate of unemployment (or the NAIRU).[5] 'True' macroeconomic unemployment, on the other hand, is assumed to be dependent on 'hysteresis' on the basis of which long periods of macroeconomic restraint, such as those prevailing in Europe during the disinflationary period, led to a gradually rising NAIRU. These interpretations eventually tie up with those based on labour market rigidities.

Microeconomic explanations of unemployment emphasise the importance of market behaviour. Of course, the labour market is the principal market concerned but, as we shall see below, this is useful only as a first approximation.

Microeconomic causes of unemployment originate from the demand as well as from the supply side of labour markets. In this framework structural unemployment is defined as an equilibrium resulting from the intersection of the labour demand and supply curves.[6] In this context, then, the causes of unemployment are those which determine the positions of these curves. On the *supply* side, labour union behaviour is relevant, to the extent that it supports

Table 4.4 Labour market regulation in OECD countries

	Legal constraints on hiring and firing	Labour standards	Replacement rate of unemployment benefits (%)	Duration of unemployment benefits (years)	Active labour market policies (%)	Union coverage ratio (%)	Union coverage index	Trade union coordination in wage bargaining	Employers' coordination in wage bargaining	Labour taxes by employers (%)	Overall labour taxes (%)
Austria	16	5	50	2.0	8.3	46.2	3	3	3	22.6	53.7
Belgium	17	4	60	4.0	14.6	51.2	3	2	2	21.5	49.8
Denmark	5	2	90	2.5	10.3	71.4	3	3	3	0.6	46.3
Finland	10	5	63	2.0	16.4	72.0	3	2	3	25.5	65.9
France	14	6	57	3.0	8.8	9.8	3	2	2	38.3	63.8
Germany	15	6	63	4.0	25.7	32.9	3	2	3	23.0	53.0
Ireland	12	4	37	4.0	9.1	49.7	3	1	1	7.1	34.3
Italy	20	7	20	0.5	10.3	38.8	3	2	2	40.2	62.9
Netherlands	9	5	70	2.0	6.9	25.5	3	2	2	27.5	56.5
Norway	11	5	65	1.5	14.7	56.0	3	3	3	17.5	48.6
Portugal	18	4	65	0.8	18.8	31.8	3	2	2	14.5	37.6
Spain	19	7	70	3.5	4.7	11.0	3	2	1	33.2	54.2
Sweden	13	7	80	1.2	59.3	82.5	3	3	3	37.8	70.7
Switzerland	6	3	70	1.0	8.2	26.6	2	1	3	14.5	38.6
UK	7	0	38	4.0	6.4	39.1	2	1	1	13.8	40.8
Canada	3	2	59	1.0	5.9	35.8	2	1	1	13.0	42.7
USA	1	0	50	0.5	3.0	15.6	1	1	1	20.9	43.8
Japan	8	1	60	0.5	4.3	25.4	2	2	2	16.5	36.3

Notes:
Column 1: scale from 1 to 20, higher values indicate stricter regulation
Column 2: includes working hours, limited contracts, employers' rights. Scale from 0 to 10, higher values indicate stricter regulations
Column 5: value indicates ALMP expenditure for unemployed as GDP share per unemployed
Column 7: values from 1 to 3 indicate a trade union coverage of 25%, between 25% and 70% and 70% respectively, above 70% respectively
Column 8: scale from 1 to 3, larger values indicate increasing amount of coordination
Source: Nickell (1997).

wage levels of the employed rather than the employment opportunities of the jobless; in addition the availability and duration of unemployment compensation and minimum wages discourage workers from entering the labour market. These factors shift the labour supply curve to the left, thus raising equilibrium unemployment for a given demand. On the *demand* side, factors that boost firing and hiring costs and those that raise capital intensity per unit of product, as well as high labour taxation, technical progress (to the extent that it promotes lower labour intensity and/or greater demand for skilled labour), and market power of the firms, all shift the firms' demand for labour to the left, thus raising equilibrium unemployment for a given level of supply. In sum, the greater the weight of the rigidities, the more the two curves shift to the left and increase the rate of equilibrium unemployment.

THE ROLE OF RIGIDITIES

The term 'rigidities' is widely used but often abused. The literature identifies two ways of considering rigidities, at least from an empirical point of view. A first approach measures rigidity directly by appropriate indicators. In this case, the conceptual problem is whether there is a causal relation between rigidity and unemployment. A second approach consists of estimating the parameters of labour market equations, and measuring the degree of rigidity on the basis of these parameters. In this second case, the conceptual problem consists of explaining why the values of the parameters differ among national cases. In practice, we are dealing with two largely complementary approaches.

Nickell (1997) offers a good example of the first approach when he suggests evaluating the impact of labour market regulations on the trend of unemployment. Indicators of flexibility are constructed to this end, based on observation of characteristics – identified as sources of rigidity – of the different labour markets. Based on the intensity of their application, he assigns a scale value to each measure. The rate of total unemployment and the rates of long-term and short-term unemployment are regressed on a series of indicators of regulation of the labour market, reported in Table 4.4. Nickell's results may be summarised as follows. The rate of unemployment is positively influenced by: duration of unemployment compensation, especially in the absence of incentives for workers to accept jobs at compensation levels and in sectors other than the previous ones; a high degree of unionisation in the absence of co-ordination with employer organisations for wage setting; high labour taxation,[7] especially if associated with high levels of minimum wages; low quality of skills. But there also exist labour market 'rigidities' that, according to Nickell's results, do not affect unemployment: worker protection legislation and labour market standards; unemployment compensation, even if generous, if it is associated with solid incentives for workers to seek new jobs; high levels of unionisation if accompanied by an equally high degree of wage-setting co-ordination with employers.

These results are relevant above all for one aspect. Even if certain institutional characteristics of the labour market may affect unemployment more than others, what seems important is their interaction, so much so that one single factor (such as unemployment compensation or the degree of unionisation) may have opposite effects on unemployment depending on the presence or absence of other factors of rigidity. In addition, as can be noted from the figures in Table 4.4, the European countries exhibit degrees of rigidity that often differ significantly among one another and that, with the exception of the UK, indicate a greater overall rigidity than in the USA.

We now come to the second approach. The analysis in terms of 'measured' rigidity are based on two alternative hypotheses:

1. When a shock hits the economy, the unemployment rate settles at a higher level than its 'natural' one; the cause of the unemployment rate's persistence at such a level is a low speed of adjustment; according to this interpretation, unemployment is the symptom of protracted disequilibrium.
2. An increase of the unemployment is not a temporary deviation from equilibrium but a permanent rise of the unemployment level compatible with a constant rate of inflation; this is the hysteresis case, i.e. the past level of unemployment affects the current equilibrium rate; thus, we are dealing with an equilibrium that does not adjust towards the previous value; in other words, each new level of unemployment is a new equilibrium. This different way of conceiving rigidity (flexibility) is based on a conceptual framework itself largely based on a Phillips curve.

In the analyses that follow this approach[8] to wage and employment elasticities provides direct information on the speed at which the labour market adjusts to exogenous shocks. Indicators are constructed from the estimated coefficients of the wage equation, specifically:

- the elasticity of wages to unemployment (real flexibility);
- the elasticity of wages to changes in inflation (nominal flexibility).

The two variables are used to construct an indicator of flexibility, defined as a ratio where the numerator and denominator represent the wage response, respectively, to prices and to the rate of unemployment. A low numerator and high denominator indicate high overall wage elasticity; the smaller the indicator, the faster the adjustments.

Another indicator of flexibility is obtained by estimating the employment elasticity to changes in aggregate demand (productivity elasticity of output changes). A low elasticity implies a high employment response to changes in output since – *ceteris paribus* – increases (declines) in output will be generated by increases (declines) in the level of employment rather than by changes in productivity.

A comparison of the two indicators offers the following results:

- in the USA, we see pronounced employment response and a low long-term wage elasticity (not very far from European levels);
- in Japan, limited employment changes in response to output variations are offset by substantial wage flexibility;
- the EU displays what is defined as 'the worst of the two situations' in view of the high rigidity of both wages and employment. This leads clearly to longer adjustment periods since the time required to bring the rate of unemployment back to equilibrium is longer in Europe than in the other cases.

The conditioning role played by rigidity in the adjustment processes, according to these analyses, also leads to an increase in the equilibrium unemployment rate (NAIRU) and, in the case of Europe, slow adjustments accompanied by persistence of unemployment. In other words, the greater European rigidity evidenced by low elasticity of wages and employment leads to longer adjustment periods. Moreover, following a shock, the persistence of unemployment not only prevents the system from returning to the preceding NAIRU level but also causes a rising NAIRU trend; thus, persistence entails not only a cyclical, but also a structural, increase in the rate of unemployment.

To sum up: (a) flexibility indicators show that the European labour market is more rigid than the American and Japanese ones; (b) the studies that were reviewed lead, via different methodologies, to the common conclusion that structural unemployment has been rising; (c) the latter is to be attributed – rather than to hysteresis or equilibrium phenomena – to slow adjustment accompanied by persistence effects; (d) changes in the NAIRU are attributed to a decreasing growth rate of productivity, to repercussions from the oil shocks, and to increasing rigidity of the labour market, but also to stagnant aggregate demand. However, inasmuch as the first two causes are also common to Japan and the USA – both of which have experienced a contained rise of the NAIRU – we might come to the conclusion that European *rigidities are the main sources of rising unemployment.*

EMPLOYMENT AND PRODUCTION STRUCTURE

The comparison between the European and US cases highlights a relevant fact that is emphasised in macroeconomic approaches as well as in those which focus on the role of rigidities: it is the difference between the two economies in the production–employment–productivity link. There is ample documentation[9] of the difference between the European and US cases. In the former, the growth of output is often slower than that of productivity, with the resulting destruction of employment; in the latter, the growth of productivity is slower than that of output, with the result that employment rises. The macroeconomic approach explains this pattern by the reaction of European economies to the loss of competitiveness following an increasingly tight exchange constraint. According to the rigidities approach, the explanation lies in the difficulty of compressing labour costs for a given productivity trend. Both points of view regard as relevant the role of investments, which paradoxically are excessive in the European case – to the extent that firms increase capital intensity per unit of output owing to a distortion of relative factor prices – and too limited to the extent that they are compressed by the monetary environment that does not encourage an expansion of capacity. In both cases growth prospect as well as the employment content of growth decline. This calls for more accurate investigation of the relations between investment and employment. While this will be dealt with in chapter 5, we can observe that, in this case, too, there are significant national differences within the EU. But these reflections suggest above all that the distinction between macroeconomic and microeconomic determinants of unemployment is largely misleading: microeconomic causes of unemployment imply the absence of adjustments in various markets that in the end are reflected in – as well as being themselves determined by – unsatisfactory macroeconomic performance. This point can be further explained by considering the *sectorial* aspects of unemployment.

The debate over the microeconomic causes of unemployment (or of equilibrium unemployment) largely ignores product composition even though this could be quite relevant for determining equilibrium unemployment and its evolution over time. This point can be clarified by considering labour demand and supply effects. To the extent that labour demand is determined by product demand, the sectoral product composition affects demand for labour in that different products or sectors display different rates of growth of demand. The references commonly found in the literature relate to the distinction between mature and new products and between industrial and service products. The demand for labour should grow faster in new sectors and in services, and the available evidence confirms that the larger growth-elasticity of employment is found in services, in Europe as well as in the USA, even though in the latter case the growth elasticity of employment is high even in the manufacturing sector. The main theoretical reference of this approach, in fact, is not new: we find it in the analysis of structural growth suggested by Pasinetti (1993).[10]

On the other hand, as shown in the literature on endogenous growth and on the service economy,[11] a well developed advanced services sector generates positive externalities for the industrial sector. In the second place, given that productivity growth in services is lower than in industry, the employment content of growth[12] is enhanced by a higher share of services in output.

A service orientation of employment has been under way for some time in the industrialised economies at approximately the same rate as that of the share of value added in industry and services.[13] The main difference between the USA – where the process is more advanced – and Europe lies in the underlying mechanisms: the rise in prices of services compared to the prices of industrial products due to stagnant productivity in the former[14] is met in the USA mostly by the downward flexibility of service wages, whereas in Europe it is dealt with by covering higher costs via taxation and public expenditure. The limit to the American solution lies in the risk of gradually debasing employment in the service sector and qualitative deterioration. The limit to the European solution consists of the heavy reliance on the transfer via the public budget, which has not contained the opportunistic behaviours and distorted resource allocations.

Product composition matters in determining the position and the evolution over time of demand for labour; however, the technological intensity for a given sectoral composition is also relevant. It is not obvious that sectors of high demand growth or high technological innovation are also those with the greatest growth of employment.[15] Table 4.5 shows average annual growth rates of employment by manufacturing sectors for the European countries. The sectors are classified according to the level of added value (high=a, medium=m, low=b) and to demand growth (greater=1 or smaller=2 than the average).[16] These data do not confirm that the greater contributions to employment creation (or the smaller contributions to its destruction) are provided by high demand-growth or high added-value sectors. The only clear evidence that emerges is that the employment trend is worse in the so-called traditional sectors, and that some of the high technology sectors display the best employment performance. The sectoral employment dynamic within the manufacturing sector is highly variable, while the sector's overall trend is negative. The main implication is that the production specialisation of a country and its evolution are relevant for structural unemployment. This is another element of diversification among

Table 4.5 EU: 1970–92 (percentage variation and annual average of employment by sectors) [a]

		1970–92	Annual average			1980–92	Annual average
M1 356	Plastic products	86.71	3.77	M1 356	Plastic products	23.24	1.79
B1 332	Furniture & fixtures	16.03	0.70	M2 342	Printing and publishing	4.87	0.37
A1 352	Other chemicals	13.75	0.60	B1 385	Professional goods	1.05	0.08
M2 342	Printing & publishing	12.26	0.53	A1 352	Other chemicals	−1.81	−0.14
M2 311.2	Food	8.40	0.37	B2 361	Pottery, china etc.	−6.33	−0.49
B2 361	Pottery, china etc.	1.19	0.05	M2 311.2	Food	−6.83	−0.53
B1 385	Professional goods	0.68	0.03	M2 341	Paper & products	−11.60	−0.89
M1 384	Transport equipment	1.96	−0.09	M2 381	Metal products	−12.03	−0.93
M2 381	Metal products	−5.89	−0.26	M2 362	Glass & products	−12.24	−0.94
M1 383	Electrical machinery	−8.61	−0.37	B1 332	Furniture & fixtures	−12.25	−0.94
M1 382	Non–electrical machinery	−9.62	−0.42	M1 382	Non–electrical machinery	−12.58	−0.97
M2 362	Glass & products	−10.72	−0.47	M1 383	Electrical machinery	−13.74	−1.06
	Total manufacturing	−11.24	−0.49	A2 351	Industrial chemicals	−14.84	−1.14
A2 351	Industrial chemicals	−14.89	−0.65		Total manufacturing	−15.81	−1.22
M2 341	Paper & products	−16.22	−0.71	A2 372	Non–ferrous metals	−16.55	−1.27
B2 331	Wood products	−16.58	−0.72	M1 384	Transport equipment	−17.29	−1.33
A2 354	Petroleum & coal prod.	−18.03	−0.78	B2 331	Wood products	−20.11	−1.55
B1 324	Footwear	−18.37	−0.80	M1 355	Rubber products	−25.11	−1.93
A2 372	Non–ferrous metals	−19.14	−0.83	A2 369	Non–metallic products	−26.18	−2.01
A2 369	Non–metallic products	−20.67	−0.90	A2 354	Petroleum refineries	−26.75	−2.06
A2 354	Petroleum & coal prod.	−22.42	−0.97	B1 322	Wearing apparel	−27.56	−2.12
A2 313	Beverages	−28.36	−1.23	A2 313	Beverages	−28.32	−2.18
M1 355	Rubber products	−28.41	−1.24	B1 324	Footwear	−28.58	−2.20
B1 322	Wearing apparel	−32.73	−1.42	A2 354	Petroleum & coal prod.	−30.68	−2.36
B1 323	Leather & products	−33.43	−1.45	B1 323	Leather & products	−32.04	−2.46
B2 321	Textiles	−41.39	−1.80	B2 321	Textiles	−33.39	−2.57
M2 371	Iron & steel	−43.92	−1.91	M2 371	Iron & steel	−38.42	−2.96
A1 314	Tobacco	−48.86	−2.12	A1 314	Tobacco	−43.63	−3.36

Note: [a] Excluding Ireland and Greece.

European countries (and regions) which will be examined in greater detail in the following chapters.

The above considerations make it difficult to evaluate the role of the so-called *technological* component of unemployment, i.e., whether the introduction of technology intensive products – which, *per se*, diminishes employment per unit – offsets the greater absolute employment created by larger output. Available empirical evidence seems to confirm that employment growth tends to be positive, or at least more sustained, in high-tech sectors. Moreover, there is evidence [17] of a positive relation between innovation effort – as measured in terms of R&D expenditure as well as patenting – and employment. Of course, employment growth induced by technological innovation will be possible to the extent that an adequate, highly trained labour force will be available, i.e., to the extent that a recomposition of labour demand is matched by a recomposition of supply.

The theoretical justification of the positive relation between innovation and employment may be clarified by recalling the links between international competitiveness, growth and employment.[18] To the extent that technological accumulation increases the world market share of a country, it raises the rate of growth consistent with balance-of-payments equilibrium, i.e., equilibrium which is financially sustainable in an open economy. The greater the product-innovation intensity, the higher the rise in the growth rate. Hence, inasmuch as the higher-technology sectors display a faster growth of employment, improved competitiveness in a high-tech sector entails a higher employment content of growth.

The consideration of the sectoral product composition allows the introduction of an additional aspect that has been singled out as a possible cause for unemployment in (*inter alia*) Europe, *globalisation*. Two aspects will be mentioned here under this – widely used as well as generic – label: the consequences of greater *trade integration* and those of the higher mobility of capital, particularly of *direct investment*.

Greater trade integration and liberalisation bring factor markets and, hence, the labour markets of the trading countries into competition with one another. This aspect is well-known in international trade theory, as international trade may be considered as a process of exchange of goods as well as of factor contents. The impact on employment is straightforward. To the extent that industrialised countries are exposed to competition from developing countries where labour cost is lower, the labour factor in the former becomes relatively more abundant. Two alternative results follow which depend on the degree of labour market rigidity in the developed countries.[19] Where the labour market is more flexible, such as in the USA, greater trade openness induces a wage decline; conversely, where the labour market is more rigid, as in continental Europe, the result is declining employment.

Product composition, or rather specialisation, plays a crucial role in determining the extension of these effects. They will be broader where specialisation is oriented towards labour-intensive sectors because these are more exposed to competition from developing countries.[20] Available evidence does not yet allow us to draw unequivocal conclusions regarding its relevance for European employment. Further evidence on this point is examined in chapter 7.

The second effect of globalisation arises from plant relocation in countries and regions where labour supply conditions are more business-friendly. In this case, as well, the theoretical and empirical debate has not led to any final conclusions. It might be recalled that, in this case as well, sectoral composition is relevant. The propensity for investing abroad is not uniform across industrial sectors; in general it is more relevant in the more technology intensive ones and where firms enjoy specific proprietary and organisational advantages. These sectors display a high propensity to relocate abroad lower value added segments.[21]

THE GEOGRAPHY OF EMPLOYMENT

The above considerations highlight that employment and production specialisation are linked. This has relevant implications for employment prospects in Europe, especially after the introduction of the single currency. As the 'new economic geography'[22] shows, a region's production specialisation also depends on its geography, that is on its location in relation to other regions. This depends on the fact that, under conditions of high capital mobility, production clusters in some locations – the 'central' ones – to the detriment of others (the 'peripheries'). One consequence is that, *ceteris paribus*, the employment prospects at the centre are better than at the periphery, and that this effect is greater the higher the mobility of labour. A second result is that the tendency to locate at the 'centre' is stronger for high-tech and higher value added sectors[23] inasmuch as the benefits of economies of scale and of locational externalities are more relevant for these sectors. It must be added that these sectors are increasingly classified as services, which, as pointed out above, enjoy the greatest rise in employment. It follows that, in central locations, there will be higher specialisation in these sectors, greater demand for skilled labour, and higher growth of demand for the goods produced within the region.

The geography aspects of employment are largely linked to the regional dimension, inasmuch as[24] (a) it is the regional components that – jointly with the continental components – explain European unemployment, and (b) above all, because the evolutions of Europe's production specialisation has increasingly taken a regional, rather than a national scale.[25] These aspects are fraught with consequences with respect to the evolution of the EMU. If, in fact, the relevant spatial dimension is the regional one, an asymmetric shock that affects a given sector does not require a change in the exchange rate, a country level variable, but rather the implementation of regional policies.

NOTES

1. Among the several contributions (CEPR, 1995; Begg, 1996; Nickell, 1997; Ciocca, 1997).
2. For a recent reconsideration of the theory of optimal currency areas, see Bayoumi and Eichengreen, 1998.
3. A description of the differences is found in CEPR (1995). See also Vinals and Jimeno, (1996).
4. See, for instance, Modigliani (1997).
5. Defined as the rate of unemployment compatible with price stability.
6. To be exact, we are dealing with 'pseudo'-curves of demand and supply. See CEPR (1995), Vinals and Jimeno (1996), Blanchard and Katz (1997) for a description of the reference model.
7. See also Daveri and Tabellini (1997).
8. Elmeskow (1993); McMorrow (1996); Symposium on NAIRU (1997).
9. See e.g. S. Collignon, *Sustaining Monetary Stability*, 1998, as well as the studies cited in the preceding note.
10. Pasinetti (1993).
11. Cf., for example, Solow (1985); De Vincenti and Montebugnoli (1997); Boitani and Pellegrini (1997).
12. This is one of the determinants of the difference between GDP growth rates required to maintain constant employment in the USA and in Europe as estimated by *European Economy* (n. 2, 1966), respectively amounting to 0.69% and 1.97% for the years 1974–96.
13. Cf. Baumol, Blackman and Wolff (1991).
14. This is a case of the well-known 'cost disease' originally explained by Baumol (1967).
15. We ignore the role of services. This aspect will be dealt with in chapter 8.
16. A detailed description is offered in chapter 7.
17. Antonelli (1995).
18. For an analysis of these aspects, see Padoan (1998).
19. Rodrik (1997).
20. It must be recalled that this is a long-term impact since in the short run greater liberalisation supports the labour-intensive sectors even in the industrial countries to the extent that it entails improved access to other industrial countries' markets.
21. See Padoan (1997)
22. Krugman (1991).
23. Guerrieri and Manzocchi (1996); Padoan (1997).
24. Vinals and Jimeno (1996) and chapter 8.
25. Fatas (1997).

5. Macroeconomic performance, investment and employment

Stefano Fantacone and Paola Parascandolo

INTRODUCTION

The present chapter and the following one look in more detail at the relationship between monetary integration and employment from a macroeconomic perspective. The analysis is carried out as follows: in the first section we identify and describe the characteristics of the European cycle. The second section analyses the relation between employment and investments over the European cycle. The following chapter looks at the relationship between export growth and the euro exchange rate in more detail.

One of the results of the process of monetary integration is the establishment of a European economic cycle which leads to a clear separation between the countries of continental Europe and those of the Anglo-Saxon area. This chapter presents new evidence on the nature of the European cycle and looks at the question of whether the process of cyclical convergence has coincided with a decline in the demand for labour and a rising rate of unemployment. Specifically, we investigate whether the dynamics of the European cycle beginning at the end of the 1970s have modified the relation between employment and investment, and stimulated a more rapid substitution of capital for labour.

THE CONVERGENCE OF ECONOMIC CYCLES IN EUROPE

The approach to EMU's costs and benefits based on the theory of optimum currency areas underlines that one of the preconditions for monetary union is the convergence of the participating countries' growth cycles. Lack of such convergence is an indication of differences in sensitivity of the individual economies to exogenous (asymmetric) shocks.[1] Other authors have suggested, on the contrary, that the optimum preconditions for a currency area can be obtained as a consequence of its creation establishment. In practice, monetary

Table 5.1 Coefficients of correlation of the business cycle in Euroland countries

	1972–79	1980–92	1992–98
With German cycle			
Austria	0.62	0.79	0.92
Belgium	0.46	0.58	0.53
France	0.87	0.38	0.49
Italy	0.79	0.39	0.36
Netherlands	0.73	0.57	0.39
Portugal	0.82	0.47	0.65
Spain	–0.14	0.37	0.62
Average	0.59	0.51	0.57
Deviation [a]	0.59	0.30	0.34
With US cycle			
Austria	0.30	–0.20	–0.39
Belgium	0.20	0.14	0.13
France	0.70	0.15	0.19
Italy	0.67	0.42	0.00
Netherlands	0.67	0.48	0.39
Portugal	0.62	–0.01	0.02
Spain	–0.22	0.36	0.06
Average	0.42	0.19	0.06
Deviation [a]	0.82	1.28	4.11
With French cycle			
Austria	0.77	0.77	0.76
Belgium	0.76	0.92	0.98
Italy	0.84	0.83	0.80
Netherlands	0.72	0.69	0.90
Portugal	0.96	0.87	0.90
Spain	–0.14	0.88	0.92
Average	0.65	0.83	0.88
Deviation [a]	0.61	0.10	0.09

Note: [a] Coefficient of variation.

Source: Based on OECD, *Economic Outlook*, Statistical Appendix, Dec. 1998.

integration would increase both trade integration and cyclical convergence of the countries participating to the process.[2] This approach is known as the hypothesis of endogeneity of optimum currency areas.

Table 5.1 presents some preliminary evidence in this respect; the coefficients of correlation among GDP cycles within Europe are compared for three different sub-periods. Specifically, we consider the cycles of Euroland's largest countries compared to Germany – the 'centre' economy of the currency area – and to the USA.[3] In addition, since the measurement of the German cycle is complicated by the unification years, we also compute the correlation with the French cycle. The results are summarised in Figures 5.1 and 5.2. The points shown on the curves, read from right to left, indicate a clear diversification over time from the US cycle. Note that, in the case of France, the curve also shifts upwards, indicating a higher coefficient of correlation between this cycle and that of the other European economies. This is not as clear in the German case precisely owing to the consequences of unification which, in the 1990s, introduced a bias in the German trends with respect to those of the rest of Europe. We also note that the increasing correlation among the European cycles was accompanied by a smaller dispersion; conversely, the latter increased in comparison with the USA. Tables 5.2 and 5.3 extend the analysis by considering the different components of demand. They show that the increase of cyclical correlation affects all demand components, but especially consumption and exports.

The data confirm the presence of a European economic cycle following the deepening of monetary integration. This is made clear by looking at the three sub-periods, reported in the tables, associated with different economic policy regimes in Europe: an initial period of flexible exchange rates introduced after the collapse of Bretton Woods regimes (1972–79); a second period of exchange rate agreements under the EMS (1980–92), and the last period (1992–96) marked by the depreciation of several currencies but also by an acceleration of the process of convergence towards the single currency. The data also show that cyclical convergence was obtained towards declining, not rising, growth rates. Data reported in Table 5.4 show the decline of the European GDP's growth rate during the period in question (3.3 in 1972–79, 2.4 in 1980–92, 1.6 in 1992–98). It appears that the countries with faster initial rates of expansion gradually adapted to the German economy's slower growth rate. Specifically, while the French and Italian GDP grew, respectively, at 3.3 and 3.7% in the 1970s as against 2.9% in Germany, the German economy expanded faster in 1980–92, when the Italian economy was growing more slowly.

The disaggregration of the components of demand also shows a gradual slowing of the growth rates of consumption and investment, but this is less

Figure 5.1 Business cycle correlation of European countries

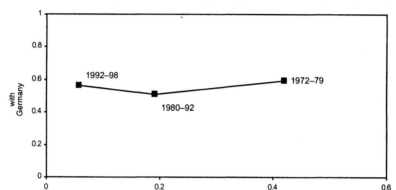

Figure 5.2 Business cycle correlation of European countries

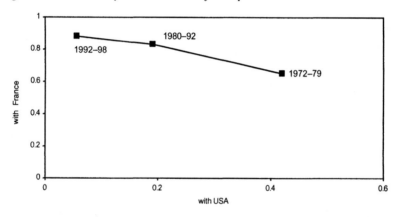

evident for exports. Two aspects are notable in this regard. In the first place, German exports rose faster than those of France and Italy in the 1980s; this is especially evident from the West German trend. Figure 5.3 compares the data for Germany as a whole with those for West Germany. It is clear that unification has had an expansionary effect on the internal components of demand, while the opposite happened in the case of exports. The latter increased over the period at an average rate of less than 4 percent in Germany as a whole, but of close to 6 percent in West Germany.

In the second place, exports are the only accelerating component of demand during the 1990s, which indicates greater dependence of the European economic cycle on foreign trade. This effect is clearly attributable

Table 5.2 Cycle of GDP components in Euroland countries (coefficient of variation with Germany)

	1972–79	1980–92	1992–98
Consumption			
Austria	–0.08	0.57	0.83
Belgium	0.14	0.70	0.72
France	0.72	0.28	0.68
Italy	0.34	–0.32	0.62
Netherlands	0.66	0.57	0.62
Portugal	–0.84	0.65	0.93
Spain	–0.60	0.52	0.76
Average	0.05	0.42	0.74
Deviation [a]	12.31	0.84	0.15
Investment			
Austria	0.54	0.73	0.62
Belgium	–0.16	0.54	0.75
France	0.52	0.57	0.77
Italy	0.31	0.62	0.34
Netherlands	0.29	0.21	0.00
Portugal	n.a.	n.a.	n.a.
Spain	–0.40	0.53	0.59
Average	0.18	0.53	0.51
Deviation [a]	2.08	0.33	0.57
Exports			
Austria	0.49	0.57	0.85
Belgium	0.74	0.55	0.65
France	0.65	0.49	0.89
Italy	–0.19	0.76	0.00
Netherlands	0.63	0.57	0.93
Portugal	0.18	0.41	0.84
Spain	0.22	–0.30	0.71
Average	0.39	0.44	0.70
Deviation [a]	0.86	0.78	0.46

Note: [a] Coefficient of variation.

Source: Based on OECD, *Economic Outlook*, Statistical Appendix, Dec. 1998.

Table 5.3 Cycle of GDP components in Euroland countries (coefficient of variation with France)

	1972–79	1980–92	1992–98
Consumption			
Austria	0.05	0.60	0.66
Belgium	0.58	0.75	0.91
France	0.72	0.28	0.67
Italy	0.58	0.80	0.78
Netherlands	0.59	0.60	0.91
Portugal	0.25	0.87	0.79
Spain	−0.34	0.91	0.89
Average	0.35	0.69	0.80
Deviation [a]	1.10	0.31	0.13
Investment			
Austria	0.63	0.88	0.71
Belgium	0.61	0.96	0.88
France	0.52	0.57	0.77
Italy	0.71	0.92	0.78
Netherlands	0.05	0.50	0.49
Portugal			
Spain	0.52	0.96	0.94
Average	0.51	0.80	0.76
Deviation [a]	0.46	0.26	0.21
Exports			
Austria	0.89	0.95	0.85
Belgium	0.90	0.86	0.59
France	0.65	0.49	0.89
Italy	0.03	0.49	−0.31
Netherlands	0.79	0.71	0.85
Portugal	0.84	0.44	0.83
Spain	0.82	−0.46	0.41
Average	0.70	0.50	0.59
Deviation [a]	0.44	0.94	0.74

Note: [a] Coefficient of variation.

Source: Based on OECD, *Economic Outlook*, Statistical Appendix, Dec. 1998.

Table 5.4 Growth rates of GDP and GDP components in Euroland countries

	1972–79	1980–92	1992–98
GDP	3.3	2.4	1.6
Germany	2.9	2.9	1.6
– West Germany	2.3		
Italy	3.7	2.1	1.1
France	3.3	2.1	1.7
Consumption	3.7	2.6	1.4
Germany	3.3	3.2	1.4
– West Germany	2.3		
Italy	4.2	2.7	0.9
France	3.5	2.5	1.5
Investment	2.1	3.1	0.5
Germany	0.9	4.3	–0.4
– West Germany	1.9		
Italy	2.9	2.1	0.2
France	1.4	2.3	0.2
Exports	6.3	3.9	5.9
Germany	5.2	3.6	4.4
– West Germany	5.7		
Italy	7.6	2.9	6.6
France	7.0	3.8	5.5

Source: Based on OECD, *Economic Outlook*, Statistical Appendix, Dec. 1998.

to the deeper real integration that has taken place in Europe and is in line with the analysis suggested by Frenkel and Rose. These aspects are examined in detail in the next chapter. We now look at the relationship between employment and investment.

EMPLOYMENT AND INVESTMENT IN EUROPEAN MONETARY INTEGRATION

As discussed in chapter 1, shortage of investment may be considered the main macroeconomic problem in the EU. It remains to be seen to what extent this is related to European unemployment. Indeed, according to some

Figure 5.3 Growth rates: Germany and West Germany, 1980–92

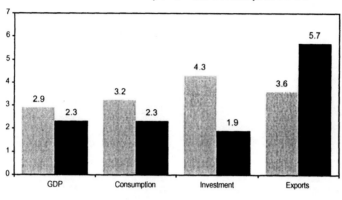

interpretations, the high level of European unemployment is directly related to the shortage of investment.[4] Table 5.5 shows that – net of the housing component – the investment share of GDP has been stable in most of the EU countries at the level of the 1970s and that it shrank in 1980–89. A constant share of investment in GDP indicates a weak process of accumulation if we consider, on the one hand, the share's net increase in the USA and, on the other hand, the fact that the share's stabilisation occurs against a gradual slowing of the growth rate of both components. Spain and Portugal are the exceptions: having started from an initially lower level of economic development, investments display a faster rise than GDP.

Furthermore, the evidence shows a qualitative recomposition of investment, i.e. an increase in the share of 'intensive' investment. This is illustrated by Table 5.6, which breaks total investment down into an 'intensive' and an 'extensive' component; the former includes expenditures for machinery, equipment, vehicles and land improvement; the latter includes expenditures for non-residential construction. This extensive component, implemented to expand production capacity, increases when the degree of capacity plant utilisation exceeds the equilibrium value and in connection with the expectation of a steady rise of demand: in other words, extensive investment, *ceteris paribus*, grows along with employment. The intensive component, conversely, depends on the flow of innovations that become available, but it may also increase in response to a shock to relative factor prices. In other words, this component of investment – in addition to reflecting technical progress – is driven by capital/labour substitution. *Ceteris paribus* it does not expand capacity but it boosts the growth rate of productivity. The evidence in Table 5.6 shows significant changes in the

*Table 5.5 Share of investment in European GDP
(excluding residential construction)*

	1972–79	1980–89	1992–96
Austria	0.20	0.18	0.20
Belgium	0.14	0.13	0.14
Denmark	0.09	0.08	0.07
Finalnd	0.20	0.18	0.14
France	0.16	0.15	0.16
Germany			0.16
West Germany	0.15	0.14	0.14
Ireland	0.14	0.14	0.11
Italy	0.15	0.14	0.14
Netherlands	0.17	0.15	0.15
Portugal	0.04	0.14	0.26
Spain	0.09	0.16	0.19
Weighted average	0.15	0.15	0.16

Source: Based on OECD, *National Accounts*, Detailed Tables (1998).

composition of investment in 1980–89. With the exception of Spain, Portugal and the UK, all countries show a shrinking of the share of extensive investment. Conversely, there are significant differences among countries in the 1990–96 sub-period, during which the intensive component of investment has risen only in Germany, Italy and the Netherlands.

The reasons behind such a rise in the share of intensive investments (*Qint*) are analysed econometrically by estimating the following equation:

$$DQint = c(1)+c(2)DY+c(3)t+c(4)d1+c(5)d2+c(6)d3+c(7)d4 \qquad (5.1)$$

where *DY* is the rate of output change, *t* is a time trend that approximates technical progress, and *d*1, *d*2, *d*3, *d*4 are dummies through which we have tried to take into account specific effects of the monetary regime.

The results are summarised in Table 5.7. The increase in the intensive component of investment is explained for approximately 50% by the variance of the time trend, whose coefficient becomes significant for all countries but Spain.

A priori, it could be expected that intensive investment type accumulation is negatively correlated with the cycle. However the negative correlation is confirmed only in the case of Germany, suggesting that, in the other

Table 5.6 Intensive and extensive investments (% of total)

	1972–79	1980–89	1992–96
Austria			
extensive investments	48.60	42.20	42.30
intensive investments	51.40	57.80	57.70
Belgium			
extensive investments	56.80	42.90	41.80
intensive investments	43.20	57.10	58.20
Denmark			
extensive investments	51.40	42.00	36.60
intensive investments	48.60	58.00	63.40
Finland			
extensive investments	53.40	51.40	51.60
intensive investments	46.60	48.60	48.40
France			
extensive investments	44.90	41.80	40.80
intensive investments	55.10	58.20	59.20
Germany			
extensive investments			40.60
intensive investments			59.40
West Germany			
extensive investments	48.10	42.50	35.80
intensive investments	51.90	57.50	64.20
Ireland			
extensive investments	40.80	38.10	38.30
intensive investments	59.20	61.90	61.70
Italy			
extensive investments	49.10	37.00	32.00
intensive investments	50.90	63.00	68.00
Netherlands			
extensive investments	47.60	40.10	35.90
intensive investments	52.40	59.90	64.10
Portugal			
extensive investments	26.40	29.20	32.70
intensive investments	73.60	70.80	67.30
Spain			
extensive investments	51.50	54.60	58.70
intensive investments	48.50	45.40	41.30
UK			
extensive investments	39.40	35.60	41.20
intensive investments	60.60	64.40	58.80
USA			
extensive investments	45.30	44.00	37.20
intensive investments	54.70	56.00	62.80

Source: Based on OECD, *National Accounts* Detailed Tables (1998).

Table 5.7 Share of intensive in total investments: econometric specification 1973–96 [a]

	Germany	Italy	France	Austria [b]	Belgium [c]	Netherlands [d]	Spain [e]
Constant	0.27	0.31	0.34	0.33	0.16	0.24	0.31
	(3.59)	(10.31)	(4.43)	(11.01)	(2.35)	(4.20)	(9.40)
DY	–0.63	0.48	0.51	0.35	–0.27	0.52	0.71
	(–2.59)	(3.56)	(1.08)	(2.18)	(–0.83)	(1.38)	(3.95)
trend	0.01	0.01	0.00	0.00	0.01	0.01	0.00
	(2.85)	(6.09)	(0.07)	(2.91)	(3.55)	(3.73)	(0.12)
d1980–86	0.08	–0.01	–0.01	0.01	0.06	0.06	
	(1.15)	(–0.46)	(–1.73)	(0.29)	(1.01)	(1.33)	
d1987–92	0.04	0.02	0.00	0.03	0.10	0.06	0.01
	(0.86)	(1.21)	(–1.42)	(2.04)	(2.36)	(1.93)	(2.10)
d1992–98	0.06	0.02	0.00	0.04	0.09	0.38	0.02
	(2.43)	–2.66	(–0.71)	–3.68	–3.77	–2.00	–0.54
Corrected R square	0.75	0.97	0.97	0.88	0.87	0.86	0.75
S. E. regression	0.030	0.010	0.000	0.010	0.020	0.020	0.010
D.W. stat.	0.96	1.00	2.16	1.42	1.09	1.55	1.57
F stat.	14.74	132.89	182.84	29.56	29.87	24.05	12.75

Notes:
[a] t statistic in parentheses.
[b] 1976–96.
[c] 1975–96.
[d] 1977–96.
[e] 1980–96.

Source: Based on OECD, *Economic Outlook*, Statistical Appendix, Dec. 1998.

countries, the process of accumulation is labour-saving regardless of the prevailing demand conditions.

Three period dummies were also inserted into the equation, with reference to the behaviour of the different European monetary regimes, to test whether monetary integration has contributed to a decline in the extensive component of investment. Results support this hypothesis only in part. The 1980–86 dummy is never significant; the 1987–92 dummy is significant for Austria and Belgium; the 1992–98 dummy is significant for Germany, Italy, Belgium, and Spain. Overall, there does not seem to be any employment-reducing effect linked to monetary integration.

We now look more closely at the relationship between the evolution of employment and monetary integration. As was mentioned above (see also chapter 6), the approach to the single currency was accompanied by an increase in the contribution of exports to growth and by a marked real appreciation of European currencies against the D-mark. Let us consider whether these evolutions have produced an impact on the employment – investment relationship. To this purpose, we estimate equations where the change in employment (*DO*) is regressed against the change in private investment (*DI*). We then add, to this basic structure, other exogenous variables that take into account the increase in the degree of openness – captured by the ratio between exports and GDP (*DX/Y*) – the trend of an index of real exchange rate (*r*) vis-à-vis the dollar in the case of Germany and vis-à-vis the D-mark for the other EU countries, and the four time dummies included in equation (5.1). Formally:

$$DO = c(1) + c(2)\,DI + c(3)\,DX/Y + c(4)r + c(5)d1 + c(6)d2 + c(7)d3 + c(8)d4 \quad (5.2)$$

Estimation results are reported in Table 5.8. The basic structure of the equation captures adequately the German model. The elasticity of employment to investment (0.16) is positive and the correlation between employment and the (rising) degree of openness is also positive and significant (0.2) while the correlation with the real (mark/dollar) exchange rate is negative and significant. As discussed in detail in chapter 6, these results confirm the validity of the export-led model for Germany, and the economy's sensitivity to the changes of the extra-EU exchange rate.

In the case of France, the employment–investment elasticity is also 0.2% but there is no significant correlation between the change in employment, exports and the real exchange rate. On the other hand, the 1980–87 dummy is significantly negative. This suggests that the decision to join the EMS may have produced a negative impact on employment creation. Such a result flies in the face of the widely accepted consideration of the initial EMS period as one of moderate monetary tightening. Our estimation results show that, despite the several successive realignments that took place in those years, the evolution of the exchange rate system exerted a negative impact on the relation between investments and employment.

The case of Italy is, to some extent, more interesting. The employment–investment elasticity is 0.07%. The change in the degree of openness, the real exchange rate vis-à-vis the D-mark and the three period dummies are all significant and with a negative sign. These results suggest that the changing

Table 5.8 Employment/investment elasticity: econometric specification 1973–96 [a]

	Germany	Italy	France	Austria	Belgium	Netherlands	Spain
Constant	–0.01	0.01	0.00	0.00	0.01	0.00	0.00
	(–2.57)[a]	(3.83)	(1.43)	(0.17)	(–3.90)	(0.53)	(–0.65)
DI	0.19	0.00	0.21	0.26	0.11	0.14	0.24
	(4.11)	(3.34)	(6.23)	(7.08)	(4.52)	(2.93)	(5.19)
DX/Y	0.20	–0.08	0.02	0.15	0.09	0.15	–0.03
	(2.39)	(–2.71)	(0.39)	(2.23)	(1.49)	(1.70)	(–0.34)
Dr	–0.05	–0.04	0.03	0.11	–0.03	–0.13	–0.08
	(14.78)	(–2.19)	(1.01)	(0.87)	(–0.67)	(–0.62)	(2.07)
d1980–86	0.00	–0.01	–0.01	–0.02	0.00	0.00	–0.12
	(1.06)	(–3.36)	(–1.96)	(–2.18)	(–0.44)	(0.02)	(–1.74)
d1987–92	0.00	–0.01	0.00	0.01	0.01	0.02	0.00
	(1.07)	(–3.80)	(–0.62)	(–0.64)	–2.71	–2.71	(–0.12)
d1992–98	0.00	–0.01	0.00	–0.01	0.01	0.01	0.00
	(–0.42)	(–3.21)	(–0.56)	(–0.69)	–2.32	(1.51)	–0.70
Corrected R square	0.97	0.82	0.77	0.85	0.80	0.63	0.83
S. E. regression	0.010	0.000	0.010	0.010	0.010	0.010	0.010
D.W. stat.	1.72	1.58	1.31	1.75	1.51	1.56	1.48
F stat.	107.48	10.32	9.91	15.72	11.23	4.62	14.12

Notes:
[a] t statistic in parentheses.
[b] Data for 1971–78; the variable associated with coefficient $c(4)$ is the real dollar exchange rate

Source: Based on OECD, *Economic Outlook*, Statistical Appendix, Dec. 1998.

nature of the European cycle, which implies a greater degree of openness, has produced unfavourable developments in the Italian labour market. Moreover, the negative impact of the real exchange rate vis-à-vis the D-mark also suggests that the evolution of the European exchange rate agreements have had their share in affecting the investment–employment relationship. Finally, the significant period dummies also point to an additional negative impact on employment linked to the different phases of monetary integration which presumably have prompted a faster substitution of capital for labour as suggested by the previous analysis.

CONCLUSIONS

In this chapter we have asked whether monetary integration has contributed to generate a specific European cycle and is characterised by a specific European accumulation process. We have discussed to what extent Europe's investment shortage – EU's most relevant macroeconomic problem – is related to European unemployment. More specifically, we have tested whether and to what extent European investment has slowed down and whether its intensive, labour-saving component has increased. According to this hypothesis, which has been extensively advanced to discuss convergence towards EMU, the European macroeconomic system has increasingly taken on a restrictive stance, so as to meet the inflation and public finance requirements. As this has coincided with a structural decline of labour demand, monetary convergence is, consequently, considered one of the causes of high unemployment in Europe.

Our analysis has confirmed the convergence of the European growth cycles and has highlighted that this has been associated with declining growth rates and with a greater weight of exports in demand creation. The rising weight of exports seems to have partially affected Europe's capacity to create employment. As far as investment is concerned, what has contributed to a deterioration of employment opportunities is not so much the slow–down of investment/output ratios as the increase of its intensive, labour-saving component. Econometric estimation shows that this trend is partly associated with the launching of the EMS, i.e. with the imposition of an exchange constraint on the European economies as a whole.

On the whole, the process of (increasing) European monetary integration seems to have had a negative impact on employment. The transmission mechanisms are, however, different. In the case of Germany, where an export-led growth model is apparently at work, the constraint has operated through the gradual slowing of demand in Europe which feeds back on a lower rate of export growth.[5] In the peripheral countries, the constraint has fed through the channels of productivity increases to recover competitiveness in the face of appreciating currencies, via substitution of capital for labour. The next chapter looks in more detail at the role of exports and competitiveness in the EU member states as well as at the consequences of the introduction of the single currency on the macroeconomic model of EMU.

NOTES

1. Bayoumi and Eichengreen (1998).
2. Frenkel and Rose (1996).
3. A similar analysis is developed by Artis and Zhang (1995).

4. The scarcity of investment, in turn, can be attributed to general lack of aggregate demand, or it can be interpreted as the result of a process of adjustment of productivity and capital stock to change in factor prices. For the first interpretation, see Muet (1997). For the second interpretation, see Gordon (1995).
5. See chapter 6 for a further analysis of this point. This interpretation reflection is offered in G. Nardozzi, 'La disoccupazione europea e il capitalismo tedesco', in Ciocca (1997).

6. Exchange rate, trade and growth

Stefano Fantacone and Claudio Vicarelli

INTRODUCTION

We argued in chapter 1 that in order to solve Europe's macroeconomic problem, i.e. the shortage of investment, and in order to exploit the benefits of a perspective 'currency region' EMU should pursue a policy of a stable exchange rate of the euro vis-à-vis third currencies. Even before the launching of the euro the European Monetary Institute (EMI) explicitly suggested that the exchange rate not be used as an intermediate objective of monetary policy, seeing that in an area as large as the euro's such an approach would be ineffective with respect to the final objective of price stability, 'the evolution of the exchange rate will be less important for the ECB than it is currently for many national central banks' (EMI, 1997). This approach, it is sometimes argued, might clash with pressures to use the exchange rate to support growth and exports.

The present chapter is concerned with these aspects; it attempts to assess whether the determinants of export of the major EMU countries might actually set off a conflict of objectives within the European Central Bank (ECB). The higher sensitivity of some economies to exchange rate dynamics might, in fact, generate a demand for real depreciation in contrast with the price stability imperative. Since the Mediterranean economies have the highest exchange rate variability, we test the hypothesis that the latter's admission into EMU will bear on the euro's external value and jeopardise its stability.

The following section offers a description of past trends of the real exchange rate in Europe in general and in individual member countries; next, we present estimates of the determinants of exports, and an analysis of the exchange rate export elasticity of the European countries; we then compare the role of exports in the growth process of individual European countries. Lastly, we consider Europe as a whole and estimate the export functions to the rest of the world.

Figure 6.1 Real exchange rates: EU and USA (1970=100; producer prices)

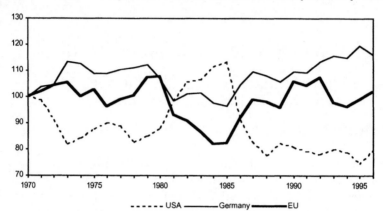

EXCHANGE RATE COMPETITIVENESS IN EUROPE

Let us first recall the performance of real exchange rates in Europe before EMU and look at the competitive conditions in which the member countries have joined the single currency. Consider, in the first place, the evolution of real exchange rates in the USA, the EU as a whole and in Germany between 1970 and 1996 (Figure 6.1). If we compare values at the beginning and the end of the period we see a devaluation of the dollar, a stable EU rate and the (gradual) real appreciation of the D-mark.[1] The latter starts in 1985, following the Plaza Agreements, and continues almost uninterruptedly until 1995, when a renewed strengthening of the dollar and the gradual nominal revaluation of a number of European currencies – the lira, peseta and sterling – reversed the trend.

The D-mark's real appreciation is explained partly by the dollar's movements and partly by the wide fluctuations of real intra-European rates. The trends of the latter are examined in more detail in Table 6.1. Several interesting features arise. Germany's competitiveness vis-à-vis other European economies over the period declines by about 20% but this occurs only in the initial and final sub-periods characterised by the free floating of all or some of the EU currencies. Under the EMS (1979–91) the real exchange rate of the D-mark remains stable, with a slight depreciation during the years of the 'hard EMS' (January 1987–September 1992). The trend of German competitiveness during the EMS period is explained by the real appreciation of the lira and, to a lesser degree, of the French franc, following the steady revaluation of the peseta and British pound. From the second half of the 1980s intra-EU competitiveness favours France, whose currency

Table 6.1 Real intra-EU exchange rates (% changes)

	Germany	France	Italy	Spain
1970–79	11.4	2.0	–13.9	–18.8
1979–87	1.8	4.6	10.3	–7.4
1987–91	–2.0	–3.3	3.2	10.1
1991–97	4.5	–1.4	–10.7	–14.9
1970–97	16.1	1.7	–12.6	–29.5
1979–97	4.2	–0.3	1.6	–13.2

Source: Banca d'Italia.

follows a large real depreciation in 1987–91. This is partly offset by the devaluation of the lira, peseta and sterling following the EMS 1992 crisis. The overall evolution of the real exchange rates of France, Italy and Spain is shown in Figure 6.2; the competitive positions of the three countries at the end of the period are no worse or more favourable than the initial levels as well as the levels prevailing at the launching of the EMS.[2]

As the data show, Germany has benefited from the European exchange rate agreements in the form of a stabilisation of the real exchange rate; besides, it is well-known that the other EMS countries have used the exchange rate to fight inflation through real appreciation at the expense of balance-of-payments equilibrium.[3] On the other hand, over the free floating period

Figure 6.2 Real exchange rates of selected European countries (1970=100; producer prices)

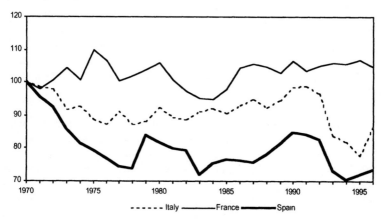

following the 1992 crisis the D-mark appreciated in real terms. Consequently, and as a first approximation, the adoption of the single currency should preserve Germany from a loss of competitiveness vis-à-vis other European economies. Nevertheless, while, in the case of Germany, the final fixing of the (intra-European) exchange rate takes place under conditions of real over-valuation, the same is not true for the other EMU countries, whose competitiveness has remained unchanged (France) or has improved slightly (Italy and Spain). Neither can the different levels of competitiveness be corrected by the vanished inflation differentials.

The evidence leads to a first conclusion. The final fixing of nominal exchange parities among the EMU currencies is not associated with real misalignments such as those observed during the EMS and which eventually led to its breakdown.[4]

EXPORTS AND REAL EXCHANGE RATES IN SOME EUROPEAN COUNTRIES

We now proceed to the econometric analysis. Consider an initial, quite general, specification (see eq. (6.1)) where exports of five European countries – Germany, France, Italy, Spain and the UK – are expressed as a function of the respective real exchange rates and of a uniform variable for world demand:[5]

$$x_i = c + \beta r_i + \gamma m + u_i \qquad (6.1)$$

The results are shown in Table 6.2.[6] Demand elasticity is positive in all cases and shows similar values for Germany, France and Italy. The two extremes are held, respectively, by the UK, with a particularly low coefficient, and Spain, which shows a demand elasticity greater than one probably owing to its late-comer integration into the international economy.

The differences among exchange rate elasticities – with unexpected results – are more interesting. They are highest and greater than one in Germany and lowest in Italy, with France and Spain in the middle. The UK's exchange rate coefficients are not significant.[7]

The results indicate that the incentive for using the exchange rate in supporting export could be greater in the centre country than in the peripheral economies. In practice this incentive has been more than offset by the great importance that the control of inflation has held for the German central bank, as results in chapter 2 show. It is also possible that the higher exchange rate elasticity of German exports may reflect the lower variability of the D-mark, whereas the fluctuations of other currencies have often smoothed over the

Table 6.2 Estimate of export functions in selected countries: first specification: 1975–96 (index number logarithms) [a]

	Germany	France	Italy	Spain	UK
Constant	4.98	3.28	2.65	3.82	0.53
	(9.9)	(3.94)	(5.24)	(2.89)	(1.51)[b]
Real exchange rate	−1.19	−0.72	−0.56	−0.79	−0.10
	(−9.94)	(−3.94)	(−5.17)	(−2.79)	(−1.44)[b]
OECD imports	0.76	0.80	0.87	1.16	0.68
	(38.98)	(38.45)	(47.46)	(24.88)	(36.37)
du_{90}	0.11				
	(4.26)				
Adjusted R squared	0.99	0.98	0.99	0.97	0.99
S. E. regression	0.025	0.031	0.029	0.073	0.025
D.W. stat.	2.00	0.64	0.87	0.42	0.80
F stat.	604.70	762.92	1186.70	331.18	888.90

Notes:
[a] t statistic in brackets.
[b] The coefficient is statistically not different from zero.

Source: OECD for exports and imports; Banca d'Italia for real exchange rates.

cumulative inflation differentials. Nevertheless, the evidence presented – this is our second conclusion – does not seem to indicate a potential weakening of the euro owing to greater exchange-rate sensitivity of the Mediterranean economies.

EUROPEAN EXPORTS AND EXCHANGE-RATE AND DEMAND SHOCKS IN THE REST OF THE WORLD

We have noted that, given the specification used, Germany shows a higher real exchange rate sensitivity than the other EU economies. In this section we examine the impact of the EU external demand and the EU exchange vis-a-vis the rest of the world on European exports for a given configuration of intra-European competitiveness.

We concentrate on the specific shock factors arising from the non-European area. In fact, it needs to be recalled that intra-European exchange-rate

*Table 6.3 Construction of the real extra-EU exchange rate: 1970-96
(dependent variable; real exchange rate; logarithms of index numbers)*

	Germany	France	Italy	Spain	UK
Constant	0.34	-0.07	0.47	-0.07	0.90
	(0.76)[a]	(-0.12)[a]	(1.66)[a]	(-0.3)[a]	(3.33)
Real intra-EU exchange rate	0.93	1.02	0.89	1.02	0.80
	(9.41)	(7.94)	(14.76)	(17.98)	(13.8)
Adjusted R squared	0.77	0.70	0.89	0.92	0.88
S. E. regression	0.027	0.020	0.019	0.024	0.031
D.W. stat.	0.48	0.48	0.54	0.56	0.67
F stat.	88.60	63.20	217.90	323.40	190.30

Note: (*) The coefficient is statistically not different from zero.

variability is often accompanied by variability with respect to third-country currencies,[8] while the synchronisation of the international cycle generates an obvious correlation between demand in Europe and in the rest of the world.

In order to eliminate such problems of collinearity, we have adopted a simple econometric procedure. The real exchange rate – r – for each country has been regressed against a constant and a real exchange rate index computed for the remaining European countries.[9] Formally for country i:

$$r_i = c + re_i + \varepsilon_i \tag{6.2}$$

where *re* is the real intra-European exchange rate. The residual ε of equation (6.2) has been used as an index of the real extra-EU exchange rate (rxe_i):

$$\varepsilon_i = rxe_i \tag{6.3}$$

The real extra-EU exchange rate obtained with the above procedure and with least squares is non-correlated to the regressor and may therefore be used to measure competitiveness shocks generated from outside the EU area. Table 6.3 shows the results. The R^2 values confirm that, as expected, in all countries a large part of the real exchange rate's variability is explained by the intra-EU movements. In any case, the lowest R^2 obtained for Germany and France show a stronger dependence for these two countries on the competitiveness trends external to the area. Graphic analysis (Figure 6.3) illustrates that the well-known phenomena of asymmetry operating within European exchange rate relations over the past decades have had an impact. The D-mark's real extra-EU depreciation during the first half of the 1980s,

Figure 6.3 Real extra-EU exchange rates in selected countries (% changes)

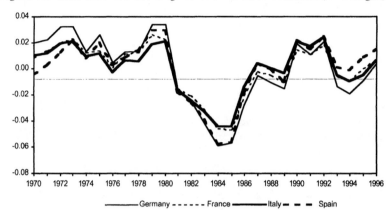

and its subsequent appreciation in the second half of the decade, both clearly attributable to the independent dynamics of the dollar, are more relevant than in the other countries.

A similar procedure was used to obtain an extra-EU demand variable as the residual of an equation in which OECD import demand (m) is regressed on a European import demand index:

$$m = c + me + \phi \qquad (6.4)$$

$$\phi = mxe \qquad (6.5)$$

where me is the index numbers of aggregate European imports and mxe the aggregate extra-EU imports. Results are shown in Table 6.4; the high R^2 value indicates that the share of world demand variability attributable to the non-European economies is quite low. Figure 6.4 illustrates these trends.

Total exports of the individual countries are thus expressed as a function of both indicators of intra-European demand and exchange rates, and of the same indicators constructed for the rest of the world. Results are reported in Table 6.5. The importance of the real exchange rate for German exports is confirmed. Not only is intra-EU exchange-rate elasticity higher than for other countries, in addition the extra-EU exchange rate has a higher estimated coefficient than that of the other countries with the exception of Spain. The extra-EU exchange-rate elasticity is higher than the EU's with the exception, in this case, of France. We also obtain a confirmation of the importance of price-competitiveness with respect to the non-European area for all countries, and not only for the Mediterranean economies. For the UK, neither of the two exchange rate indicators, on the other hand, showed coefficients statistically different from zero.

Table 6.4 Construction of the extra-EU import demand: 1975–96 (dependent variable; total OECD imports; logarithms of index numbers)

Constant	0.02
	(2.65)
EU imports	1.16
	(63.2)
Adjusted R squared	0.99
S. E. regression	0.031
D.W. stat.	0.84
F stat.	3.991

Table 6.5 Estimation of export functions in selected countries: second specification: 1975–96 (index number logarithms) [a]

	Germany	France	Italy	Spain	UK
Constant	4.01	3.91	2.30	3.69	0.12
	(5.06)	(3.70)	(4.44)	(3.33)	(0.42)[b]
Real intra–EU exchange rate	–0.91	–0.84	–0.48	–0.75	–0.02
	(–5.21)	(–3.68)	(–4.33)	(–3.19)	(–0.30)[b]
Real extra–EU exchange rate	–1.41	–0.81	–0.86	–2.82	0.12
	(–5.41)	(–2.45)	(–2.19)	(–6.23)	(0.58)[b]
EU imports	0.88	0.95	1.00	1.36	0.76
	(32.41)	(43.49)	(42.2)	(37.38)	(29.8)
Non–EU imports	0.24	0.24	0.86	0.47	1.12
	(1.19)[b]	(1.18)[b]	(3.48)	(1.12)[b]	(5.49)
du_{90}	0.11				
	(4.30)				
du_{76}				–0.15	
				(–3.06)	
Adjusted R squared	0.99	0.99	0.99	0.99	0.99
S. E. regression	0.023	0.027	0.027	0.044	0.023
D.W. stat.	1.62	0.87	1.58	1.09	1.43
F stat.	461.72	533.15	547.70	368.70	512.20

Notes:
[a] Figures in brackets are t statistic.
[b] The coefficient is statistically not different from zero.

Sources: OECD for exports and imports; Banca d'Italia for EU exchange rates; authors' computation for extra-EU exchange rates.

Figure 6.4 Extra-EU import demand (% changes)

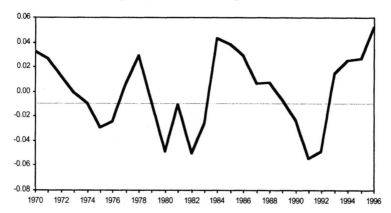

In the second place, there are important differences in demand elasticity. European demand elasticity is lower for Germany than for the other countries, while extra-EU demand displays significant coefficients for Italy only.

On the whole, these results offer some answers to the questions of sustainability of a common exchange rate policy. Ultimately, shocks originating outside the area might actually produce asymmetrical effects. A slowing of extra-EU imports, for example, could affect Italy more markedly than other major countries. If a weaker extra-EU demand were to be accompanied by a devaluation of the dollar, and thus by a real appreciation of the euro, Germany would also be affected significantly. Similarly, if the shocks were to affect real exchange rates and not demand, the centre economy would suffer more substantial consequences.

This leads to a third conclusion. Concerns expressed on the basis of the theory of optimal currency areas might be well-founded, but for more complex reasons than usually considered. Specifically, the consequences of external shocks for the euro area can be different depending on whether the affected variable is external demand or the real exchange rate.

THE EXCHANGE RATE AND ECONOMIC GROWTH: IS THERE AN EXPORT-LED MODEL IN EUROPE?

A further aspect to be investigated regards the role of exports in the growth process of the European countries. As noted by Gros (1996), the weight assigned to the exchange rate in the authorities' objective function should be directly proportional to the contribution of exports to growth. In other words, the cost associated with giving up the exchange rate tool would be higher for those countries where there is a clearly identifiable link between exports, employment and long-term economic growth, according to the standard export-led model.

The following relations were estimated in order to check whether such a model is applicable to the European economies:

$$n_i = c + n_i(-1) + x_t + \phi_i \tag{6.6}$$

$$nm_i = c + nm_i(-1) + x_i + \nu_i \tag{6.7}$$

$$i_i = c + i_i(-1) + x_t + \mu_i \tag{6.8}$$

$$\pi_i = c + \pi_i(-1) + x_t + \theta_i \tag{6.9}$$

$$\pi n_i = c + \pi n_i(-1) + x_i + \zeta_t \tag{6.10}$$

$$x_t = c + x_i(-1) + \pi m_i + \psi_i \tag{6.11}$$

where n_i is total employment, nm_i is employment in manufacturing, i_i is private sector gross fixed capital formation, (π_i) is total private sector productivity, (πm_i) is productivity in manufacturing, and the remaining Greek letter symbols are the residuals. All variables are from OECD and are expressed as logarithms. The results of the estimations are presented in Table 6.6.

With reference to employment, Germany is the only country for which export elasticity is statistically significant, even though this is not valid where manufacturing employment is considered. In Germany, statistically significant relations are found for gross fixed capital formation functions as well – at a 10% probability level – and for manufacturing productivity; in the latter case, the relation is bi-directional. The German case, then, exhibits typical features of the export-led model, according to which employment, gross fixed capital formation and productivity are positively affected by exports, which, in turn, are affected by productivity.

Such evidence is not obtained for other countries, the tested relations for which are almost always insignificant. Only for Italy do we find elasticities that are not statistically different from zero for the two–way relationship between exports and productivity.

To complete the analysis, Granger tests have been carried out to check the presence of statistical links between exports, employment and productivity.[10] Table 6.7 shows the results. The null hypothesis of non-causality is rejected for Germany insofar as relations between exports, on the one hand, and employment and gross fixed capital formation, on the other, are concerned. In

Table 6.6 Exports and economic growth in selected countries: econometric estimation 1970–96 (logarithms of index numbers) [a]

	Germany	France	Italy	Spain	UK
Total employment					
Constant	7.80	1.50	1.97	–0.69	3.20
Total empl. (–1)	0.54	0.90	0.90	0.90	0.80
Total exports	0.06	–0.009[b]	0.01[b]	–0.01[b]	–0.0[b]
Manufacturing employment					
Constant	2.60	0.19	0.86	1.30	–0.03
Manuf. empl. (–1)	0.71	0.97	0.90	0.83	1.00
Total exports	0.03[b]	–0.02[b]	–0.05[b]	0.02[b]	0.04[b]
Private gross fixed capital formation					
Constant	4.70	1.80	6.20	2.90	2.20
Investmt. (–1)	0.60	0.90	0.70	0.80	0.80
Total exports	0.2[a]	0.02[b]	0.1[b]	0.0[b]	1.7[b]
Total productivity					
Constant	–0.20	0.44	0.50	0.60	0.70
Tot. prod. (–1)	1.00	0.90	0.90	0.90	0.85
Total exports	–0.07[b]	0.03[b]	0.04[b]	0.06[b]	0.07[b]
Manufacturing productivity					
Constant	3.23	0.14	1.30	–	0.50
Manuf. prod. (–1)	0.25[b]	0.43[b]	0.66	–	0.80
Total exports	0.27	0.35[a]	0.32	–	0.21[b]
Total exports					
Constant	–3.10	–4.50	–1.30	–	–0.75
Tot. exports (–1)	0.65	0.46	0.68	–	0.68
Manuf. product.	0.72	0.81	0.34	–	0.27

Notes:
[a] The coefficient is statistically not different from zero.
[b] The null hypothesis of non-significance of the coefficient is rejected with a 10% probability.

turn, there is Granger causality between gross fixed capital formation and productivity, and between the latter and exports, confirming the export-led model. However, it must be noted that non-causality is rejected for the relation between productivity and gross fixed capital formation as well, so the former variable apparently follows a pattern not entirely attributable to exports.

*Table 6.7 Exports and economic growth in selected countries: Granger causality tests: 1970–96 (logarithms of index numbers) **

	Germany	France	Italy	Spain	UK
Exports → employment	11.3*	0.7	1.5	4.2**	1.7
Exports → gross fixed capital formation	7.9*	0.5	2.7***	0.1	1.5
Exports → productivity	0.0	1.6	0.7	0.8	2.0
Gross fixed capital formation → exports	0.6	0.1	1.6	1.6	0.1
Productivity → exports	8.6*	0.3	0.2	0.8	3.5**
Gross fixed capital formation → productivity	3.0***	0.2	4.7	2.6	1.3
Productivity → gross fixed capital formation	8.4*	1.2	6.3*	1.4	4.6**

Notes:
The asterisks indicate cases for which the null hypothesis of non-causality is rejected:
* = 1% of significance
** = 5% of significance
*** = 10% of significance

Causality tests do not lead to equally clear results for other countries. Again, some evidence of a relationship between exports and growth is found for Italy, through gross fixed capital formation, while a relation between exports and employment is present in the case of Spain.

The elasticity estimates and the Granger tests were repeated for extra-EU exports. No significant result was obtained, which is not surprising if we consider the low degree of openness of the European economy when intra-area trade is excluded.

To sum up, for most European countries the loss of the exchange rate should not affect long-term growth, which seems to depend only marginally on exports. This is the fourth conclusion arising from the analysis. Germany is the significant exception inasmuch as its exports appear to be a major determinant of growth. Nevertheless, this applies only to intra-EU exports. The impact of the German model on the euro's exchange rate should thus be limited.

EUROPEAN EXPORTS AND THE DOLLAR EXCHANGE RATE

Let us now consider the European area as a single unit to test whether the composition of EMU would affect the behaviour of exports, and specifically whether the presence of the Mediterranean economies might affect exchange rate elasticities.

Figure 6.5 Real exchange rates: Banca d'Italia (BdI) and authors compared

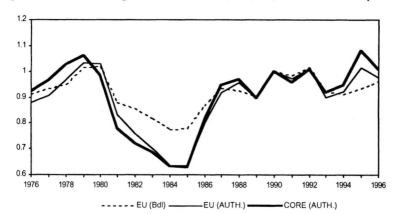

These aspects are analysed by comparing the results of two different aggregates: the first one – named Core – includes Germany and those countries for which compliance with the Maastrich parameters has never been in doubt (France, Belgium, Luxembourg, Netherlands, Denmark, Ireland); a second aggregate – named EU12 – includes the Mediterranean economies (Italy, Spain, Portugal, Greece) as well as the UK.[11]

We estimate the extra-EU export function; for this purpose, a data source (EUROSTAT) different from that used above was utilised. EUROSTAT data include export quantities by country of destination.

We first estimate the following equation:

$$x_j = c + r_j + mw + d_{95} + d_{96} \qquad (6.12)$$

where j = Core, EU12; where mw now includes imports of developing countries, and d_{95} and d_{96} are two time dummies.[12]

The real exchange rate vis-à-vis extra-EU countries is calculated as the ratio between producer price indexes – one internal and one external to the area – and the trend of the effective nominal exchange rate vis-à-vis the dollar, which was chosen as external reference currency. The internal price index as well as the nominal exchange rate were weighted by the individual country shares in total extra-area exports. The index of US producer prices was used as proxy for foreign prices.[13]

Figure 6.5 shows the real exchange rate constructed for the aggregates EU12 and Core and compares it with the Banca d'Italia's data for the EU countries. The main differences concern the 1980s and the years 1994–95. Our real exchange rate indexes, based on the movements of the US currency

Table 6.8 Estimation of the extra-EU export function for two different European aggregates: first specification: 1980–96 (logarithms of index numbers) *

	EU12 equation	Core equation
Constant	19.49	18.96
	(1339.23)	(1165.25)
Real exhange rate	–0.41	–0.19
	(–5.79)	(–2.33)
World demand	0.60	0.53
	(14.34)	(10.00)
du_{95}	–0.21	–0.25
	(–4.57)	(–4.79)
du_{96}	0.26	–0.29
	(5.50)	(–5.29)
R squared	0.98	0.91
Adjusted R squared	0.97	0.88
Durbin–Watson	1.73	1.14
S.E. of regression	0.038	0.044

Note: [a] t statistic in brackets.

alone, obviously show wider fluctuations than those of the BdI index which includes other non-EU currencies (Canadian dollar, yen and Swiss franc).

Estimation results for the period 1980–96 are shown in Table 6.8. All coefficients are statistically significant and the signs are as expected. The independent variable 'real exchange rate' shows a higher coefficient in the EU12 equation than in the Core equation; in both, world demand elasticity is higher than that of the real exchange rate.

The lower real exchange-rate elasticity found in the Core equation compared to the EU12 equation is not fully consistent with the results discussed in the preceding paragraphs. We therefore proceed to check whether the two equations might have been poorly specified.

As a first test, the components of the real exchange rate were considered separately. The real exchange index was constructed as the ratio between the domestic prices of the relevant area and the product of foreign prices times the nominal exchange rate. It is thus possible that estimating the two

Table 6.9 Estimation of the extra-EU export function for two different European aggregates: second specification: 1980–96 (logarithms of index numbers) [a]

	Eu12 equation	Core equation
Constant	19.47	18.92
	(1097.58)	(1345.58)
Internal prices	−0.77	−0.99
	(−3.39)	(−5.13)
Foreign prices x exchange rate	0.46	0.35
	(6.32)	(5.42)
World demand	0.78	0.76
	(6.86)	(11.94)
du_{95}	−0.24	−0.30
	(−5.14)	(−8.39)
du_{96}	0.23	−0.36
	(4.71)	(−9.30)
R squared	0.98	0.97
Adjusted R squared	0.97	0.95
Durbin–Watson	1.77	2.34
S.E. of regression	0.035	0.028

Note: [a] t statistic in brackets.

components with a single coefficient introduces distortions. The two equations were therefore re-estimated disaggregating the real exchange rate as follows:

$$x_j = c + p_i + (e_j * p_{usa}) + mw + d_{95} + d_{96} \qquad (6.13)$$

where e_j is the effective nominal rate vis-à-vis the dollar. The results are reported in Table 6.9.

In both equations, the coefficients of world demand are higher than in the previous estimation. In the EU12 equation, the coefficients of the two components of real exchange rate are not significantly different; on the other hand, in the Core equation the internal price elasticity is markedly higher than that of the product of nominal exchange rate times foreign prices (0.99 against 0.35), also world demand elasticity is higher than the former (0.76).

Table 6.10 Estimation of the extra-EU export function for two different European aggregates: third specification: 1980–96 (logarithms of index numbers) [a]

	Eu12 equation	Core equation
Constant	19.47	18.96
	(1666.79)	(1098.16)
Real exchange rate	−0.24	−0.19
	(−3.42)	(−1.69?)
World demand	0.98	0.54
	(8.67)	(2.76)
Internal demand	−1.01	−0.05
	(−3.45)	(0.09)
du_{95}	−0.30	−0.26
	(−7.11)	(−3.84)
du_{96}	0.15	−0.29
	(3.33)	(−4.23)
R squared	0.99	0.91
Adjusted R squared	0.98	0.86
Durbin–Watson	2.18	1.13
S.E. of regression	0.027	0.046

Note: [a] t statistic in brackets.

Hence, in the case of the EU12 equation the real aggregate exchange rate does not seem to introduce any distortions, as the standard errors of the two specifications are virtually identical. For the Core group, by contrast, separating the two components of the real exchange rate leads to a clear improvement of the estimation results, as shown by the higher R^2 and the lower standard error.

Given the importance of the share of intra-European trade in the trade of the member countries, as a second step we consider the role played by the internal market. For this purpose, a new independent variable (the area's internal demand) was introduced as follows:

$$x_j = c + r_j + mw + d \, \text{int}_j + d_{95} + d_{96} \qquad (6.14)$$

where $d\,\text{int}_j$ represents internal demand. The results of the estimation are shown in Table 6.10.

The independent variable 'internal demand' is not statistically significant in the Core equation, but it is significant, with the expected sign, in equation

EU12. In the latter case, the new specification has led to a lower standard error in the equation. In addition, the real exchange rate coefficient is now very close to that of the Core equation.

Having taken into account the role of the internal market, we obtain practically identical exchange rate elasticities in the two country groups. The size of the coefficient, furthermore, is modest. We may conclude that the broader the internal European market, the smaller is extra-European exports' dependence on the exchange rate and, thus, the lower is the incentive to use it as an instrument for 'active' demand support policies. Note that this result is consistent with the approach suggested by Collignon (1997) to evaluate the net benefits of a currency area discussed in chapter 1.

CONCLUSIONS

In this chapter we have presented some tests of the determinants of exports of the large European countries. The hypothesis that was tested was whether the inclusion of Mediterranean countries in EMU might jeopardise the euro's stability due to the greater variability of exchange rates. To address these questions, we have considered different specifications of the individual countries' export functions; moreover, we have compared the export determinants of two different groups of countries, defined as Core and EU12. The conclusions can be summarized as follows:

- the euro will replace currencie of countries whose competitive conditions are basically in equilibrium. This lowers *ex ante* the cost associated with the loss of the exchange rate tool;
- export exchange rate elasticity is higher in Germany than in the other countries; hence, it is not correct to attribute to the Mediterranean economies a stronger pressure for using the euro exchange rate to support competitiveness;
- the asymmetrical effects of shocks originating outside Europe should be limited and could be relevant only in special circumstances. Rather, the impact of such shocks on the euro would be unclear and would, in any case, not be likely to cause relevant policy conflicts within EMU;
- Germany is the only economy for which the export-led model seems to be consistent with empirical evidence. In the other countries, giving up the exchange rate tool should not jeopardise growth which depends only marginally on export pull;
- estimation results for an aggregate of European exports show that real exchange rate elasticity is not significantly different for a smaller group of countries and for a wider one that includes the Mediterranean economies.

From this point of view, the larger the number of countries in the EMU, the smaller the propensity to use the euro's exchange rate to support competitiveness. This result is consistent with the approach evaluating the net benefits of a currency area discussed in chapter 1.

Overall, the fear that the Mediterranean economies will put pressure on the ECB for a real depreciation of the euro seems unfounded. Such a concern reflects a distinction more appropriate to the European monetary system (EMS). The structure underlying the European exchange rate mechanism was clearly asymmetrical: German interest to limit intra-European exchange rate fluctuations was coupled with other countries' desire for a nominal anchor.

In EMU this asymmetry is no longer justified because, to the extent that inflation has been checked, the European countries face the same objectives: to re-establish durable conditions for growth and to lower the high levels of unemployment. The above analyses underscore that it is the enlargement of the EMU and of the single market that will facilitate attainment of these objectives.

NOTES

1. Real exchange rates are computed on producer prices. EU's computation based on labour costs confirm the real devaluation of the dollar and a substantial appreciation of the D-mark (European Commission, 1997).
2. The same scale as for Figure 6.1 was used to simplify comparison.
3. The steady growth of Germany's favourable intra-EU trade balance during the EMS period and, conversely, the deterioration of the Italian and French balances, are analysed in Bini Smaghi and Vona (1986).
4. For a more detailed description of this disequilibrium, see CER (1995).
5. The assumption of an identical demand variable for all countries allows us to concentrate the comparison on exchange rate elasticity.
6. All the equations show low Durbin–Watson values, as is to be expected from the use of a simple specification. In any case, the residuals pass the Dickey-Fuller test and thus satisfy the necessary stationarity conditions.
7. The lack of significance of the exchange rate in the UK's export function is quite surprising. At the beginning of the 1980s, there was an extensive debate regarding the de-industrialisation induced by the sterling appreciation. Hence, the equation might have been badly specified. Nevertheless, even British commentators are surprised by the lack of real effects associated with the current sterling revaluation. See NIESR (1997).
8. For example, a lira/mark depreciation may be accompanied by a lira/dollar depreciation.
9. Both exchange rate indexes are taken from Banca d'Italia.
10. Similar tests are also presented in Gros (1996).
11. Greece, UK and Denmark have not joined EMU in the first wave. The exclusion of these countries from the estimates does not change the results reported below. Lack of data, on the other hand, has prevented the inclusion of Austria, Finland and Sweden.
12. As of 1995, Austria, Sweden and Finland are members of the EU. Exports to these countries, previously included in the extra-EU aggregate, are now included in intra-EU trade. The discontinuity in the dataset was corrected by introduction of the two dummies.
13. A more detailed account of the construction of real exchange rates and of the other variables is provided in the Appendix.

APPENDIX: CONSTRUCTION OF THE DATASET AND ESTIMATION OF THE EQUATIONS

The independent variables used in the estimates were constructed as follows:

Real exchange rates is the ratio between internal price index of area concerned i (P_i) and the product of the index of nominal exchange rate (e_j) times the price index of the extra-EU area (P_{usa}):

$$r = \frac{P_i}{(e_j * P_{usa})}$$

The index of internal prices P_i

$$P_i = \prod_k (PPI_k^{qk})$$

is given by the product over of the index numbers of producer prices *PPI* (sources: IMF and OECD) of the k countries belonging to the aggregate, each weighted by the individual country's share (q_k) of total exports of the aggregate to non-EU countries.

To obtain prices of the extra-EU area:

$$P_{usa} = PPI_{usa}^{q\ usa})$$

a proxy was chosen consisting of the US producer price (PPI_{usa}) weighted by the share of the aggregate's exports to the non-EU area of the aggregate's total exports.

The index of effective nominal exchange rate e_j

$$e_j = \prod_k (e * \$^{qk})$$

was constructed as the product over the bilateral exchange rate indexes of the individual countries (k) vis-à-vis the dollar, each weighted by the country's share of exports (q_k) of the aggregate's total exports to the non-EU area.

Increases (decreases) of the real exchange rate indicate a loss (gain) of competitiveness. Increases (decreases) of the index of nominal exchange rate indicate a devaluation (revaluation) and hence a gain (loss) of competitiveness: the bilateral exchange rates vis-à-vis the dollar are expressed as the number of units of national currency per unit of foreign currency.

World demand is the index number of imports of the main trading partners other than Europe, weighted by the respective shares of world trade.

Internal demand:

$$D\,\text{int} = \prod_k (D\,\text{int}\,_k^{qk})$$

product over the indexes of internal demand (*D*int) of the single *k* countries belonging to the aggregate (source: OECD), each weighted by the individual country's export share (q^k) out of total exports of the entire aggregate to the non-EU area.

The dependent variable is the volume of total exports, expressed in physical quantities, towards non-EU countries (source: EUROSTAT); hence, the exports of the aggregates (Core, EU12) to non-EU countries are given by the sum of the exports of the individual countries belonging to each aggregate. Data for exports from Austria, Finland and Sweden were not available and were not included in the two aggregates.

The method of estimation is ordinary least squares. Significant distortions were present in the first four observations of the export series (1976–79); i.e., a large part of the estimation errors is concentrated in this period. The results shown in the tables, therefore, are obtained for the 1980–96 period of estimation; the equations of the Core aggregate are better than those obtained for the 1976–79 period, while the equations of the EU12 aggregate display similar results for the two periods concerned.

7. Specialisation and flexibility

Stefano Manzocchi, Pier Carlo Padoan and Claudio Vicarelli

In this chapter we explore the sectoral dimension of industrial (un)employment in Europe. The main idea is that, even though the macroeconomic dimension has been crucial in generating differences in employment performance on the two sides of the Atlantic, European industry presents sectoral specificities that have hampered employment growth. In fact, as discussed in chapter 8, while it is uncontroversial that economic development and employment in the advanced countries depend increasingly on the service sector, industrial production remains crucial for the support of per-capita income growth. In addition, as we will see, the EU countries are far from being a homogeneous grouping, and national specificities in the EU help explain much of employment and growth performance.

The differences within the EU stand out also when we consider the changes in the national specialisation models. The European countries have displayed different degrees of mobility and flexibility in the industrial structure as well as different directions in the process of change itself. This has consequences for employment prospects as well as for the management of economic policies following the introduction of the single currency.

SECTORAL ASPECTS OF INDUSTRIAL EMPLOYMENT IN EUROPE

As we saw in chapter 1, the moderate rates of growth and rising unemployment in Europe are clearly in contrast to recent trends in the USA. On the whole, the US unemployment rate fell three percentage points from 1992 to 1998, to a low of 4.5%, while in the EU it fluctuated around 10%. The difference is even more relevant in the manufacturing sector; from 1985 to 1997 industrial employment fell by 1.1% per year in the EU, an overall decline of 13%, while the annual rate of contraction was only 0.2% in the USA and was nearly zero in Japan, until 1997.[1] Two aspects are evident: first, industry in general tends to expel labour even when the growth rate is sustained, as in the case of the USA; second, employment dynamics in European industry have been particularly negative in the past decade.

A number of interpretations of these facts have been suggested. Technology and social organisation have been invoked[2] to explain the long-term decline of manufacturing employment, and its recent acceleration. The assumedly negative effect of expanding world trade on employment and wages in the industrial countries has also been widely discussed.[3] Even though they consider several aspects of the evolution in the industrial countries, these interpretations are not fully satisfactory. For example, in the USA, where the so-called 'information revolution' started earlier and has been more widespread than in Europe, the contraction of industrial employment since 1970 has been smaller. This begs for an explanation of the negative performance of western Europe; as recalled in chapter 1, one hypothesis is that the consequences of international integration in Europe have been absorbed through changes in employment levels, while in the USA the adjustment has operated through wage changes.[4] An alternative explanation is that the excessive fiscal burden on labour in Europe has led to a more capital intensive restructuring of European industry.[5] Even though these interpretations are partially supported by the data, they do not offer a full explanation for the decline of industrial employment in Europe. A different interpretation can build on the characteristics and sectoral dynamics of the models of specialisation.[6]

The sectoral dynamics of industrial employment are differentiated in both Europe and the USA (Tables 7.1 and 7.2). While the number of employed grew in some sectors in absolute terms or in relation to the industrial average, in others the relative and absolute decrease in employment has been even greater. In general, the relative growth of employment has been greater, or the decrease smaller, in part of the chemical sector, food, electrical and non-electrical machinery (which includes consumer electronics and computers), professional instruments and plastic products. The greatest decrease has occurred in textiles and clothing and leather and footwear, in petrochemicals and in steel, and in beverages and tobacco and in glass and rubber products.

These trends can be ascribed to a number of factors. On the one hand, the dynamics of world demand and of trade volumes have differed greatly across sectors and affected the sectoral employment dynamics; on the other hand, the evolution of the international division of labour may have produced, in the various countries, different impacts on employment associated with the specific features of national specialisation models. Finally, the restructuring processes have impacted industrial sectors with different intensity, inducing changes in labour intensity – and in value added per worker – with respect to

Table 7.1 Sectoral employement in eight European countries: 1980–94 [a]

		% change	
ISIC code	Sector	Total	Annual average
356	Plastic products	18.81	1.25
342	Printing & publishing	3.70	0.25
352	Other chemicals	–2.30	–0.15
385	Professional goods	–5.89	–0.39
332	Furnitures & fixtures	–8.93	–0.60
311.2	Food	–10.33	–0.69
381	Metal products	–15.65	–1.04
383	Electrical machinery	–17.34	–1.16
341	Paper & products	–18.85	–1.26
382	Non–electrical machinery	–20.19	–1.35
331	Wood products	–22.81	–1.52
3000	Total manufacturing	–23.50	–1.57
361	Pottery, china, etc.	–24.23	–1.62
384	Transport equipment	–24.67	–1.64
372	Non–ferrous metals	–26.42	–1.76
369	Non–metallic products	–26.46	–1.76
362	Glass & products	–28.87	–1.92
351	Industrial chemicals	–29.68	–1.98
353	Petroleum refineries	–37.73	–2.52
355	Rubber products	–48.76	–3.25
322	Wearing apparel	–51.26	–3.42
313	Beverages	–52.21	–3.48
354	Petroleum & coal products	–71.06	–4.74
324	Footwear	–73.21	–4.88
321	Textiles	–74.16	–4.94
323	Leather & products	–75.51	–5.03
371	Iron & steel	–86.40	–5.76
314	Tobacco	–108.39	–7.23

Note: [a] Austria, Finland, Germany, Netherlands, Portugal, Spain, Sweden, UK.

industry as a whole. The interaction among the three aspects (composition of national industrial product, world demand dynamics, and labour intensity) may explain the unsatisfactory European performance. In analytical terms, the employment impact of changes in demand depends on the amount of labour employed in the production processes; if L is the logarithm of

Table 7.2 Sectoral employment in the USA: 1980–94

		% change	
ISIC code	Sector	Total	Annual average
356	Plastic products	59.25	3.95
342	Printing & publishing	26.32	1.75
332	Furnitures & fixtures	11.71	0.78
331	Wood products	8.62	0.57
311.2	Food	4.28	0.29
352	Other chemicals	2.14	0.14
341	Paper & products	0.73	0.05
321	Textiles	−4.78	−0.32
383	Electrical machinery	−7.92	−0.53
384	Transport equipment	−7.97	−0.53
3000	Total manufacturing	−8.62	−0.57
361	Pottery, China, etc.	−10.98	−0.73
355	Rubber products	−12.35	−0.82
354	Petroleum & coal products	−12.91	−0.86
381	Metal products	−13.14	−0.88
372	Non–ferrous metals	−13.74	−0.92
385	Professional goods	−16.39	−1.09
369	Non–metallic products	−16.99	−1.13
382	Non–electrical machinery	−21.58	−1.44
351	Industrial chemicals	−24.21	−1.61
362	Glass & products	−25.70	−1.71
322	Wearing apparel	−29.67	−1.98
313	Beverages	−30.74	−2.05
353	Petroleum refineries	−31.70	−2.11
314	Tobacco	−37.31	−2.49
323	Leather & products	−46.95	−3.13
371	Iron & steel	−48.86	−3.26
324	Footwear	−62.00	−4.13

employment in one sector, C is the logarithm of world demand for sectoral output and v is the logarithm of the ratio between the number of workers and value added (the inverse of unit productivity of labour) we obtain, through a first-order approximation :

$$(dL/dt) \ \text{v} \ (dC/dt) + C \ (dv/dt) \qquad (7.1)$$

where the expressions in parentheses represents, respectively, the growth rates of employment in the sector concerned, of world demand, and of labour intensity.

With this simple relationship in mind, we can examine the average sectoral dynamics of employment according to the variation in world demand and in labour intensity in the production process. In the case of a reduction in sectoral employment, we have three cases:

$(dL/dt)<0$ if: (a) $(dC/dt)<0$; $(dv/dt)>0$ and $v(dC/dt) > C(dv/dt)$
                (b) $(dC/dt)>0$; $(dv/dt)<0$ and $v(dC/dt) < C(dv/dt)$
                (c) $(dC/dt)<0$; $(dv/dt)<0$ (7.2)

In the first case, demand dynamics is negative (or, in relative terms, lower than the manufacturing average), but labour intensity rises (in absolute terms, or in relation to industry in general); however, the second, positive, effect is not large enough to offset the first. The opposite occurs in case (b), where growth of world demand is insufficient to offset the decline in the labour content of the production process. Lastly, in case (c), both effects depress average sectoral employment (in absolute terms or in relation to industry as a whole). Similar considerations apply in case of rising employment in a sector:

$(dL/dt)>0$ if: (d) $(dC/dt)<0$; $(dv/dt)>0$ and $v(dC/dt) < C(dv/dt)$
                (f) $(dC/dt)>0$; $(dv/dt)<0$ and $v(dC/dt) > C(dv/dt)$
                (g) $(dC/dt)>0$; $(dv/dt)>0$ (7.3)

We would therefore expect a better employment balance, absolutely or relatively, in those sectors where demand increases at a sustained pace and/or the labour content of the production process expands or does not contract.

With some elaboration on medium–long–term data, it is possible to quantify these components of sectoral heterogeneity. The dynamics of world demand are frequently associated with traditional (or mature) sectors with low growth rates of demand, and innovative segments (often those with a high value added) with high growth rates.[7] Nevertheless, several studies offer a more complex picture.[8] In a longer time-horizon we can discard cyclical components and concentrate on the growth of international trade volumes (exports and imports of the main OECD countries) as reference, and we note that some medium to high-added-value sectors have shown percentage growth rates lower than the industrial average in 1980–94 (and in 1970–94); this is the case of the petrochemical and steel segments, construction materials, and food and beverages. On the other hand, trade volume have grown at a sustained pace in 'traditional' segments such as furniture, footwear and clothing, in addition – as is to be expected – to chemistry (including pharmaceuticals), machinery (including computers, consumer electronics and telecommunications) and vehicles (see Table 7.3). Thus, the equation 'traditional equals static' is not always valid. This can help explain the relative employment creation performance of segments such as furniture, but it runs up against tangibly negative employment data in other traditional sectors (even in those with sustained trade growth).

One explanation is that the dynamics of international trade of the industrial countries is an incentive to the transfer segments (or whole lines) of production to non-OECD countries as a response to the competitive pressures from emerging economies. Hence, trade expansion reflects the growth of net imports of the OECD area (for instance, in the shoe and clothing sectors). The ability of European and US producers to compete in markets where the technological or dimensional barriers to entry are low is often based on restructuring to salvage profit margins through the reduction of labour intensity in the production process or in some of its segments.[9] This process has occurred in traditional sectors, where the pressure of the newly industrialised countries is felt more strongly [10] but also in some of the advanced sectors (e.g., semiconductors or PCs, where some emerging Asian economies have gained considerable competitive advantage in the 1980s and 1990s)[11]. As regards the case of the EU, several studies have shown that the completion of the Internal Market has intensified competition and 'vertical' specialisation in the European industrial systems which spurs the search for higher-added-value and more skilled-labour-intensive products even in the traditional sectors.[12] A statistical check on the importance and intensity of the restructuring processes implemented in the 1980s and the first half of the 1990s is obtained from an analysis of value added per worker at constant prices in manufacturing industry. Sectors which show higher value added per worker compared to the industrial average display increased intensity of physical or human capital, or of R&D, and where therefore, *ceteris paribus*, there is a decline in the relative intensity of unskilled labour (which, in the case of the traditional sectors, can be assimilated with the variable v in equations (7.1)–(7.3)).

The data for 'apparent' labour productivity or value added per worker must be interpreted from two different points of view. On the one hand, a high value added per worker denotes (physical or human) capital – or R&D – intensive segments characterised by high unit wages; on the other hand, *higher* value added per worker can be obtained via labour–reducing restructuring processes as other factors of production are held constant.

Several studies allow classification of the industrial sectors on the basis of a few parameters such as market concentration, the share of the factors of production in value added, returns to scale, intensity of R&D, and the number of patents.[13] A first group of sectors with high R&D and skilled-labour

Table 7.3 OECD countries: ratio of growth rate of international trade by sector to total manufacturing

ISIC code	Sector	1994–80	1994–70
3000	Total manufacturing	1.00	1.00
31	Food, beverages & tobacco	0.72	0.63
311.2	- Food	0.69	0.59
313	- Beverages	0.81	0.72
314	- Tobacco	1.07	2.46
32	Textiles, apparel & leather	1.04	0.85
321	- Textiles	0.75	0.65
322	- Wearing apparel	1.56	1.10
323	- Leather & products	1.06	1.04
324	- Footwear	1.17	1.14
33	Wood products & furniture	0.95	0.95
331	- Wood products	0.75	0.71
332	- Furnitures & fixtures	1.42	1.94
34	Paper, paper products & printing	0.82	0.70
341	- Paper & products	0.79	0.67
342	- Printing & publishing	0.98	0.85
35	Chemical products	0.70	1.18
351	- Industrial chemicals	0.82	1.12
352	- Other chemicals	1.65	1.98
3522	- Drugs & medicines	2.13	1.77
3529	- Chemicals products	1.42	2.13
353	Petroleum refineries	–0.11	0.63
354	Petroleum & coal products	0.18	0.51
355	Rubber products	1.02	1.12
356	Plastic products	1.64	1.80
36	Non-metallic mineral products	0.78	0.87
361	Pottery, china etc.	0.69	0.71
362	Glass & products	0.99	0.94
369	Non-metallic products	0.74	0.92
37	Basic metal industries	0.27	0.40
371	Iron & steel	0.32	0.41
372	Non-ferrous metals	0.21	0.39
38	Fabricated metal products	1.38	1.26
381	Metal products	0.78	1.03
382	Non-electrical machinery	1.36	1.09
3825	Office & computing machinery	3.85	2.75
3829	Machinery & equipment	0.85	0.78
383	Electrical machinery	1.95	1.79
3832	Radio, TV & communic. equip.	2.25	1.96
3839	Electrical apparatus	1.59	1.58
384	Transport equipment	1.27	1.19
3841	Shipbuilding & repairing	0.52	0.28
3842	Railbroad vehicles	1.52	1.51
3843	Motor vehicles	1.36	1.31
3844	Motorcycles & bicycles	0.51	0.70
3845	Aircraft	1.21	1.44
3849	Transport equipment	0.81	0.83
385	Professional goods	1.39	1.46
39	Other manufacturing	0.88	1.36

intensity is also associated with high rates of growth of world demand (computers, telecommunications, other chemicals and some segments of the transport equipment). Among the capital-intensive sectors, we must distinguish between skilled–labour intensive ones (food, motor vehicles) and those which employ mostly unskilled labour (textiles, steel, glass, rubber and plastics). Finally, we identify sectors, respectively of high–skilled labour intensity (machinery, professional instruments, electrical equipment) and unskilled labour intensity (clothing, furniture, leather, some metal products).[14] In the high-tech and high added-value sectors, Europe as a whole displays a low 'quality' of production specialisation, i.e., ability to generate value added and to reward factors of production with high returns (Table 7.4). While, in fact, only the USA and Japan are specialised, respectively, in computers and telecommunications equipment,[15] both are also specialised in vehicles (together with Germany and Spain), some EU countries are specialized in chemicals (including Germany, France, UK and the Netherlands) and in industrial machinery (Germany, France, Italy, UK, Sweden and the Netherlands). Europe's limited presence in the high-tech sectors should be ascribed to a generally modest intensity of R&D in many European countries (excluding Scandinavia, as well as non-EU Switzerland), measured both by low input levels of R&D and low output levels of patents.[16] There is, however, another relevant aspect that concerns the *dynamics* of labour productivity (i.e., value added per worker), which can be related to the inverse of variable v as defined in equations (7.1)–(7.3). In fact, a rise in value added per worker, *ceteris paribus*, coincides with a drop in average labour intensity which could depend on the nature of the restructuring processes. These processes can develop in two directions: a virtuous one of upgrading and introduction of skilled labour, and a vicious one, of downsizing and reduction of the labour force. A comparative analysis shows that the two aspects are both present and that these trends are common to both Europe and the USA.[17]

Table 7.5 summarises two sets of evidence concerning, respectively, trade dynamics and the trend of value added per worker (at constant prices) in ten EU countries between 1980 and 1993–94.[18] The sectors that show a sustained trade dynamics and a decline of the unit value added (i.e., an increase in v) are those in which – see equation (7.3) – one expects a better employment performance than the manufacturing average. This is the case with the plastics and furniture segments but also with motor vehicles (in the USA) and non-electric machinery (in Europe), while in the case of footwear the trade dynamics are pulled by the *imports* of the OECD countries and thus do not, on average, lead to higher employment in the industrial countries (Tables 7.1 and 7.2). The case of sectors which show weak trade dynamics and rising unit

Table 7.4 Comparative sectoral specialisation in 12 OECD countries: 1970–93 [a]

ISIC code	Sector	USA	Jap	Ger	Fra	UK	Ita	Esp	Por[a]	Swe	Nl	Den	Fin
356	Plastic products						S	S				S	
332	Furnitures & fixtures						S	S				S	
352	Other chemicals	S		S	S	S					S	S	
342	Printing & publishing	S				S		S				S	S
311.2	Food	S			S			S			S	S	
361	Pottery, china etc.		S	S			S	S	S				
385	Professional goods	S	S	S		S							
384	Transport equipment	S	S	S				S					
381	Metal products			S	S			S	S				
383	Electrical machinery		S	S									
382	Non-electrical machinery	S	S	S	S	S	S			S			
362	Glass & products				S			S		S			
351	Industrial chemicals	S		S		S				S			
341	Paper & products	S								S	S		S
331	Wood products									S	S		S
353	Petroleum refineries						S			S			
324	Footwear						S	S	S				
372	Non-ferrous metals							S					S
369	Non-metallic products						S	S	S			S	
354	Petroleum & coal products			S						S			
313	Beverages					S	S	S	S	S			
355	Rubber products		S			S		S					
322	Wearing apparel							S	S				
323	Leather & products							S	S	S			
321	Textiles							S	S				
371	Iron & steel			S	S	S		S		S			
314	Tobacco	S				S					S	S	

Notes: [a] The sectors of specialisation (indicated by S) are those where the Balassa index of comparative advantage is higher than one, and the contribution to the trade balance is positive for the period reviewed (1980–93). In the case of Portugal, only the index of comparative advantage is used.

The contribution to trade balance index of country *j* for a given product *i* is the following:

$$Ics_{i,j} = \left[\frac{(x_{i,j} - m_{i,j})}{(x_j + m_j)/2} - \frac{(x_j - m_j)}{(x_j + m_j)/2} \times \frac{(x_{i,j} + m_{i,j})}{(x_j + m_j)} \right] \times 100$$

where $x_{i,j}$ = exports of product i by country *j*;
$m_{i,j}$ = imports of product *i* by country *j*;
x_j = total exports by country *j*;
m_j = total imports by country *j*.

The Balassa index of revealed comparative advantage is the following:

$$B_{i,j} = \left(X_{i,j} / \textstyle\sum_i X_{i,j} \right) / \left(\textstyle\sum_j X_{i,j} / \textstyle\sum_i\sum_j X_{i,j} \right)$$

where: X = exports,
    i = product
    j = country

Table 7.5 A classification of industrial sectors according to demand and value added patterns

---

(1)   *Sectors with high growth of international demand and with value added per worker declining more than average:*

Footwear (324)
Furniture & fixtures (332)
Plastic products (356)
Non-electrical machinery (382)
Transport equipment (384)

(2)   *Sectors with high growth of international demand and with value added per worker increasing more than average:*

Other chemicals (352)
Electrical machinery (383)
Professional goods (385)

(3)   *Sectors with low growth of international demand and with value added per worker declining more than average:*

Wood products (331)
Printing & publishing (342)
Petroleum & coal products (354)
Pottery, china etc. (361)

(4)   *Sectors with low growth of international demand and with value added per worker increasing more than average:*

Textiles (321)
Petroleum refineries (353)
Industrial chemicals (351)
Iron & steel (371)
Non-ferrous metals (372)

Sources: Author's calculations, based on OECD (1998). Growth rates of world demand (1980–94) as of Table 7.3; average variations of value added per worker (at constant prices) computed for ten EU countries over 1980–93.

value added (i.e., a decline of v) is symmetrical. In these conditions, equation (7.2) indicates that the relative employment performance should be below average. This is the case of steel, industrial chemistry and, at least in Europe – to which the value added data refer, in textiles. The two intermediate cases are equally interesting. On the whole, sectors with strong demand dynamics,

Table 7.6   Changes in total manufacturing employment in OECD countries: 1980–94

Finland	-33.45
UK	-28.28
Sweden	-25.25
France	-24.83
Belgium	-23.96
Italy	-23.17
Austria	-19.97
Spain	-16.69
Netherlands	-13.26
Germany	-12.66
Portugal	-11.07
USA	-8.62
Denmark	-2.57
Japan	9.72

where one also observes rising value added, show excellent employment performance (with the exception of professional instruments in the USA); this is the case with industries with high intensity of R&D and skilled labour, in which the effect of expanding demand prevails over the reduction of labour intensity (as in case (f) of equation (7.3)). There is less homogeneity in the group of industries where international trade growth is below average while relative value added per worker is shrinking (v increases). This group includes resource-intensive sectors with high economies of scale, such as oil and coal, that are affected by a deep and widespread decline in employment (case (a) of equation (7.2)), but also sectors in which increasing labour intensity produces positive employment growth (case (d) of equation (7.3): for example, publishing and wood products).

The above description raises two questions: (a) Up to what point do the restructuring processes require the relocation of highly labour-intensive segments and downsizing if the sector is to be kept alive in advanced countries? (b) What is the relative weight of individual sectors in the national specialisation models? By combining the data in Table 7.4 (sectors of national specialisation) and Table 7.5 (sectoral dynamics of demand and value added) with the data illustrated in Table 7.6 (changes in industrial employment in the main countries), we note that the international division of labour, for a given macroeconomic profile, explains (a) the greater resilience of industrial employment in the USA compared to the EU as a whole (wider presence of dynamic sectors of the high-tech group; and of capital-intensive industries where stagnant or modestly shrinking 'apparent' labour productivity is observed, such as the food sector); (b) in the European context, industrial employment resilience in some countries compared with others.

For instance, Denmark, which contained the employment decline after 1980 (Table 7.6), is specialised in segments of high demand growth (furniture, plastics) or where labour intensity was deepened (food, publishing). This also is the case, in part, of the Netherlands (specialised in food, chemicals and machinery) and of Germany (chemicals, vehicles and machinery).[19] The picture is more complex for countries such as France, Finland, Sweden or the UK, where specialisation in some segments in which employment creation has been satisfactory (other chemical products, publishing, machinery) is counterbalanced by other sectors where employment has been declining markedly (beverages, tobacco, steel); the overall result has been a strong lay-off of workers during the 15 years from 1980 to 1994. In the case of the Mediterranean countries, we observe two phenomena: on the one hand, the gradual decline of sectors with declining employment (textiles), accompanied by specialisation in the food and vehicle sectors, has allowed Spain to limit the loss of employment in industry. This has not been the case in Italy, whose position in sectors such as furniture, plastics or machinery has not been sufficient to offset the constant dwindling of the traditional lines of textiles and clothing and leather and footwear. Above all, what bears on the Italian experience is the gradual de-specialisation in industries where world demand has been buoyant, such as office machines (computers) and motor vehicles. The second phenomenon, which concerns Portugal, is connected with its entry into the EU in the mid-1980s; this economy has exploited the favourable cost differentials in the domestic market and strengthened its specialisation in a number of labour-intensive sectors (with positive employment balances in footwear and clothing and contained losses in beverages). This has allowed Portugal to attain better employment dynamics than the European average from 1980 to 1994 (Table 7.6).

As we have argued, the national specialisation model is relevant for industrial employment as world demand trends and labour intensity vary across sectors. In the following section, we analyse the changes that have taken place in the specialisation models, with respect to aggregate mobility and flexibility as well as to the direction towards which the individual industrial systems have evolved.

MOBILITY AND FLEXIBILITY: ADAPTATION OF THE SPECIALISATION MODELS

This section discusses the capacity for active change, or, alternatively, of passive adaptation, in European industry. We return to the issue of the process of industrial (de)specialisation as measured by indicators of revealed comparative advantage (Table 7.4), but we also construct synthetic indices of overall mobility and flexibility of European industrial systems.

In our terminology, *mobility* means remodelling the *hierarchy* of comparative advantages of a given nation by abandoning or reducing specialisation in some segments and gaining it in others. *Flexibility*, on the other hand, means gradually to modify the *distribution* of the set of specialisation indices; this does not necessarily imply substituting sectors of specialisation but rather gradually to transform one's structure of comparative advantages. An analytical definition of the indicators of mobility and flexibility employed in this study, as well as a discussion of their merits and limits from the viewpoints of statistical method and of economic interpretation, will be found in the Appendix to this chapter. A joint evaluation of the two indices offers an appraisal of the overall change that has taken place in specialisation models in Europe since 1980

Tables 7.7 and 7.8 show, respectively, the indices of mobility and flexibility of the main OECD industrial systems, calculated for the period 1980–1994 on the basis of the Balassa indices of comparative advantage for sectoral exports (see extended note to Table 7.4) Some results appear evident, as, for example, that the North American countries have transformed the hierarchy of their comparative advantage considerably during the 1980–94 period, while several European countries that have joined the EU during this period (Portugal, Denmark, Finland and Spain) have reoriented their specialisation model. Specifically, as emphasised at the end of the preceding section, adaptation of the specialisation model has been remarkable in the Iberian countries, even though the changes have followed different directions. Germany, France and the UK display comparable values of indices of mobility and – with the exception of France – of flexibility; Italy ranks among the lowest in terms of both indicators, exhibiting a notable immobility of the specialisation model.[20]

Moving on to the indicators of mobility and flexibility, calculated from the indices of relative comparative advantage, of sectoral employment between 1980 and 1992 (Tables 7.9 and 7.10), we note that, while the ranking of mobility tends to reproduce that of Table 7.7, except for the countries at the lower end which display higher indices, overall flexibility is tangibly lower (compare Tables 7.8 and 7.10), thus confirming a more stable sectoral distribution of employment with respect to exports. In fact, one can expect

Table 7.7 Index of mobility of export structure in OECD countries: 1980–94 (%) [a]

USA	53.80
Finland	53.70
Canada	50.80
Portugal	49.90
Denmark	48.00
UK	48.70
Germany	47.50
Spain	46.40
Netherlands	43.80
France	43.20
Austria	41.00
Belgium	35.10
Sweden	33.30
Italy	22.00
Japan	16.20

Note: [a] Definition: see Appendix.

Table 7.8 Index of flexibility of export structure in OECD countries: 1980–94 (%) [a]

Portugal	10.20
Spain	8.00
UK	7.80
USA	7.80
Germany	7.70
Austria	6.90
Belgium	4.30
Japan	3.60
Netherlands	3.10
Finland	3.10
Canada	2.60
France	2.40
Sweden	1.70
Denmark	1.60
Italy	1.50

Note: [a] Definition: see Appendix.

Table 7.9 Index of mobility of employment structure in OECD countries: 1980–92 (%) [a]

UK	58.56
Finland	54.45
Spain	49.54
USA	44.02
Belgium	43.13
Austria	45.42
France	44.92
Japan	49.00
Italy	43.28
Canada	44.68
Denmark	45.96
Sweden	39.39
Portugal	38.54
Germany	37.95

Note: [a] Definition: see Appendix.

Table 7.10 Index of flexibility of employment structure in OECD countries: 1980–92 (%) [a]

UK	13.63
Portugal	5.57
Finland	4.91
Denmark	4.68
Japan	4.39
Italy	4.21
Austria	4.01
France	3.52
Sweden	3.16
Spain	2.48
Canada	2.36
Belgium	2.32
USA	2.31
Netherlands	2.15
Germany	1.77

Note: [a] Definition: see Appendix.

that, as trade specialisation changes, transformation of the sectoral distribution of labour will be more modest, provided that labour is a near-fixed (or immobile, in the short run) factor of production. The data on mobility of the structure of employment (Table 7.9), which apparently contradict those on flexibility, can be interpreted in the sense that even countries where export comparative advantage has remained stable over time have faced restructuring processes that may have altered the hierarchy of sectoral employment in industry. On the whole, nevertheless, the earlier reflections regarding the *relative* intensity of the industrial transformation in the OECD countries do not lose their validity.

These results must be qualified in the sense of understanding the direction sought by the process of change (or of consolidation of what existed); to do so the indices must be linked to the sectors in which (de)specialisation or consolidation have been observed. In this respect the taxonomy of the first section allows a *qualitative* assessment regarding the direction, as well as the intensity, of industrial changes.

In general, positions of comparative advantage in the high value-added and demand-dynamic sectors (high-tech sectors with large economies of scale) tend to reinforce themselves; the countries which already had an established specialisation in the early 1970s have preserved it subsequently, with few exceptions (for instance, the de-specialisation in Italy and Sweden in computers and office machines, and in France in motor vehicles; the gradual specialisation of Spain in vehicles). This relative stability in the high-value-added segments is not surprising if we consider that production is characterised by dynamic increasing returns, economies of scale and oligopolistic markets, which represent high entry barriers for new competitors.

Conversely, the transformation of the international division of labour has been more intense in the 'mature' segments with high capital and energy intensity (petrochemicals and steel) and in the 'traditional' sectors. In the former case, specific events have changed the international picture (the discovery of the North Sea oil fields has substantially strengthened the British position in the refining segment, and that of the Netherlands in the segments of petroleum derivatives and coal). In the case of traditional sectors, we observe a widespread tendency to de-specialisation. Specifically, the UK loses positions in textiles and leather, Germany in furniture and ceramics, France in the leather and footwear and textile and clothing lines, and Spain in textiles and clothing, footwear, and beverages. Two European countries have moved in the opposite direction: Portugal, by substantially strengthening its specialisation model in the traditional sectors (clothing, footwear, ceramics) and Italy, by maintaining its comparative advantage in the segments of leather and footwear, textiles and clothing, and furniture.

The appraisal of the stability or transformation of national industrial structures is closely connected to the direction in which they move. At least three models can be singled out in Europe: first, that of the countries that occupied (and kept) positions of comparative advantage in dynamic, high-added-value sectors (Denmark, Netherlands, Germany) and have transformed their industrial structure by downsizing the weight of the traditional segments. Even though these economies have suffered losses of employment these have been limited through a process of moderate redefinition of the hierarchy of comparative advantages (Tables 7.7 and 7.9).

In the second place, some countries have altered the sectoral structure of industry more radically: the UK, Finland, Spain and Portugal. The first two underwent a vigorous contraction of industrial employment, connected in part with specialisation in resource-intensive sectors that were substantially restructured (petroleum, paper mills) and in part, in the case of the UK, to more intense tertiarisation of the economy. The Iberian countries, on the other hand, have modified their production structures in opposite directions: Spain has downsized the weight of several traditional sectors while specialisation in high-economies-of-scale segments has increased, while the Portuguese industry has deepened the comparative advantages in the labour-intensive segments. Both Iberian experiences seem to have been rewarding in terms of employment, even though the one-off effect of joining the EU and, in the case of Portugal, the modest size of the (virtually regional) economy must be emphasised.

Among the countries where the industrial structure has changed the least, we find France and, above all, Italy. Nevertheless, while the French economy has lost its comparative advantage in the traditional sectors (but also in motor vehicles), it has preserved its competitive advantage in a few segments – of both dynamic (other chemicals) and 'mature' (steel) types – with large economies of scale. Conversely, Italy has maintained its specialisation in several traditional sectors. As noted above, employment trends are unsatisfactory in many specialised sectors of these two economies, regardless of whether they are 'mature' and highly capital-intensive, or traditional (the main exceptions are other chemicals in France and furniture and plastic products in Italy). The gradual abandonment of industries with strong international demand, such as vehicles and office equipment, and the trends in the sectors subjected to major restructuring processes have contributed to falling industrial employment in these two countries.

To sum up, the sectoral dynamics of industry and the national models of specialisation have medium and long-term impact on manufacturing employment. It is interesting to note that econometric estimates reported below confirm the greater sensitivity of employment and industrial wages to international competition in those segments where the relative position of a

Monetary union, employment and growth

Table 7.11 Sectoral elasticities of employment and wages: Germany [a]

ISIC code	Sector	Dependent variable			
		Employment		Wages	
3843	Motor vehicles (MV)	——	——	——	——
3829	Machinery & equipment (MI)	——	——	——	——
354	Petroleum & coal products (PC)	0.02	(2.45)		
381	Metal products (MP)	0.08	(2.04)	0.22	(1.98)
3839	Electrical apparatus (EL)	——	——	——	——
3522	Drugs & medicines (FA)	——	——	——	——
385	Professional goods (PG)				
371	Iron & steel (IR)	0.06	(2.08)[b]	0.30	(2.77)[b]
384	Transport equipment (TR)				
361	Pottery, china etc. (PO)	0.04	(0.19)	0.24	(2.04)
351	Industrial chemicals (CH)	0.07	(2.79)	−0.11	(2.05)
3529	Chemical products (OPC)	——	——	——	——
341	Paper & products (PR)	0.07	(2.93)	−0.18	(−2.68)
362	Glass & products (GL)	0.07	(3.59)	0.17	(2.01)
356	Plastic products (PI)	0.07	(2.79)	0.11	(1.73)
332	Furnitures & fixtures (FU)	0.07	(2.78)	0.08	(2.67)
372	Non-ferrous metals (NF)	0.07	(2.78)	0.08	(2.67)
321	Textiles (TE)	0.10	(4.16)	0.17	(2.23)
322	Wearing apparel (WE)	0.14	(1.13)	0.11	(2.21)
323	Leather & products (LE)	0.15	(3.28)	0.21	(2.15)
331	Wood products (WO)	0.12	(2.39)	0.17	(2.47)
314	Tobacco (TO)	0.16	(2.47)	0.20	(2.26)
3832	Radio. TV & communic. equip. (TV)	——	——	——	——
369	Non−metallic products (NMP)	0.24	(3.74)	0.33	(2.68)
324	Footwear (FT)	0.10	(0.65)	0.15	(2.21)
311	Food (FO)	−0.07	(−2.41)	−0.10	(−1.38)
313	Beverages (BE)	0.04	(1.65)	0.20	(2.74)
355	Rubber products (RU)	0.17	(3.26)	0.20	(1.02)
341	Paper & products (PA)	0.05	(2.40)	0.19	(4.65)
3825	Office & computing machinery (CO)	——	——	——	——
353	Petroleum refineries (PE)	0.17	(3.41)	0.25	(4.65)[b]

Notes:
[a] t statistic in brackets.
[b] Indicates co-integration.

given country is weakest (or rather, where there exists *de-specialisation,* i.e. absence of comparative advantages and negative contributions to the trade balance). Tables 7.11 to 7.14 report estimates of employment and wage elasticity as functions of an indicator of the competitive pressure sustained by each sector for the four largest EU economies. Our indicator of competitive pressure is the sector import price.

The reported results are focused on the sectors in which the country concerned enjoys a strong or moderate comparative advantage (the first two groups of sectors in Tables 7.11–7.14) during the period under review (1970–92). In most of the cases, employment and wage elasticities are on average higher (a drop in import prices has a greater depressing impact on wages and/or employment) in the sectors in which the country has no comparative advantage. This result is largely independent of the specific sector, inasmuch as the four economies have different models of specialisation. This result is not surprising and indeed it matches the definition of the sector of specialisation as that sector where competitive advantages are sustained over time – and have been firmly established – and allow the pressure of international competition to be faced.

On the other hand we have argued that different models of specialisation expose the national industrial systems to different medium to long-term trends arising from the dynamics of world demand, of productivity and labour intensity and, hence, of employment and wages. An efficient response to world competition in a segment with strong demand dynamics, and where global employment is expanding, is fundamentally different from success in a sector whose market is shrinking and where the relative use of labour in the production process is declining.

In the following section we turn our attention to another dimension of the sectoral heterogeneity of industry, namely to the differences in the sensitivity of industrial sectors to co-movements originating, respectively, in the dynamics of *sectoral* or *national* demand and supply. In other words, we investigate whether industrial production follows sectoral or country-level trends.

ASYMMETRIES AND SHOCK: THE CO-MOVEMENTS OF PRODUCTION IN INDUSTRIAL SECTORS

In this section we discuss the outlook for the EU's stabilisation and cohesion policies in the light of the structural asymmetries identified in the preceding sections. In fact, it is not only the starting positions and the relative propensity for change in domestic industries that condition the medium to

Table 7.12 Sectoral elasticities of employment and wages: France [a]

		Dependent variable			
		Employment		Wages	
ISIC code	Sector				
313	Beverages (BE)	0.06	(2.09)	——	——
355	Rubber products (RU)	0.07	(1.73)	——	——
3522	Durgs & medicines (FA)	——	——	——	——
371	Iron & steel (IR)	0.07	(2.18)	——	——
362	Glass & products (GL)	0.16	(2.28)	——	——
3529	Chemical products (OCH)	——	——	——	——
3829	Machinery & equipment (MI)	——	——	——	——
311	Food (FO)	−0.005	(−0.31)	——	——
381	Metal products (MP)	0.05	(2.44)	——	——
342	Printing & publishing (PR)	0.08	(8.36)	——	——
322	Wearing apparel (WE)	0.09	(3.46)	——	——
3832	Radio, TV & communic. equip. (TV)	——	——	——	——
323	Leather & products (LE)	0.10	(3.76)	——	——
321	Textiles (TE)	0.11	(3.52)	——	——
384	Transport equipment (TR)	0.11	(2.29)	0.26	(2.31)
351	Industrial chemicals (CH)	0.10	(5.08)	——	——
356	Plastic products (PI)	0.11	(2.45)	——	——
353	Petroleum refineries (PE)	0.04	(2.44)	——	——
369	Non-metallic products (NMP)	0.16	(5.14)	——	——
372	Non-ferrous metals (NF)	0.16	(3.44)	——	——
381	Metal products (MP)				
324	Footwear (FT)	0.13	(2.39)	——	——
331	Wood products (WO)	0.18	(3.23)	——	——
332	Furnitures & fixtures (FU)	0.21	(2.91)	——	——
341	Paper & products (PA)	0.03	(1.45)	——	——
385	Professional goods (PG)	0.21	(2.53)	0.35	(2.63)
361	Pottery, china etc. (PO)	0.27	(3.47)	——	——
314	Tobacco (TO)	−0.33	(−3.22)	——	——
3825	Office & computing machinery (CO)	——	——	——	——
3839	Electrical apparatus (EL)	——	——	——	——

Note: [a] t statistic in brackets.

Table 7.13 Sectoral elasticities of employment and wages: Italy [a]

ISIC code	Sector	Dependent variable			
		Employment		Wages	
321	Textiles (TE)	0.07	(0.18)[a]	0.14	(0.97)[b]
332	Furnitures & fixtures (FU)	0.08	(2.12)	−0.47	(−2.34)
313	Beverages (BE)	0.10	(0.48)[b]	0.14	(0.97)[b]
322	Wearing apparel (WE)	0.11	(2.13)	0.51	(4.50)
355	Rubber products (RU)	0.11	(2.45)	0.11	(1.09)[b]
323	Leather & products (LE)	0.12	(3.26)	−0.47	(−2.78)[b]
324	Footwear (FT)	0.15	(2.60)	−0.22	(−1.78)
356	Plastic products (PI)	0.13	(2.09)[b]	0.16	(1.27)
361	Pottery, china etc. (PO)	0.13	(2.01)	0.17	(2.46)
362	Glass & products (GL)	0.16	(2.15)	0.10	(2.28)
369	Non-metallic products (NMP)	0.11	(2.83)	1.14	(2.39)
381	Metal products (MP)	0.12	(2.39)	0.13	(3.44)
3829	Machinery & equipment (MI)	——	——	——	——
3839	Electrical apparatus (EL)	——	——	——	——
353	Petroleum refineries (PE)	1.14	(3.55)	0.31	(2.69)
342	Printing and publishing (PR)	0.16	(3.47)	1.15	(2.44)
371	Iron & steel (IR)	0.29	(4.02)	0.32	(1.46)
3522	Drugs & medicines (FA)	——	——	——	——
311	Food (FO)	0.22	(6.52)	0.21	(2.90)
341	Paper & products (PA)	0.22	(3.21)	0.44	(1.24)
354	Petroleum & coal products (PE)	0.21	(2.45)	0.20	(2.81)
372	Non-ferrous metals (NF)	0.21	(3.88)	0.33	(2.36)
3825	Office & computing machinery (CO)	——	——	——	——
3832	Radio, TV & communic. equip. (TV)	——	——	——	——
3843	Motor vehicles (MV)	0.22	(4.29)	0.38	(1.94)
385	Professional goods (PG)	0.22	(4.55)	0.51	(2.18)
3529	Chemical products (OCH)	——	——	——	——
331	Wood products (WO)	0.30	(2.41)	0.30	(2.61)
351	Industrial chemicals (CH)	0.31	(3.55)	0.27	(3.09)
384	Transport equipment (TR)	0.28	(3.74)	0.17	(1.06)

Notes:
[a] t statistic in parentheses.
[b] Indicates co-integration.

Monetary union, employment and growth

Table 7.14 Sectoral elasticities of employment and wages: UK [a]

ISIC code	Sector	Dependent variable			
		Employment		Wages	
313	Beverages (BE)	0.10	(2.55)[b]	0.31	(2.23)
385	Professional goods (PG)	0.09	(4.00)	0.350	(2.66)[b]
314	Tobacco (TO)	–0.14	(–1.23)	–0.41	(–1.08)
3522	Drugs & medicines (FA)	——	——	——	——
342	Printing & publishing (PR)	0.10	(3.25)	0.19	(2.15)
3529	Chemical products (OCH)	——	——	——	——
3829	Machinery & equipment (MI)	——	——	——	——
361	Pottery, china etc. (PO)	–0.29	(–3.00)	0.29	(3.09)
351	Industrial chemicals (CH)	0.23	(2.41)	0.35	(2.38)
353	Petroleum refineries (PE)	0.21	(3.74)	0.63	(2.31)
355	Rubber products (RU)	0.26	(3.11)	0.55	(2.30)
354	Petroleum & coal products (PE)	0.13	(2.16)	——	——
371	Iron & steel (IR)	0.21	(2.12)	0.37	(1.96)
369	Non-metallic products (NMP)	0.25	(2.52)	0.76	(4.25)
372	Non-ferrous metals (NF)	0.26	(2.18)	0.40	(2.42)
381	Metal products (MP)	0.27	(2.67)	0.28	(2.34)
3832	Radio, TV & communic. equip. (TV)	——	——	——	——
3839	Electrical apparatus (EL)	——	——	——	——
384	Transport equipment (TR)	0.16	(2.06)	0.38	(3.15)
3825	Office & computing machinery (CO)	——	——	——	——
321	Textiles (TE)	0.35	(2.49)	0.29	(3.30)
322	Wearing apparel (WE)	0.18	(1.42)	0.40	(5.49)
362	Glass & products (GL)	0.28	(3.32)	0.37	(2.45)
323	Leather & products (LE)	0.29	(3.78)	0.59	(2.33)
3843	Motor vehicles (MV)	0.31	(2.15)	0.44	(2.25)
324	Footwear (FT)	0.25	(2.35)	0.47	(2.69)
331	Wood products (WO)	0.33	(2.80)	0.21	(0.95)
332	Furnitures & fixtures (FU)	0.07	(1.85)[b]	0.09	(0.94)
341	Paper & products (PA)	0.30	(6.19)	–0.88	(–3.19)
311	Food (FO)	0.22	(4.56)	0.41	(4.40)[b]
356	Plastic products (PI)	0.29	(2.41)	0.37	(4.33)

Notes
[a] t statistic in brackets
[b] Indicates co-integration.

long-term outlook for manufacturing employment, but also the impact of the new macroeconomic economic policy 'environment' in Europe on different specialisation structures

Two aspects are relevant in the assessment of the issue. In the first place, we must consider whether the *national* or the *sectoral* dimension prevails in the determination of the co-movements of production (or of exports) in the manufacturing sectors. In the second place, we must determine the European industrial sectors' *relative weight* as well as their degree of *dispersion*.

A few examples may clarify the matter. If, for example, the correlation between cyclical movements of production is high across one sector where the sector concerned reflects a symmetrical incidence of the shocks in Europe. In such a case, *if* the sector's weight is relevant and homogeneous in the countries of the Monetary Union, such a behaviour suggests the need for centralized, or at least 'co-ordinated' economic policy interventions in response to a negative shock (case A). If, conversely – even assuming symmetrical co-movements of sectoral production in different countries – the sector is concentrated in only a few regions (or countries), a specific policy of structural or regional support for the critical areas may be more appropriate (case B). If, finally, industrial dynamics are related to the country, rather than to the sectoral, dimension (asymmetrical co-movements), a centralised monetary policy intervention at the EU level is to be excluded; it remains to be seen what are the most appropriate instruments to face the decline of industrial production (case C).

Two aspects need to be investigated: the size of the sectoral co-movement of industrial production relative to the size of the national co-movement, and the sector's weight and dispersion in the EU. The literature on the decomposition of the fluctuations (or of the shocks) of industrial production is impressive; in this section we diverge from the approach of a large part of the existing literature for two reasons.

First, numerous studies on the decomposition of manufacturing shocks in Europe consider the costs and benefits of the creation of a Monetary Union and the composition of the group of countries that are qualified to join.[21] However, once the single currency is introduced, these issues need to be redefined in the sense of asking which policies are appropriate for assuring stability and welfare for all partners in the Monetary Union.

Second, as mentioned in chapter 2, several studies have emphasised that the criterion of optimal currency areas used to establish the ideal extension of the Monetary Union, should be interpreted dynamically because the very membership in a process of currency integration changes the underlying national economic structures and hence the parameters for evaluation.[22]

Table 7.15 Sectoral incidence of national shocks in nine European countries

	Percentage of sectors where country-level shocks prevail over sector-level shocks
Austria	37.04
Belgium	51.85
Finland	88.89
France	70.37
Germany	96.30
Italy	77.78
Netherlands	40.74
Portugal	66.67
Spain	70.37

The following analysis does not consider the role of the asymmetrical co-movements in the various countries (industrial dynamics 'pulled' by the country size), which might depend on past divergent national macroeconomic policies; in fact, centralization of monetary policy and the constraints on fiscal policy within the EMU could, *per se*, decrease the role of the country component of industrial dynamics. Rather, we ask in what *segments* the national component has been more, or less, relevant than the sectoral one.

The analysis of the co-movements of industrial production is performed by calculating the coefficient of correlation of the annual growth rate of output of each sector in each country for the period 1980–94 with two alternative aggregates: (a) the growth rate of one sector in the aggregate of the remaining eight EMU members;[23] (b) the growth rate of aggregate industrial production of the remaining 26 (3-digit) industrial sectors in one country. The consideration of a sectoral aggregate of the euro area, and of a national industrial aggregate, avoids the measurement of *bilateral* co-movements (for example, Italian chemicals vs. Dutch chemicals, or Italian chemicals vs. Italian textiles) and then calculating the mean, which might lead to distortions due the absence of a weighting procedure.

The evaluation of the relative weight of national and sectoral co-movements is performed as follows. For each *country* the percentage of sectors where the national dimension of shocks prevails over the sectoral one (Table 7.15) is computed; similarly, for each *sector* the percentage of countries in which the national dimension of shocks prevails over the sectoral one (Table 7.16) is computed. A value close to 100% indicates a prevalence

Table 7.16 Incidence of national shocks on selected sectors in nine European countries

ISIC code	Sector	Percentage of sectors where country-level shocks prevail over sector-level shocks
311	Food	55.56
313	Beverages	55.56
314	Tobacco	66.67
321	Textiles	55.56
322	Wearing apparel	77.78
323	Leather & products	66.67
324	Footwear	66.67
331	Wood products	77.78
332	Furnitures & fixtures	77.78
341	Paper & products	88.89
342	Printing & publishing	66.67
351	Industrial chemicals	33.33
352	Other chemicals	66.67
353	Petroleum refineries	55.56
354	Petroleum & coal products	66.67
355	Rubber products	55.56
356	Plastic products	55.56
361	Pottery, china etc.	66.67
362	Glass & products	88.89
369	Non-metallic products	66.67
371	Iron & steel	77.78
372	Non-ferrous metals	88.89
381	Metal products	55.56
382	Non-electrical machinery	66.67
383	Electrical machinery	44.44
384	Transport equipment	77.78
385	Professional goods	77.78

Table 7.17 Relative size and dispersion of industrial sectors in the euro area

ISIC code	Sector	Relative weight of production in total industrial output (%)	Coefficient of variation of relative national weight
311	Food	14.22	0.10
313	Beverages	2.17	0.14
314	Tobacco	0.88	0.18
321	Textiles	4.10	0.20
322	Wearing apparel	2.02	0.24
323	Leather & products	0.49	0.29
324	Footwear	0.80	0.42
331	Wood products	2.08	0.22
332	Furnitures & fixtures	2.02	0.14
341	Paper & products	3.93	0.29
342	Printing & publishing	3.63	0.12
351	Industrial chemicals	6.10	0.16
352	Other chemicals	4.23	0.12
353	Petroleum refineries	4.46	0.14
354	Petroleum & coal products	0.39	0.24
355	Rubber products	0.81	0.15
356	Plastic products	2.59	0.14
361	Pottery, china etc.	0.61	0.36
362	Glass & products	0.95	0.09
369	Non-metallic products	2.70	0.14
371	Iron & steel	4.50	0.08
372	Non-ferrous metals	2.04	0.07
381	Metal products	5.60	0.07
382	Non-electrical machinery	9.23	0.12
383	Electrical machinery	8.70	0.10
384	Transport equipment	9.46	0.14
385	Professional goods	1.30	0.21

of national over sectoral dynamics, while values close to 50% indicate substantial equilibrium between the two components.

Table 7.15 shows that, as was to be expected, the larger economies are dominated by the country dimension, while the 'satellite' economies are dominated by the sectoral dimension. This is evident above all in the case of the D-mark area (Austria and Netherlands), while the Finnish anomaly can be explained by belated membership of the EU and by the predominant role played by resource-intensive sectors in Finnish industry. Table 7.16, conversely, shows that the *sectoral* co-movements are more relevant in high-economies-of-scale segments such as food, industrial chemicals and electrical equipment, while the *national* dynamics prevail in the case of the traditional sectors (clothing, footwear, furniture), of the wood and paper and of ceramics and glass, but also in high-capital-intensity industries such as steel and automobiles.

This evidence has to be interpreted in the light of relative weight, and dispersion, of the sector within the overall industrial production of the euro area so as to distinguish among the three cases outlined above. Table 7.17 shows the percentage weight of the 27 sectors in EMU's industry, as well as a measure of the relative (dis)homogeneity of their weight in different countries (the coefficient of variation of the national percentages). Food, electrical equipment and industrial chemicals present a large weight (together, they represent almost 30% of industrial production of the nine countries), as well as substantial homogeneity within the European industrial systems. Thus, these segments are associated with case A, i.e. sectors in which the production cycles are symmetrical within the euro area and that, at the same time, are important and uniformly distributed in many countries. Hence, cycles in these sectors appear compatible with centralised, or co-ordinated, policy interventions. Conversely, many traditional sectors such as clothing and leather and footwear, or resource-intensive ones like the wood and paper line, petroleum derivatives and coal, or ceramics and glass, are either too small or too concentrated to call for centralised economic policy instruments, no matter whether they are characterised by symmetrical (case B) or asymmetrical shocks (case C). Finally, Tables 7.16 and 7.17 show that some manufacturing segments, largely present and homogeneously distributed in the Union (motor vehicles, non-electrical equipment and refineries), have in the past exhibited national rather than sectoral, output dynamics (case C); if these dynamics were to persist after the launching of EMU, the policy dilemma posed by case C, the absence of appropriate policy instruments, is likely to emerge.

In conclusion, this section suggests that the specialisation models not only condition the medium to long-term outlook for Europe's national industries, based on different sectoral trends (connected to demand, to international competition and to labour intensity), but that they will have a major impact on economic policy management within EMU. Thus, 'what and where to produce' will not be irrelevant from the viewpoint of stabilisation and cohesion policies.

NOTES

1. Source: European Commission (1998).
2. See Rifkin (1995).
3. For a review, see IMF (1997).
4. On this point, see *Neven* and *Wyplosz* (*1996*).
5. See Daveri and Tabellini (1997).
6. See, for instance, European Commission (1998); CER, Centro Europa Ricerche, Rapporto 5/95; and Rapporto 3/98.
7. See again, European Commission (1998), p. 16.
8. See CER-Svimez (1998).
9. We refer to the intensity of *non-specialised* labour, while the employment of specialised labour may increase after restructuring has taken place.
10. See, for example, Audet (1996).
11. See Lall (1998); Ernst and Guerrieri (1997).
12. Fontagnè, Freudenberg and Péridy (1998); De Nardis and Traù (1998).
13. Among recently published studies, see Davies and Lyons (1996) and to OECD (1996). A comparison of the sectoral dimension of R&D in Europe and in the USA is presented in Eaton, Gutierrez and Kortum (1998).
14. Neven and Wyplosz (1996) suggest a similar classification.
15. These areas are identified as subsectors, respectively, of Non-electric equipment (ISIC 3825) and Electric equipment (ISIC 3832), which do not appear separately in Table 7.4.
16. Eaton *et al.* (1998).
17. With regard to Europe, see *Neven* and *Wyplosz* (*1996*) and *CER, Centro Europa Ricerche* (*1998*), Chapter 3. Regarding the USA, see 'The strange life of low-tech America', *The Economist*, October 17, 1998.
18. In some cases the variation of value added per worker displays contrasting trends which have made it impossible to ascribe some sectors to one of the four groups.
19. Data for Germany do not include the eastern Länder.
20. See also Guerrieri and Manzocchi (1996). Similar conclusions are found in studies that utilise data for industrial production rather than for exports; see, for example, De Nardis and Malgarini (1998).
21. See, among others: Bayoumi and Eichengreen (1992); IMF (1997b), (Chapter 3); Helg, Manasse, Monacelli and Rovelli (1995).
22. Frankel and Rose (1996); Paci and Rovelli (1997).
23. Data for Ireland and Luxembourg were not available.

APPENDIX: MEASURES OF MOBILITY AND FLEXIBILITY

Corrado Pollastri

Measurement of mobility

In this approach, changes in the sectoral hierarchy over time are considered to be relevant for the evaluation of mobility in specialisation. To this end, we used only the ordinal component of the series of Balassa indices (for a definition, see extended note to Table 7.4). For example, the fluctuations in the sectors placed at the tail end of the ranking (more and less specialised sector) are not considered a factor of mobility, regardless of their magnitude.

The position of a sector in the ranking in a given year is interpreted as a variable included in a stochastic discrete process in which the probability function controlling the process takes on the form of a transition matrix.

Based on the Proudman and Redding[1] formulation, we consider the stochastic variable that describes the quartile in which a sector belongs at time $t X_t$ and we analyse its probability function. The probability of belonging at time t to a given state x (defined by the quartile of belonging) is represented via a stochastic difference equation, expressing the probability as a function of the probability of falling into different states in the preceding period:

$$P(\widetilde{X}_t = x) = p_t$$

$$p_t = P(p_{t-1} + \varepsilon_t)$$

$$(7A.1)$$

Intuitively, we may consider operator P as a matrix (transition matrix) that describes the transition of variable X over time. For example, the probability of being in state i at time t may be calculated as the sum of the probabilities of being at time $t-1$ in states $j=1...k$, multiplied, respectively, by the transition probabilities from state j to state i. In our case, the reference distribution considered is that of all of the sectoral observations; the states are identified by their belonging to a quartile of the total distribution.

By making a few simplifying hypotheses on function P it is possible to obtain its estimate on the basis of the transitions that have occurred over a period in the series of data available for the analysis.

The transition matrices that are estimated in this way for each country supply the basis for measuring mobility over time. *Minimum mobility* results in the extreme case in which the matrix is an identity matrix; mobility increases as the probabilities placed along the main diagonal shift away from unity. Different indicators of mobility have been suggested which synthesise the phenomenon on the basis of the transition matrix; we describe one of them here (*IM*, due to A.F. Shorrocks)[2] calculated as the difference between unity and the determinant of the transition matrix (see equation (7A.2)):

$$IM = 1 - Det\,[P] \qquad\qquad (7A.2)$$

On the one hand, this approach presents robustness problems due to the simplifying hypotheses for the equation which defines the transition matrix; in addition, the subdivision of the transition process into a predetermined number of stages (four, in this case) is highly discretional. The discretisation of the stochastic process entails an unequal evaluation of the fluctuations of the index numbers, which are considered factors of mobility only if they cause a shift in the state from one period to another. In some cases, there may occur fluctuations of some sectors located close to the limits of separation of the quartiles which give rise to an over-estimation of mobility for the country involved.

On the other hand, this method allows the measuring mainly of the large fluctuations in time of the sectoral rankings. In this sense, the information supplied by this index may be useful if *mobility* in specialisation is interpreted solely as a major structural change in relative positions; conversely, to capturing the overall variation of the distribution of the Balassa indices (of exports or of employment), it is more appropriate to consider the measurement of *flexibility* specified below.

Measurement of flexibility

The index of *flexibility* of specialisation measures a distance among the sectoral distributions of the Balassa indices over time. An approach may be suggested that derives the measurement of *flexibility* from the analysis of the breakdown of overall variability into functions of the two variables, *sector* and *time*. It is possible to define a model of breakdown of the variance by identifying the fraction of information concerning sector and time (simple effects) and the sector–time interaction. The variability which becomes an expression of mobility in time is given by the sum of the effect 'time' and the effect 'interaction sector–time'. The former reflects the shift (upwards or downwards) of the sectoral distributions over time. The latter, conversely, reflects the variability that occurs sectorally from year to year. The residual portion that does not reflect variability over time is the simple effect of the sector variable which, as we have seen, is highest when there is no mobility over time.

Analytically, the model of variance analysis may be specified as follows:

$$V_a = \text{Var}\{b_a\} : \text{simple effect of time variable}$$
$$V_s = \text{Var}\{b_s\} : \text{simple effect of sector variable} \qquad (7A.3)$$
$$V_{a,s} = \text{Var}\{b_{a,s}\} - (V_a + V_s) : \text{effect of sector–time interaction}$$

$$a = \text{year}$$
$$s = \text{sector}$$

where *ba, s* is the index of comparative advantage (Balassa) for a given sector and a given year. The simple effect of the time variable is calculated as the variance of the sectoral means for each year, while the simple effect of the sector variable is measured by the variance of the annual means for each sector. Since the model is deterministic (the number of observations equals the number of degrees of freedom), the effects specified in the model completely capture the entire variability of the population, and the effect of the interaction can be deduced from the difference from total variance. An index of flexibility (*IF*) may be obtained by relating the measurement of time variability to overall variability. In formal terms, this can be written as follows:

$$IF = 1 - \frac{\text{Var}\{b_s\}}{\text{Var}\{b_{a,s}\}} \qquad (7A.4)$$

$$\varepsilon\,(0;1)$$

This index would be nil if there is no sectoral variability, inasmuch as the entire variability of the distribution would be expressed by the differences of the values among sectors, which are identical for all years.

Relation of time variability to overall variability has the two-fold effect of yielding the relative index (comprised between zero and 1 and thus homogeneous among countries) and to account implicitly for the specific sectoral distribution. Independently of the structure of sectoral distributions in the individual countries (large or small structural differences between the indices of different sectors that persist over time), the relation between the time variables (simple time effect and composite sector–time effect) and the overall variability allows obtaining a measurement of *flexibility (IF)* which, time variability being equal, is intensified in the case of the countries with a homogeneous structure (low sectoral structural variability and thus low total variability), while it is reduced for the countries with high sectoral variability. In this way, one does not risk underestimating a reduced variability in absolute terms but which is significant with respect to the sectoral profile of the individual country. This procedure is required in order to be able to deal with cases of countries whose sectoral specialisation structure differs extremely. Consider for example Germany and Spain (Table 7.9): the former shows a substantially homogeneous export specialisation with values close to 1 in many sectors, while the latter displays some highly specialised sectors (footwear, for instance), with Balassa index values even approaching 10. Only the use of a relative index such as *IF*, which accounts for the different sectoral specialisation structure, allows the evaluation of the level of *flexibility* of specialisation in countries with such different structures.

Notes

1. Proudman and Redding (1998).
2. Shorrocks (1978).

8. Employment and European regions

Stefano Manzocchi, Pier Carlo Padoan, Paola Parascandolo and Massimo Tozzi

REGIONAL DIFFERENCES AND CONVERGENCE: THE DEBATE AND THE POLICIES

Few terms have received greater attention by economists, and become more popular even among laymen, than the term 'convergence' during the past decade. A reasonable estimate might be that several hundred theoretical and applied papers dealing with this term have been published in the leading economic journals. The debate regarding the definition and relevance of the issue is still very much alive.[1] The controversy revolves around the question of what should be studied (convergence among income levels or rates of growth, towards an equilibrium position of the economic system, or convergence of the distribution of per capita income among different countries or regions?), as well as around the importance to be attributed to the different aspects of convergence. Thus framed, the debate has not ended; neither does the need for more research seem to be felt in view of the abundance of the existing material. Nevertheless, the issue's policy dimension can hardly be overstated with respect to the disparity between rich and poor countries (which affects aid and development policies) and to discussion of regional convergence in the integrated areas, i.e., the topic of this chapter.

The main results of the existing studies of per capita income convergence among the European regions can be summarised in a few lines:

- the divergence between the 25 wealthiest and the 25 poorest regions has been almost constant between 1983 and 1993;[2]
- if the inequality between European regions is broken down into an 'internal' component, reflecting the inequality between regions within a given country, and an 'external' component, reflecting the inequality between regions of different countries, the former increased while the latter diminished;[3]
- in a number of countries, such as Spain, Portugal, Germany (even without the new Länder) and Belgium, there has been divergence

139

between the per capita incomes of different regions between 1983 and 1993.[4] There has also been divergence in terms of regional unemployment rates.[5] This calls for the opportunity to maintain structural and cohesion policies in the EU, while the issue of the appropriate decision and intervention level (Community, national, regional) becomes crucial.

These results are substantially confirmed by the econometric specifications offered in this chapter, with an important qualification that is fraught with economic policy implications. Our estimates show that the convergence among regional incomes in Europe is almost trivial unless a variable is introduced that accounts for the structural differences between groups of homogeneous regions. More precisely, if each region is identified on the basis of product composition according to a cluster analysis, convergence among the regions increases. In other words, we identify a case of conditional convergence in the sense that not all regions move towards the *same* income level, but rather towards *different levels* according to their structural characteristics. The relevance of this result lies, on the one hand, in highlighting the role of the production structure for medium-term macroeconomic performance and, on the other hand, in stressing the importance of cohesion policies to reduce regional disparities in the long run.

The evidence discussed below also sheds some light on the possibility that with a single currency differences in intra-national specialisation entail the risk of exacerbating the distances between 'central' and 'peripheral' regions, according to the interpretative scheme suggested by the 'new economic geography'.[6] An alternative case is the catching-up scenario, i.e., the acceleration of the growth rate of the backward regions.

Several implications for the EMU's functioning derive from a deepening of regional specialisation. One is the possible differential impact of macroeconomic and monetary policy on the regions. The negative effect of a shock could have quite diverse consequences for a Europe made up of regions with largely different production structures. Thus, there arises a demand for regional policies as an essential instrument for the success of EMU. In an effort to look at these issues, we outline a map of models of regional specialisation (groups) in the EU. In doing so we complement the available regional-level analyses which normally ignore aspects of production specialisation.

REGIONAL SPECIALIZATION IN EUROPE

Specialisation in Europe is more pronounced at the regional than at the national level. In fact, European countries display fairly homogeneous production structures – as shown by the high proportion of intra-industry trade – but relatively heterogeneous regional structures.

Starting from these considerations, this chapter identifies groups of European regions that are characteriszed by similar industrial specialisations irrespective of the country to which the region belongs. Secondly, we test for convergence in per-capita income among the European regions. We check for possible differences in adjustment speeds, which might suggest that in the EU regional economies belong to different groupings that converge only locally.

The statistical units considered are the 144 European regions of the NUTS-2 level belonging to Italy, France, UK, Germany, Spain, Portugal, Greece, Luxembourg, Netherlands, Ireland, Denmark and Belgium. The analysis was subsequently broadened to the regions of Finland and Sweden.[7.] The following variables were considered so as to identify the region's production structure: distribution of employees in the manufacturing industry (subdivided into the main NACE sectors), in the agricultural sector, in construction and in energy; distribution of employees in private services (subdivided into credit and insurance, commerce, transportation and other services) and in public sector services; per capita GDP in purchasing power parity and the rate of unemployment, the latter with separate data for youth unemployment (up to 25 years of age).

We have used multivariate factor analysis. On the basis of synthetic indicators computed as linear combinations of the above variables, we have identified groups, each of which includes regions which present the same 'model' of specialisation and by similar levels of income and employment. The analysis has produced a statistically satisfactory classification into groups of regions based on the distribution of people employed in the different economic sectors, and on specific aspects regarding the specialisations in manufacturing industry and in services.

The results are summarised in Figure 8.1 which shows, for the reference year (1991), the results of the principal components analysis. The first factor (horizontal) axis may be interpreted as the development factor (leftward-oriented = higher growth, rightward = lower growth): high per capita GDP levels and low levels of unemployment are positively correlated to the intensity of the industrial sector, specifically of the machinery, motor vehicle and electrical, electronic and precision mechanics sectors. It is interesting to note that a large service sector is positively correlated with the first factor axis but with a clear distinction between public and private services as there is a clear positive correlation with private services and virtually no relation with public services. Moreover, the position of the variable 'private services' indicates a positive link between private services and the high-tech industrial sectors while the commerce sector is negatively correlated with growth.

Figure 8.1 Principal component analysis (1991)

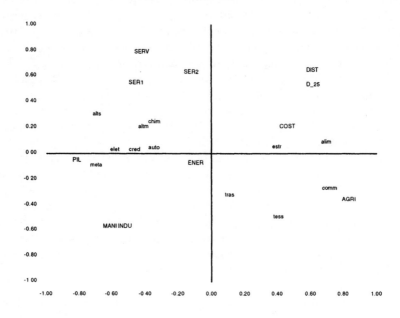

List of variables:

DIST	= Total unemployment rate
D_25	= Rate of youth unemploymtn
PIL	= Gross domestic product (GDP)
AGRI	= agricultural employment as percent of total
ENER	= energy sector employment as percent of total
MANI	= manufacturing employment as percent of total
ESTR	= mining sector employment as percent of manufacturing
CHIM	= chemical sector employment as percent of manufacturing
META	= machinery sector employment as percent of manufacturing
AUTO	= motor vehicle employment as percent of manufacturing
ELET	= electric/electronic emplmt as percent of manufacturing
ALIM	= food sector employment as percent of manufacturing
TESS	= textile sector employment as percent of manufacturing
ALTM	= other industries sector emplmt as percent of manufacturing
COST	= construction employment as percent of total
SER1	= market services employment as percent of total
COMM	= commerce employment as percent of all sevices
TRAS	= transportation employment as percent of all services
ALTS	= other services employment as percent of all services
SER2	= non-market services employment as percent of services

Conversely, at the other extreme of the factor axis, we find the characteristics of underdevelopment (high levels of unemployment and low levels of per-capita GDP), which is positively correlated with construction, mining, agriculture and the traditional industrial sectors – food, textiles, leather and clothing.

The second (vertical) factor axis may be interpreted as the factor of 'tertiarisation' (bottom-to-top orientation) independently of the level of per capita income.

The inspection of the chart suggests other relevant features: the bisector of the second and fourth quadrants may be interpreted as an indication of the level of technological development (left-to-right orientation); on the upper left section we find specialisations in chemicals, motor vehicles and electric, electronic and precision mechanics industries; at the lower right, we find agriculture associated with limited – mostly traditional – industrial development.

The bisector between the first and third quadrants represents the intensity of employment (leftward orientation = less unemployment, rightward = more unemployment); this suggests that unemployment is inversely correlated with the share of manufacturing. The analysis reveals an extremely fragmented and non-homogeneous Europe, particularly as regards the level of development and the labour market; regions with high per capita GDP and low unemployment rate – associated with an industrial model highly specialised in advanced sectors as well as in banking and other business services – contrast with marginal areas where the agricultural economy, traditional industry and commerce still weigh significantly and are associated to high unemployment. The poor regions are specialised in agriculture, construction and mining; their industrial structure is concentrated in food and in textiles, leather and clothing, while private services are strongly biased towards commerce.

A comparison between 1981[8] and 1991 indicates significant structural changes, namely:

1. the distance between highly industrialised/high employment areas, on the one hand, and areas with a backward production structure and with a high rate of unemployment, particularly among young workers, on the other, has increased;
2. the positive relationship between regional per capita income and the share of manufacturing has become more relevant;
3. other private services, including business services and particularly banking are increasingly located in regions where manufacturing is well-established.

In general, regional disparities widened in the 1980s, as confirmed by the fact that the majority of the variables considered show an increase in their coefficient of variation. These disparities, however, do not necessarily relate to the same regions. In fact, the analysis does not indicate that all of the 'poor' regions (with low industrialisation and high unemployment) fell further behind the 'wealthy' regions (the highly industrialised ones with low unemployment) or that all included in one group in 1981 were still there in 1991. Even taking into account the general divergence between 'wealthy' and 'poor' regions, there have been several cases of 'fall-back' of some of the former and cases of 'leap forward' of some of the latter.

During the 1980s, the concentration of advanced manufacturing increased substantially, with a corresponding rise in importance of traditional industrial specialisation in the less developed areas; the most important growth in the variability of the geographic distribution of employees has occurred in the chemical and machinery sectors; similar trends are noted in food, textiles, clothing and leather and in services. This was accompanied by increased geographic variability of youth unemployment rates; in 1981–91, the coefficient of variation of the total unemployment rate rose by 55.9% from 40.4% to 63%; that of youth unemployment climbed similarly, by 57.5%, from 48.3% to 76.1%.

To sum up, the inverse correlation between the level of industrial development and unemployment has become more significant; total and youth unemployment are concentrated largely on the less industrialised areas; moreover, the contrast between the developed regions with high-tech industrial sectors and business services, on the one hand, and areas specialised in traditional sectors of production, on the other, has deepened.

The widening of the regional disparities can be explained by the fact that in Europe the sectors in which the less advanced regions were specialised (in 1981) destroyed employment during the 1980s.

Table 8.1 shows that the employment share of both agriculture and industry has declined, while private services and, to a lesser extent, public services have gained importance. Within the industrial sector, sectors with increasing employment shares are chemicals, machinery, motor vehicles, and electric and electronic equipment, i.e., the sectors located in the more developed regions, while there has been a decline in the share of construction and of the traditional sectors: textiles, leather and clothing. This pattern confirms what has already been discussed in chapter 7. The difference patterns for traditional and advanced services, already evident in 1981, has sharpened. A review of the components of services shows that the commercial sector's share in tertiary employment has declined, that the banking and insurance sector's share has remained almost unchanged, and that the 'other services' sector has been the most dynamic one, with a more than five point increase in its share of total tertiary employment. Inasmuch as, in the early 1980s, the latter were already consistently located in the more developed regions of the EU, the absorption of labour in this sector has been an additional factor explaining the widening of regional disparities.

Table 8.1 Sectoral composition of European employment (% of Europe 11, excluding Greece)

	1981	1991
Agriculture	8.21	5.89
Industry	36.15	31.89
- Energy	1.60	1.36
- Manufacturing	25.03	23.58
- mining	10.30 [a]	8.47
- chemicals	6.67 [a]	7.49
- mechanical	19.65 [a]	20.52
- transport equip.	10.19 [a]	11.70
- electrical and electronics	12.54 [a]	14.05
- food	10.56 [a]	10.68
- textiles, leather and apparel	12.86 [a]	10.23
- others	17.24 [a]	16.85
- Construction	9.53	6.95
Services	55.64	62.21
- Market services	37.19	42.15
- commerce	49.30 [b]	46.61
- transport	16.42 [b]	14.30
- banking and insurance	6.79 [b]	6.42
- other	27.49 [b]	32.67
- Non market services	18.45	20.06
Total employment	100.00	100.00

Notes:
[a] % of manufacturing sector.
[b] % of market services.

Source: Authors' calculations.

The clustering procedure of the 144 European regions for 1991 has identified ten homogeneous groups (ranked by per capita GDP), each with specific industrial and production specialisation and a distinct level of per capita income and unemployment (see Appendix 1 for a full description).

The results are summarised in Table 8.2, which identifies the groups' sectors of specialisation, i.e., those sectors in which the percentage of sectoral employment is above the European average.

Lastly, we present some data concerning the changes that have taken place in the period 1981–91.

Table 8.2 Group specialisation

	1	2	3	4	5	6	7	8	9	10
Agriculture								x	x	x
Energy		x	x		x					x
Construction						x		x	x	x
Mining					x		x	x	x	x
Chemicals	x	x			x		x			
Mechanical	x		x	x	x	x				
Motor vehicles	x	x		x	x				x	
Electrical machinery	x	x	x	x						
Food						x		x	x	x
Textiles			x				x	x		x
Others			x	x		x		x		
Commerce			x					x	x	x
Transport	x	x					x			x
Banking		x		x	x	x		x		
Other services	x	x	x	x	x	x	x			

Source: Authors' calculations.

In 1991 the groups are more separate from one another, and internally more homogeneous, than they had been in 1981; this suggests that the regional differences in Europe widen in accordance with their degree of specialisation and in terms of performance (employment and per capita income). For example, while in 1981 the highest income group included 14 regions showing a combination of strong industrialisation and high degree of tertiarisation, in 1991 the highest income group includes a smaller number of regions (9) distinguished by a more marked industrial specialisation, especially in machinery sectors. All in all, during the decade – during which monetary integration in Europe has deepened – there is evidence of increasing regional specialisation, while the national component in the identification of regions loses importance.

CATCHING-UP AMONG THE EUROPEAN REGIONS

The estimation of catching-up equations at the regional level[9] allows for a dynamic interpretation of disparities among Europe's macro-regions.

The equation adopted to test the convergence hypothesis is based on the growth model of Solow (1956) and its extensions (Mankiw, Romer and Weil,

1992).[10] The model shows that economies with an initially lower per-capita capital grow faster than the wealthier economies, i.e. 'convergence' of the poor economies towards one steady state equilibrium. The possibility that the initial per-capita resource-endowment disparity would be completely eliminated, that is, that the poorer economies would 'catch up' with the wealthy ones, is based to the hypothesis that the economies have identical basic parameters: a saving rate s, a labour force growth rate n, etc. This is the case of absolute convergence. Neoclassical growth models (Barro and Sala-i-Martin, 1991 [11]) show the possibility of different steady-state capital equilibrium levels per capita for different economies. The idea is that each should converge the faster towards its own steady state the farther it is from it, i.e., the lower its initial resource endowment. Thus, there exists an inverse relation between the speed of convergence and distance from the steady-state equilibrium. This hypothesis is defined as 'conditional' convergence. If the convergence process is rapid, it will suffice to analyse the steady-state behaviour as if the economies were close to equilibrium. Contrariwise, if the convergence process is slow, the economies would be far from steady-state and their growth process would be dominated by transition dynamics.

Moreover, if the convergence among regions were both rapid and absolute, there would not be any need to implement regional development policies; short-term risk-pooling policies would suffice to offset negative shock effects. If the convergence were absolute but slow, regional policies could be useful instruments for speeding up the transition towards the steady state by helping to remove the initial differences of per-capita income at a faster rate. If, conversely, the convergence is only conditional, with regional differences that tend to persist indefinitely, then the need for active regional policies would last well beyond the short run.

We can obtain a measure of the rate of convergence in a neoclassical model of exogenous growth by log-linearising the law of capital-stock movement around the steady state; in the case of a Cobb–Douglas production function, the per-capita income-rate of growth is a fixed proportion of the per-capita capital-rate of growth, so that the convergence parameter can be estimated through an equation of the following type:

$$(1/T) \log \left(\frac{y_{i,t}}{y_{i, t-T}} \right) = a - [\log (y_{i, t-T})][(1-e^{-\beta T})/T]$$

where $y_{i, t-T}$ indicates the per capita income of the *ith* region at the beginning of the time interval (in our case, 1980–95), $y_{i,t}$ is the per capita income in the final period, and β is the measure of convergence among the regions. The method of estimation is non-linear least squares, and the result is a significant but very small convergence parameter (Table 8.3).

Table 8.3 Catching-up equation: estimation results [a]

	Coefficient
Constant	0.13
	(9.42)
β	0.00
	(5.03)
Corrected R square	0.1701
S. E. regression	0.0087
D.W. stat.	1.0044

Note: [a] t statistic in brackets.

The results suggest there would seem to be a tendency for convergence toward one level of per-capita income among the European regions, but this tendency would be quite slow and slower than the value estimated for the European countries (cf. Mankiw, Romer and Weil, 1992). If we add country dummies to the basic equation in order to account for each region the measure of convergence does not change significantly (Table 8.4).

All coefficients associated with the country fixed effects are significant (with Portugal the only exception), and all dummy coefficients have a positive sign.[12] Conversely, when we introduce groups fixed effects, the measure of convergence more than doubles (from 0.01 to 0.02) (Table 8.5).

If we take into account the grouping obtained according to the structure of production the hypothesis of convergence among subsets of regions within the EU is confirmed.[13]

Specifically, the coefficients for group 7, 8 and 9 are not significant; this indicates that these groups are not significantly different from group 10, which was used as reference. Hence, we may add, these four groups share a common steady-state equilibrium. On the other hand, the coefficients associated with groups of regions that exhibit higher per-capita income and employment are significant. This suggests a process of conditional convergence towards a limited, but different, number of long-term equilibria among the European regions and is an example of the well-known phenomenon of 'convergence clubs'. Our analysis confirms this result usually found in the literature and clarifies it by identifying the 'club' characteristics in terms of production specialisation patterns.

These results lead to an obvious but relevant economic policy implication. The transition to higher levels of employment and per capita income calls for a modification of the specialization model. They also confirm that the

Table 8.4 Catching-up equation: estimation with country fixed effect [a]

		Coefficient
Constant		0.16
		(7.27)
β		0.00
		(3.54)
β	Belgium	–0.03
		(–4.35)
β	Denmark	–0.02
		(–2.38)
β	Germany	–0.02
		(–3.50)
β	Greece	–0.04
		(–5.67)
β	Spain	–0.03
		(–4.27)
β	France	–0.03
		(–5.65)
β	Italy	–0.03
		(–4.78)
β	Netherlands	–0.03
		(–5.31)
β	Portugal	–0.00
		(–1.20)
β	UK	–0.04
		(–6.26)
Corrected R square		0.6741
S. E. regression		0.0054
D.W. stat.		1.5409

Note: [a] Excluding Luxembourg; t statistic in brackets.

regional dimension, more than the national one, explains the (conditional and limited) convergence process in the EU.

It is possible to account for both fixed effects, i.e., simultaneously group as well as country, by introducing separate dummies for each of the two

Table 8.5 Catching-up equation: estimation with group fixed effect [a]

	Coefficient
Constant	0.21
	(8.75)
β	0.02
	(5.20)
β group 1	0.02
	(4.18)
β group 2	0.01
	(2.66)
β group 3	0.02
	(4.55)
β group 4	0.01
	(2.83)
β group 5	0.00
	(1.76)
β group 6	0.01
	(3.19)
β group 7	0.00
	(1.61)
β group 8	0.00
	(1.44)
β group 9	0.00
	(1.46)
Corrected R square	0.3048
S. E. regression	0.0080
D.W. stat.	1.2927

Note: [a] Excluding group 10; t statistic in brackets.

characteristics, or multiplicative dummies including both effects. In the latter case – which is presented here – the convergence parameter is higher than the one obtained by the basic equation and similar to that obtained in the previous version; however, the goodness of fit of the model improves tangibly (R^2 equal to about 0.8) (Table 8.6).

The results confirm two facts. In the first place, the existence of a 'wealthy regions' club', whose members are not substantially different from the

Table 8.6 Catching-up equation: estimation with multiplicative fixed effects (country and group)

	Coefficient	t Student
Constant	0.21	13.94
β	0.02	8.05
β Belgium 2	–0.00	–1.01
β Belgium 3	–0.00	–1.18
β Belgium 4	–0.00	–1.69
β Belgium 5	–0.00	–1.12
β Belgium 6	–0.00	–1.13
β Belgium 7	–0.02	–5.06
β Denmark 4	–0.00	–0.38
β Germany 2	0.00	1.06
β Germany 3	–0.00	–1.30
β Germany 4	–0.00	–2.40
β Germany 5	–0.00	–2.39
β Germany 8	–0.01	–1.90
β Greece 7	–0.02	–4.51
β Greece 10	–0.03	–10.70
β Spain 4	–0.01	–3.66
β Spain 8	–0.02	–6.96
β Spain 9	–0.01	–4.16
β Spain 10	–0.02	–4.22
β France 1	–0.02	–3.57
β France 2	–0.01	–3.29
β France 4	–0.02	–7.71
β France 5	–0.02	–3.85
β France 6	–0.02	–3.29
β France 7	–0.02	–4.51
β Italy 1	–0.01	–2.46
β Italy 2	–0.00	–2.53
β Italy 3	–0.01	–3.64
β Italy 4	–0.00	–2.63
β Italy 6	–0.02	–5.69
β Italy 7	–0.02	–6.90
β Italy 9	–0.02	–5.17
β Netherlands 2	–0.02	–5.72
β Netherlands 6	–0.01	4.90
β Luxembourg 6	0.02	3.07
β Portugal 7	–0.00	–0.12
β Portugal 10	–0.00	–1.69
β UK 2	–0.02	–3.57
β UK 4	–0.02	–5.95
β UK 5	–0.02	–9.44
β UK 7	–0.02	–4.19
Corrected R square	0.8084	
S. E. regression	0.0050	
D.W. stat.	0.6601	

Table 8.7 Catching-up equation: estimation results. Breakdown by periods [a]

	Coefficient		
	1980–87	1987–92	1992–95
Constant	0.09	0.37	–0.11
	(3.44)	(13.65)	(–1.95)
β	0.00	0.04	–0.01
	(1.08)	(10.22)	(–2.32)
Corrected R square	0.0014	0.4827	0.0284
S. E. regression	0.0157	0.0161	0.0027
D.W. stat.	0.6498	0.8195	0.3507

Note: [a] t statistic in brackets.

regions of group 1 of Germany's, the reference case. In the second place, the long-term equilibrium of a region depends largely on its belonging to a group – i.e., a production specialisation – and only in part on its belonging to a country.

The last part of the analysis looks at the importance of the exchange rate regime for the convergence process. We ask whether, and to what extent, the introduction of the EMS in 1979 may have affected the regional convergence process in Europe. For this purpose, we consider three separate periods: the initial EMS period, the period of fixed exchange rates of the 'hard EMS', and the period following the 1992 crisis.

In the 1980–87 period, which was marked by a policy of moderately controlled exchange rates, no pattern of income convergence emerges among the European regions, since the estimated value of is not significantly different from zero (Table 8.7).

Conversely, there is convergence among the European regions during the period of fixed exchange rates, 1987–92. The value of β is substantially identical to that obtained from the basic equation that covers the entire period.

In the following period, 1992–95, which was marked by a more flexible exchange regime and by several devaluations of currencies within the European exchange agreements, the opposite holds: i.e. divergence among the European regions' growth rates.

This result is confirmed (Figure 8.2) if we consider another measure of

Figure 8.2 Convergence of European regions [a]

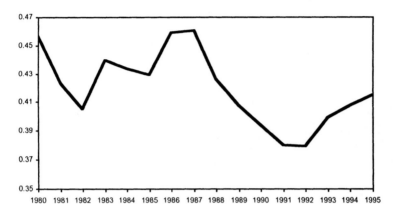

Note: [a] *A declining value indicates increasing convergence.*

convergence, the so-called σ *convergence* (Barro and Sala-i-Martin, 1992[14]) according to which two or more economic systems converge if the dispersion of their per-capita incomes decreases over time.

NOTE

1. Note, among the most recent assessments and surveys, the contributions by Durlauf and Quah (1998); and Pritchett (1997).
2. European Commission (1996).
3. De la Fuente and Vives (1995).
4. European Commission (1996).
5. Regarding the different indicators of regional disparities, see Dignan (1995).
6. Krugman (1993).
7. See Appendix 8.1. Data for the Austrian regions are not sufficient for inclusion in the analysis.
8. See CER Report 5/1995.
9. In this case, 141 statistical units are analysed. They belong to Italy, France, UK, Germany, Spain, Portugal, Greece, Luxembourg, Netherlands, Denmark and Belgium. The equations are estimated for regional per capita income expressed as purchasing power parity, as supplied by Eurostat (1998).
10. Mankiw, Romer and Weil (1992), pp. 407–437.
11. Barro and Sala-i-Martin (1991).
12. The estimated equation includes country dummies with the exception of Luxemburg. This was necessary to avoid singularity problems in estimation. The country intercept is given by the sum of the equation constant term and the dummy coefficient.
13. The equation includes nine dummy variables related to the different regional groupings, with the exception of the tenth group to avoid singularity problems in estimation. Each group intercept is given by the sum of the equation constant term and the group coefficient.
14. Barro and Sala-i-Martin (1992).

APPENDIX 1: COMPOSITION AND CHARACTERISTICS OF THE GROUPS

Region	*Country*
Group 1	
STUTTGART	Deu
KARLSRUHE	Deu
OBERBAYERN	Deu
MITTELFRANKEN	Deu
BREMEN	Deu
DARMSTADT	Deu
BRAUNSCHWEIG	Deu
FRANCHE-COMTE	Fra
PIEMONTE	Ita
Group 2	
BRABANT (94)	Bel
ANTWERPEN	Bel
HAMBURG	Deu
ILE DE FRANCE	Fra
HAUTE-NORMANDIE	Fra
PROVENCE-ALPES-COTE D'AZUR	Fra
LIGURIA	Ita
LAZIO	Ita
GRONINGEN	Ned
ZUID-HOLLAND	Ned
ZEELAND	Ned
SOUTH EAST (UK)	UK
Group 3	
WEST-VLAANDEREN	Bel
FREIBURG	Deu
TUEBINGEN	Deu
NIEDERBAYERN	Deu
OBERPFALZ	Deu
OBERFRANKEN	Deu
UNTERFRANKEN	Deu
SCHWABEN	Deu
GIESSEN	Deu

KASSEL	Deu
DETMOLD	Deu
ARNSBERG	Deu
KOBLENZ	Deu
LOMBARDIA	Ita
VENETO	Ita
EMILIA-ROMAGNA	Ita
MARCHE	Ita

Group 4

OOST-VLAANDEREN	Bel
BERLIN	Deu
HANNOVER	Deu
LUENEBURG	Deu
WESER-EMS	Deu
SCHLESWIG-HOLSTEIN	Deu
DANMARK	Dan
PAIS VASCO	Esp
NAVARRA	Esp
ARAGON	Esp
MADRID	Esp
CATALUNA	Esp
CHAMPAGNE-ARDENNE	Fra
PICARDIE	Fra
CENTRE	Fra
BASSE-NORMANDIE	Fra
BOURGOGNE	Fra
ALSACE	Fra
PAYS DE LA LOIRE	Fra
BRETAGNE	Fra
POITOU-CHARENTES	Fra
AQUITAINE	Fra
MIDI-PYRENEES	Fra
LIMOUSIN	Fra
RHONE-ALPES	Fra
VALLE D'AOSTA	Ita
TRENTINO-ALTO ADIGE	Ita
FRIULI-VENEZIA GIULIA	Ita
EAST ANGLIA	UK
SOUTH WEST (UK)	UK
SCOTLAND	UK

Group 5

LIMBURG (B)	Bel
DUESSELDORF	Deu
KOELN	Deu
MUENSTER	Deu
RHEINHESSEN-PFALZ	Deu
SAARLAND	Deu
LORRAINE	Fra
NORTH	UK
YORKSHIRE AND	
HUMBERSIDE	UK
EAST MIDLANDS	UK
WEST MIDLANDS	UK
NORTH WEST (UK)	UK
WALES	UK

Group 6

LUXEMBOURG (B)	Bel
AUVERGNE	Fra
LUXEMBOURG	
(GRANDDUCHE)	Lux
FRIESLAND	Ned
DRENTHE	Ned
OVERIJSSEL	Ned
GELDERLAND	Ned
FLEVOLAND	Ned
UTRECHT	Ned
NOORD-HOLLAND	Ned
NOORD-BRABANT	Ned
LIMBURG (NL)	Ned

Group 7

HAINAUT	Bel
LIEGE	Bel
NAMUR	Bel
NORD-PAS-DE-CALAIS	Fra
LANGUEDOC-	
ROUSSILLON	Fra
ATTIKI	Gre
IRELAND	Irl
TOSCANA	Ita

UMBRIA	Ita
ABRUZZO	Ita
PUGLIA	Ita
LISBOA E VALE DO TEJO	Por
NORTHERN IRELAND	UK

Group 8

TRIER	Deu
GALICIA	Esp
CANTABRIA	Esp
RIOJA	Esp
CASTILLA-LEON	Esp
CASTILLA-LA MANCHA	Esp
COMUNIDAD VALENCIANA	Esp
BALEARES	Esp
MURCIA	Esp
ALENTEJO	Por

Group 9

EXTREMADURA	Esp
ANDALUCIA	Esp
CEUTA Y MELILLA	Esp
CANARIAS	Esp
CORSE	Fra
MOLISE	Ita
CAMPANIA	Ita
BASILICATA	Ita
CALABRIA	Ita
SICILIA	Ita
SARDEGNA	Ita

Group 10

ASTURIAS	Esp
ANATOLIKI MAKEDONIA, THRAKI	Gre
KENTRIKI MAKEDONIA	Gre
DYTIKI MAKEDONIA	Gre
THESSALIA	Gre
IPEIROS	Gre
IONIA NISIA	Gre

DYTIKI ELLADA	Gre
STEREA ELLADA	Gre
PELOPONNISOS	Gre
VOREIO AIGAIO	Gre
NOTIO AIGAIO	Gre
KRITI	Gre
NORTE (P)	Por
CENTRO (P)	Por
ALGARVE	Por

First group: most highly developed regions
Composed of 9 regions representing 7% of the European population and 8.7% of employment.[1] It is marked by the highest average GDP per capita (about 37% higher than the European average) and by a negligible rate of unemployment (4.4% total and 6.9% below 25 years, as against the European averages of 8.6% and 17.9%).

The occupational composition of the group leans heavily towards industry, particularly manufacturing industry (32% of total employed as against the European average of 21.8%), with only 3.5% in agriculture compared with a 9.4% average for Europe.

The group is heavily specialised in the motor vehicle sector (at 24% of the industrial labour force, the highest share among all the groups, as against a 9.5% average for Europe) and in electric, electronic and precision mechanics (at 20.7% of manufacturing labour force, the highest share among all the groups, as against the European average of 11.2%) and representing around 20% of total European employment in these two sectors

Within the service sector, 'other services' are most prominent (36.3% of total employment in market services as against a European average of 30.4%) and credit and insurance.

This group includes the regions where a clear correlation (rising in 1981–91) is found between the presence of advanced industry and the development of an advanced tertiary sector.

Second group: the regions surrounding Europe's large metropolitan areas
This is composed of the 12 regions that are most densely populated (they average twice the European population), representing 15.5% of Europe's population and 16.6% of its employed labour force. It is marked by a very high per-capita GDP (28% above the European average), combined with the highest share of tertiary activities (71.4% of total employment as against the European average of 59.7%), especially in market services (51.3% against a European average of 40.5%). Moreover, these services are most concentrated in 'other services' (38.8%), credit (6.6%) and transportation (16.5%), with the

lowest share for commerce (37.5% against the European average of 49.5%).

The specialisation of the group's labour force within manufacturing industry is highest in the chemical sector (14.6% against 6.1% for Europe and 18.7% of total European employment in manufacturing), as well as in motor vehicles and electrical, electronics and precision mechanics.

Lastly, unemployment does not appear to be as low as in Group 1, although it is lower than the European average (8% of the total labour force and 16.7% under 25 years of age).

Third group: the regions with highest industrial development

It is composed of 17 regions representing 11.7% of the population and 13.5% of European employment, with per-capita GDP 11% higher than the European average and a minimal unemployment rate (3.6% of the total and 5.2% of the under-25 class).

High employment in industry (41%), specifically in manufacturing (32.7%), is strongly linked to the presence of basic machinery (maximum incidence of 16.1% of manufacturing industry employment compared with a European average of 17.4%, and 24% of total European employment in the sector), in addition to major presence in electrical, electronic and precision mechanics, 'other' manufacturing industry and textiles, leather and clothing (respectively, 14.8%, 17.5% and 13.2% of employment in manufacturing).

Finally, specialisation in services (53% of total group employment) is not very far from the European average.

Fourth group: the average European structure

This, the most numerous group, includes 31 regions. It represents 23.1% of the population and 22.7% of total European employment and is the closest to average figures for Europe.

Fifth group: the average service regions

Composed of 13 regions, it includes 13.5% of Europe's population and 13.2% of its employed labour force, with a per-capita GDP exactly in line with the European average and a lower level of unemployment, especially among the young. In addition, the group displays a high level of industrialisation and of tertiarisation, while agricultural employment is the lowest in Europe (barely 2.1% against the European average of 9.4%).

The high level of industrialisation (37% of the total employed) reflects the strong presence of manufacturing (27.4% of total employed), as well as the heaviest presence of the energy sector which employs 4.1% of the group's employed labour force (against the European average of only 1.3%), and represents 34.1% of total European employment in the sector.

Manufacturing industry is specialised in chemicals (10.8% of manufacturing employment), basic machinery (21.5%), motor vehicles (12.3%) and mining (11.4%), with the traditional sectors trailing. Lastly, the group shows a slightly higher presence of advanced services (credit and 'other services') compared to traditional services.

Sixth group: the intensive service regions
Made up of 12 regions, it represents 3.9% of Europe's population and 3.1% of employment, its per-capita GDP is close to the European average, unemployment is lower than average.

The composition of employment is strongly service-oriented (overall, 67% of total employment), especially in market services (49.3%), a solid industrial share (29.5% total and 20.3% in manufacturing, about 1.5% less than the European average).

There is a relevant presence of advanced services, with the highest share among all groups of credit and insurance (7.2% of all service employment) and of 'other services' (44.1%), and the lowest share of commerce (36.6%) and transportation (11.1%).

Industrial specialisation shows a diversified but highly specialised structure; about half of employment in manufacturing industry is located in basic machinery (22.8) and other manufacturing industry (the highest share among the groups, at 24.2%), while the food industry plays a more-than-marginal role (17.4%, the European average).

Seventh group: the intermediate areas
This includes 13 regions, 9.2% of Europe's population and 8.5% of its employed labour force; per-capita GDP is about 12% below the European average, while unemployment (at 11.2% overall and 25.7% for the under-25s) is slightly above the average.

These regions' employment is largely concentrated in the service sector (65.3%), mostly in market services (42.6%) but also in non-market services (22.7% of total employment).

Industrial presence is below average, both overall (27.4% of total employment) and in manufacturing (19.5%). Agriculture is somewhat more prominent (at 7.4%).

Industrial specialisation leans heavily towards mining (18.1% of total manufacturing employment) and textiles, leather and clothing (17.6%).

Eighth group: developing regions or with traditional industrial structure
It is composed of 10 regions comprising 4.4% of the population and 3.9% of the employed labour force; per-capita GDP is 25% below the European

average and the average level of unemployment is in line with that of group seven.

The employment composition includes 15.5% in agriculture and 30.6% in industry, 53.% in services, above all market services (35.2%). Industrial employment is relevant in construction (at 10.3% of total employment, the highest proportion among the groups), while manufacturing accounts for only 19.4%.

The food sector is most relevant (25.3% of manufacturing employment) and in 'other' manufacturing (20.7%) along with basic machinery (14.1%). Market services include mostly commerce (64% of total employment in market services), with only 16.7% in 'other' services, the lowest percentage among the groups. The traditional structure of specialisation points to the backwardness of these regions

Ninth group: the unemployment regions

Made up of 11 regions, it includes 7.7% of Europe's population and 6.1% of the employed labour force; in addition to a per-capita GDP 30% lower than the European average, it has the distinction of having the highest level of unemployment in Europe: 22% overall and 48.7% for those under 25.

Agriculture is also prominent here (14.7% of total employment), but, unlike the preceding group, employment in services is high (64.5%), especially in non-market services (at 24.2% of total employment the highest among the groups).

Industrial employment is only 20.5% of the total and manufacturing is negligible (only 8.7% of total employment), while the share of construction employment (10.5%) is the highest among the groups. Moreover, manufacturing is represented heavily by mining (15%) and by food (26.7%).

Lastly, employment in commerce is concentrated in market services (59.7%), while employment in credit and insurance is minimal (2.9%).

Tenth group: the agricultural regions

The 11 regions include 4.1% of Europe's total population and 3.8% of total employment; its GDP per capita is low (44% below the European average), but unemployment is not high (6.4% overall and 21.4% under 25 years).

This group is an exception to the general inter-relations discussed in the text above, as the inverse relation between the weight of the industrial sector and unemployment is not confirmed for these regions (mainly located in Greece), which also displays the lowest participation rate in the labour force in Europe.

Agriculture is the single most important employer (30.9% of total employment in the group and represents 17% of Europe's total labour force employed in agriculture); the modest industrial presence (24.2% overall and

14% in manufacturing), is relatively larger than services, which are at the lowest proportional level among the groups, both overall (44.6%) and in market (31.9%) and non-market services (12.4%).

Industrial employment is limited to the food sector (41.5% of manufacturing employment), to textiles, leather and clothing (23.6%) and mining (18.6%), while service specialization is mostly in commerce (58.5% of market services employment) and transportation (16.4%), leaving more advanced services far behind.

Note

1. The European averages presented here refer to the Europe of 12.

APPENDIX 2: MEASUREMENT OF THE VELOCITY OF CONVERGENCE IN AN EXOGENOUS GROWTH MODEL

The growth model by Solow (1956) and its extensions (Mankiw, Romer and Weil, 1992) states that ρ_k, the rate of growth of per-capita capital (k), is given by:

$$\rho_k = \frac{\dot{K}}{K} = sA_t k^{-(1-\alpha)} - (x + \delta + n) \tag{8A.1}$$

where k indicates the capital/labour ratio and the dot indicates the time derivative.

We note in equation (1) that higher values of per-capita capital growth are associated, *ceteris paribus*, with lower values of k. In other words, in a model of exogenous growth there exists a tendency for economies with an initially lower per-capita capital ρk to grow faster than the 'wealthier' economies.

A measure of the velocity of convergence can be obtained by log-linearising equation (8A1) around the steady state value, k^*, which gives:

$$\rho_k = \frac{d[\log k]}{dt} \cong -\beta \left[\log \left(\frac{k_0}{k^*} \right) \right] \tag{8A.2}$$

with $\beta = (1 - \alpha)(x + \delta + n)$, where β is the coefficient that determines the velocity of convergence from k (current value) to k^*. In other words, coefficient β indicates how rapidly per-capita capital approaches its steady state. In the present case, wich is a Cobb–Douglas production function, the growth rate of per-capita income is linked to the growth-rate of per-capita capital:

$$\rho_y = \alpha \rho_k$$

Therefore, equation (8A.2) becomes:

$$\rho_y \cong -\beta \log \left(\frac{y_0}{y^*} \right) \tag{8A.3}$$

where y^* indicates the level of steady state of per-capita income. Equation (8A.3) is a differential equation in $\log[y(t)]$ whose solution is:

$$\log[y(t)] = (1 - e^{-\beta t}) \log[y^*] + e^{-\beta t} \log[y_0] \tag{8A.4}$$

For each $t \geq 0$, $\log[y(t)]$ is a weighted average of the initial value $\log[y_0]$ and of the value of steady state $\log(y^*)$. Equation (8A.4) implies that the average rate of per-capita income growth in an interval from an initial value 0 to a value $T \geq 0$ is given by:

$$\frac{1}{T} \log \left[\frac{y_{iT}}{y_{i0}} \right] = \alpha + \frac{(1 - e^{-\beta t})}{T} \log(y_{i0}) + u_{i0,T} \qquad (8A.5)$$

where t stands for year, i for region or country, u_{i0}, T represents the mean error, u_{it} for the period from 0 to T, intercept α equals $x + [(1 - e^{-\beta t})/T] \log(y^*)$.

If $\beta > 0$, the poor economies grow faster than the rich ones.

9. Alternative uses of excess reserves after the introduction of the euro

Stefano Manzocchi and Pier Carlo Padoan

INTRODUCTION

As many have argued, the establishment of the euro generates a considerable amount of excess reserves. The issue was debated in the early stage of EMU and has subsequently lost some of its appeal, especially given the initial weakness of the single currency vis-à-vis the dollar. Assuming as a still realistic hypothesis that the introduction of the euro makes available for EMU a substantial amount of resources, to which we will refer to as excess reserves (ER), this chapter will look at the issue of the use of ER. It first discusses the likely amount of excess reserves determined by the introduction of the euro according to the alternative hypotheses discussed in the literature, and looks at a set of possible uses of excess reserves. Two of these uses are analysed in greater detail in the next two sections – the use of excess reserves for debt-relief operations in Central and Eastern European countries (CEECs) and the use of excess reserves as a way of financing cohesion policies in CEECs before their accession to the EU.

THE AMOUNT OF EXCESS RESERVES: SOME ESTIMATES

The elimination of EU currencies obviously eliminates the rationale for holding such currencies by monetary authorities of the EU member states.[1] This is not what is usually referred to as 'excess reserves' however. The ER we will be discussing are of non-EU currency ER, mostly denominated in US dollars. Several estimates of ER have been offered in the literature. Results vary according to the methods used to compute them. The European Commission (European Commission, 1990) estimated that between $200 billion and $230 billion could be regarded as ER of which about $85 billion would be gold. Gros and Thygesen (1992) suggest an amount of $120 billion. A more conservative estimate – Lehay (1996) – suggests $55 billion. Less

Table 9.1 International reserves: 1995 (billions of US dollars)

	Foreign currency	Other (minus gold)	Gold (market price)	Total
EU core [a]	164.5	15.9	94.6	275.2
EU 12	299.7	23.8	137.4	460.9
EU 15	349.8	26.5	144.5	520.8
USA	49.1	25.7	101.2	176.0
Industrial countries	655.6	69.3	292.0	1017.0
World	1325.7	83.9	351.0	1760.5

Note: [a] EU core includes Austria, Belgium-Luxembourg, France, Germany and the Netherlands.

Source: IMF (1996) as reported in Henning (1997a).

conservatives estimates (Goldman Sachs, 1996; JP Morgan, 1996) suggest values in the range of $150–200 billion.

At the end of 1995 the value of total reserves held by EU15[2] was $520.8 billion – see Table 9.1 – including $349.8 billion of foreign reserves (of which about $45 billion were official Ecus) and $144.5 billion of gold valued at market prices. While the currency composition of official reserves is not known, Masson and Turtelboom (1997) report that, at the end of 1995, the EU15 central banks held $90.7 billion worth of one another's currencies and $204.7 billion worth of non-EU currencies of which $171.3 billion worth constituted US dollars.

The calculation of the amount of excess reserves requires a 'theory' of demand of international reserves by monetary authorities. This runs up against two difficulties. The first is that the state of such a theory is still not fully consolidated,[3] the second is that the ECB will behave in a way that is not identical to that of any other national central bank as: (a) while not officially admitted the behaviour of the ECB will reflect the status of the euro as a key currency, and (b) its medium run behaviour will reflect the transitional problems of the euro that we mentioned in chapter 1. We will consider only one determinant of the demand of international reserves, related to the need to finance imports, the other major determinant being the function of intervention in currency markets as well as portfolio diversification. As far as this latter point is concerned, Masson and Turtelboom (1997) find that, while the demand for international reserves for diversification purposes may be relevant, a pure portfolio approach broadly overestimates the demand for reserves.

Table 9.2 Foreign exchange reserve ratio: 1995 [a]

	Foreign exchange reserves over total imports (%)	Foreign exchange reserves/GDP (%)
EU core [a]	23.8	3.4
EU 12 [a]	40.0	3.8
UE 15 [a]	46.7	4.1
USA	6.4	0.7
Industrial countries excluding EU 15	20.9	2.2
World (GDP 1993)	25.9	5.5
EU 15 excluding intra EU holdings	27.4	2.4

Note: [a] Excludes intra group imports.

Source: Hennings (1997a).

Consequently, as a first approximation, it is safe to consider import financing as the major reason for reserve holding. In such a way, by applying the 'appropriate' import reserve ratio we can obtain a reasonable guess of the initial value of ER.

The world average reserve to import ratio is 25.9%, but for the USA it falls to 6.4%. On the other hand, when one excludes intra-EU imports and cross holdings of EU currencies, the reserve to import ratio for EU15 is 27.4% (see Table 9.2). The striking difference between the USA and the EU obviously reflects a negative externality from the lack of monetary integration in the latter case or, if one prefers, the positive externality stemming, in the case of the USA, from the centralisation of monetary policy as well as the much lower degree of trade openness. In addition country-specific aspects may be relevant. Lehay (1996) finds that, over the past 20 years, the Southern members of the EU, i.e. Spain, Greece, Portugal and Italy, have held reserves much in excess of what the 'equilibrium' reserve to import ratio would require; one possible explanation is that in these countries financial markets have been less than fully developed for a long period of time. Similar results can be obtained by looking at the ratio of international reserves to GDP. External currency reserves of EU15 were 2.5% of GDP at the end of 1995, compared to 2.2% for non-EU countries and to 0.7% for the USA.

To sum up, the amount of ER can be related to the four institutional shocks associated with the creation of the euro. The first two shocks – the disappearance of a large part of international trade and of a large number of sizeable currency markets – will increase the size of ER, while the other two – the creation of a new currency and of a new monetary institution – will tend to decrease it as aspects of reputation building will tend to raise, other things being equal, the demand for international reserves by the ECB. For the latter reason it is reasonable to assume that, at least in its in early life, the ECB will hold a proportion of reserves higher than that of the USA as indeed has been the case.[4] However if, following Henning (1997), we assume that the ECB would want to hold as much as 2.5 times the US reserve ratio, up to 25% of EU reserves would be 'excess'. This is likely to be a conservative estimate as it assumes an average import to reserve ratio similar to that of the small EU member states. It is probably more reasonable to assume that the ECB would choose a reserve to import ratio more similar to that of the key countries like Germany or France which display a much lower than average figure. In the first case the calculation leads to an amount of $50 billion ER. If, making a less conservative assumption, 50% of EU reserves were considered in excess, the amount of ER would jump to $100 billion, which represents a middle range estimate taking into account the existing calculations.

ALTERNATIVE USES OF EXCESS RESERVES

Once the amount of reserves needed to cope with the transition period is determined, the problem remains of allocating the ER. Several ideas have been advanced in the literature and they can be grouped as follows:[5] (a) ER are kept with the ECB for intervention in currency markets; (b) ER are used to 'buy back' part of the public debt of EU member states; (c) ER are used for debt-relief operations in CEECs; (d) ER contribute to finance a 'convergence funds' allocation in favour of Central and Eastern European countries. This section considers a quick assessment of alternatives (a) and (b), while the next two sections will look at options (c) and (d) in more detail.

ER are kept for intervention in currency markets

According to the view long ago put forward by Machlup (1966) central banks do not have an upper limit to their desire to hold foreign reserves. In such a case, evidently, there would be no excess reserves. Several reasons can be advanced to justify the holding of ER with the ECB. One is related to the need for the ECB to build its reputation as an institution geared to financial stability both internally and externally. A very careful management of ER and its possible smooth elimination would be consistent with such a target. A second reason relates to the possibility, suggested by some scholars (Pisani, Ferri *et al.*, 1997) that the introduction of the euro might increase the variability of the euro/US\$ real exchange rate; hence it would be desirable to hold large amounts of reserves for the purpose of stabilising the bilateral exchange rate as an intermediate target. A third reason relates to the function of 'lender of last resort' of the ECB. This function may be regarded as a crucial feature of regional central banks as several experiences show. The introduction of the euro will definitely increase the role of EMU as an attraction pole for developing or transition economies. It will certainly be in the interest of the EU to stabilise financial relations with (and within) these economies, especially in the perspective of future enlargements.

Would \$100 billion be too large or too small an amount to serve these purposes? Over the long run such an amount does not seem to be extremely large: as pointed out in Lehay (1996), gross dollar purchases and sales against Deutschmarks and yen between March 1973 and December 1992 totalled \$98 billion. Looking at specific episodes one obtains different perceptions. According to Funabashi (1988) total intervention sales of dollars by the major industrial countries in September and October 1985, following the Plaza Agreement, amounted to about \$10 billion. However, the same author reports a figure of \$140 billion purchases for 1987, the year of the Louvre Accord and the New York stock market crash. In conclusion one might argue that, if monetary authorities (and not just the ECB) expect an increase in the probability of major financial breakdowns in areas of their interest, the holding of ER as a precautionary motive could not be ruled out as irrelevant. Indeed financial instability in Asia, Latin America and especially Russia strengthen this option.

ER are used to 'buy back' national debt

This option may sound unrealistic at first, especially given the prohibition on the ECB to finance the public debt of EU member countries. This objection could be bypassed as ER would be used before being handed out to the ECB. The crucial issue is a different one and it deals with the possible distributional criteria to be followed among EU members. An answer is that, given an average percentage of ER for the EU as a whole, each country could be entitled to use the same percentage of its own reserves, i.e. a 'national' approach would be followed. The issue is more delicate, though, as it faces the following trade-off: if the operation is undertaken on a EU wide basis – with a so-called 'redistribution approach' – it would be more appropriate to grant the ER to the most highly indebted countries, like Belgium or Italy, as this would increase the overall stability of the euro. This approach would require a substantial redistribution of resources within the EU. If, on the contrary, the 'national' approach is preferred, no redistribution is needed but the overall benefits would probably be smaller. In sum, this option requires the solution of a co-operation problem within the EU which may be hard to solve and may be rightly judged to be inconsistent with respect to the stability pact.

THE USE OF EU EXCESS RESERVES FOR DEBT-RELIEF OPERATIONS IN CEECS

In this section and in the next we consider two alternative systems of employing the stock of excess exchange reserves by EU countries in order to support the convergence of per capita income in Central and Eastern Europe to Western levels: a debt-relief (stock-of-debt) operation, and the allocation of 'convergence' funds. In both cases growth enhancement in Central and Eastern Europe is triggered by a rise in the investment–GDP rate made possible by the additional flow of financial resources in the region. In the case of debt relief, we rely on an estimate of the relationship between the existing stock of foreign debt and net financial inflows to compute the available amount of additional resources, while in the case of 'convergence' funds we directly allocate the stock of excess reserves among Central and Eastern European economies. The purpose of the exercise is to provide some quantitative indications of the relative effectiveness of the two systems in promoting investment and growth in the region, and of the cost of the operations for EU members. This example seems the more useful given the new challenges that the EU faces in the reconstruction of the Balkan area following the Kosovo crisis.

Note that in the perspective of the *political economy* of foreign transfers and aid, there is a *trade off* inherent in each of the two hypotheses. In the case of a stock-of-debt operation, the EU bureaucracy is only involved in the initial preparation of the operation, because once the transfer has been made a market mechanism is largely responsible of the flow of additional resources to the receiving countries: hence the role of the EU bureaucrats is limited but, on the other hand, the moral hazard problem of the use of the funds (investment versus unproductive consumption or public expenditure) is magnified (once the transfer is completed, no effective monitoring by the EU is possible). In the case of the allocation of structural funds, the EU bureaucracy is involved in a long-lasting, sequential process of transfer, monitoring of the results obtained in the recipient countries and conditional revision of the allocation criteria; therefore, the role of the bureaucracy is magnified but the moral hazard problem in Central and Eastern Europe is potentially reduced. Given this trade-off, we look at the relative economic effectiveness of the two plans in order to offer some elements for an overall evaluation of the alternative.

Excess foreign exchange reserves as resources for a debt-relief operation in Central Eastern Europe

Debt-relief operations for low- or middle-income countries have been arranged on several occasions in the last decade. What we argue here is that a debt-relief operation in Central and Eastern European countries could enhance the creditworthiness of these countries which are on the waiting list for EU accession, and could therefore trigger more financial resources to their economies and favour the convergence towards Western European per capita income levels. Therefore, it is in the interest of current EU members to (partly) employ the stock of excess foreign exchange reserves resulting from the passage to the euro for a debt-relief initiative in Central and Eastern Europe.

We will proceed as follows: given the estimation of an econometric relationship between the net inflow of financial resources in CEECs and the outstanding stock of foreign liabilities (see Appendix), we elaborate on the estimated coefficients as well as on other pieces of evidence from the literature to provide a prediction of the impact of debt relief on the growth rates of CEECs and of the financial cost of the operation for EU countries.

An estimate of the impact of the debt-relief initiative on per capita output growth in CEECs

In order to provide an approximation of the impact of the stock-of-debt reduction on per capita output growth in the CEECs, we will make the following three, admittedly strong, assumptions:

1. a reduction in the ratio of *net* foreign debt to GDP in CEECs leads to an increase in net foreign borrowing (as a share of gross output) according to the econometric estimates shown in column 6 of Table 9A.2 (see Appendix);
2. all additional net resources received from abroad are devoted to private investment; and
3. the impact of investment on growth is the one estimated by Levine and Renelt (1992) whose preferred (and 'robust') equation has been used by the IMF to forecast patterns of medium- and long-run growth in transition economies (see IMF, 1996, p. 92).

Of course, all the discussion and the resulting figures are based on a *ceteris paribus* assumption. From the panel-data estimates of Table 9A.2 in the Appendix, we infer that a reduction of 0.1 points in the net debt/GDP ratio leads to an increase of 0.015 in the annual ratio of net financial inflows over GDP (column 6) or:

Delta (net financial inflows/GDP) = (− 0.15) x Delta (net foreign debt/GDP)

If we assume that all this annual flow of additional resources is used to finance private investment (admittedly, this is quite a strong hypothesis) the increase in the investment share of GDP is exactly equal to the increase in net inflows over GDP.

We can therefore use the variation in the investment rate generated by the above procedure to estimate the growth enhancement contribution of the debt-relief operation. As reported in the 'robust' regressions of Levine–Renelt (1992, p. 946, eg. 2) the estimated coefficient of the investment share of GDP in the equation of the average annual real per capita GDP growth is 17.5; hence we find that the change in the growth rate is given by:

Delta (per capita growth rate) = (17.5) x (–0.15) x Delta (net foreign debt/GDP)

For instance, assuming that in each country the foreign debt to GDP ratio is reduced by 0.1 points we would obtain an increase in the annual growth rate equal to a quarter of a percentage point with respect to the baseline forecast:

$$0.26 = (17.5) \times (–0.15) \times (–0.1)$$

Of course, a reduction of 0.2 points in the net foreign debt/GDP rate would raise the growth rate half a percentage point and so on; it is clear that the cost of such a stock-of-debt operation varies enormously according to the dimension of the country: a reduction of 0.1 point in the debt/GDP ratio is quite expensive if gross domestic output is as large as Poland's, but quite affordable if implemented in a small economy like Latvia. Alternatively, we could set a target growth rate for all (or a subset of) the CEECs and evaluate the cost for the EU of a debt-relief operation aimed at covering the gap between the baseline forecasts and the target rate in each individual country. Notice that, under the assumptions considered here, such an increase in the growth rate lasts indefinitely.

Let us estimate the cost of raising the growth rate in the more advanced among large CEECs, namely the Czech Republic, Hungary and Poland. In the 'high-growth policies' simulations conducted by the IMF (1996, p. 92), which are based on values of the independent variables consistent with the

Table 9.3 The cost of raising the growth rate in the three CEECs

	IMF 'high-growth policies' simulated annual growth rate (%) [a]	Cost of a stock of foreign debt reduction aimed at raising the growth rate at 6% (billions of US dollars) [b]	Reduction in the number of years required for CEECs to reach industrial countries per capita income (after the stock-of-debt operation) [c]
Czech Republic	4.4	24.0	from 19 to 14
Hungary	5.0	17.0	from 22 to 18.5
Poland	4.8	60.0	from 23 to 18.2

Notes:
[a] IMF (1996).
[b] Authors' estimates; see text.
[c] Obtained comparing IMF growth-rate predictions with assumption of a 6% growth rate.

upper bound of IMF forecasts, average per capita GDP growth rates are estimated to be around 5% per year (see column 1 of Table 9.3). In order to raise the annual per capita growth rate to 6%, a reduction of net debt-to-GDP of, respectively, 0.6, 0.4 and 0.5 points is needed in the Czech Republic, Hungary and Poland: this leads to the estimate of the financial resources required for this kind of debt-relief operation reported in column 2 of Table 9.3. The global cost of the operation – about $100 billion – is high compared with the EU Commission forecast of the overall resources that will be employed for so-called Reinforced Pre-accession Strategy – about ECU 21 billion (at 1997 constant prices) – over 2000–06 (EU Commission, 1997); however the estimated cost of the operation is consistent with the non-conservative figures on excess reserves. Notice that this debt-relief operation would imply *negative* net liabilities for the Czech Republic and Poland of about $20 billion and $30 billions respectively (recall that *net* debt is defined subtracting foreign exchange reserves from gross debt, hence these figures can merely reflect an increase in reserve assets in these countries; clearly, this is conducive to higher creditworthiness and more favourable foreign borrowing conditions). A growth rate of 6% in the three advanced CEECs lowers the number of years required to reach the *current* level of industrial countries' per capita income of about five years (see column 3 in Table 9.3); moreover, as the increase in the growth rate is permanent, the contribution to catching up and development should not vanish over time.

EXCESS FOREIGN EXCHANGE RESERVES TO FINANCE A 'CONVERGENCE' FUND ALLOCATION IN CEECS

An alternative use of the stock of excess reserves stemming from the introduction of the euro is the allocation of structural funds to CEECs to favour their convergence to EU per capita income level. As mentioned before, the main differences with a stock-of-debt operation is that the allocation of structural funds directly affects investment, and that its time length is limited while the impact of the debt relief operation is prolonged. The issue of structural assistance in CEECs, and its implications for the current EU patterns of structural funds, has different facets and is a complex one (see for instance Hallet, 1997; and Baldwin *et al.*, 1997): we neglect the key questions of the political equilibria supporting EU fund allocations, and of the distribution of transfers among regions or sectors *within* a country. Instead, we investigate an option that does not interfere with the *current* pattern of EU structural funds: the allocation to the three main Visegrad countries, which are the first candidates for EU accession after the year 2000, of 'convergence funds' financed by EU excess reserves and aimed at favouring their convergence to Western income levels.

The way we will proceed is as follows: we first take from Baldwin *et al.* (1997) an informed guess on the reasonable allocation of EU Structural Funds (including the Cohesion Fund) to the three main Visegrad countries (Poland, Hungary and the Czech Republic)[6] according to the criteria currently used in the European Union; second, starting from the figure obtained above on the global cost of a debt-relief operation in the three CEECs (about US$100 billion) we compute for how many years this amount of excess reserves can finance the allocation of a 'convergence' fund in the three transition economies. Finally, we adopt a two-fold strategy for evaluating the impact of this 'convergence' fund allocation on these economies: on the one hand, we rely on the study by Levine and Renelt (1992), assuming that all the funds are employed for fostering investment in the Central and Eastern regions; on the other hand, we check our results with those obtained by de la Fuente and Vives (1995) in a study on the Spanish regions.

As far as the first point is concerned, Baldwin *et al.* (1997, pp. 151–4) offer a wide array of hypotheses concerning the distribution of EU structural funds to the three main Visegrad countries: the range of projected annual values stretches between a per-capita allocation of ECU 400, leading to an overall cost of ECU 23.6 billion (approximately US$25 billion), and a projection assuming that the aggregate amount of funds reaches 5% of the GDP estimated for the year 2000, leading to an overall cost of ECU 11.1 billion (about US$12 billion).

According to the authors, the second projection is likely to be the most reasonable one. In terms of the estimated stock of excess reserves or the required cost of the debt-relief operation mentioned before (US$100 billions), the two projections lead, respectively, to 4 and 9.3 annual allocations.

Let us now turn to the two scenarios concerning the impact of the structural allocations. Under the first scenario, all of the convergence funds received by the three CEECs would be devoted to additional investment: this means that under the higher projection the Czech Republic and Hungary would invest an additional US$5 billions and Poland an additional US$17 billions for *four* years; while under the lower projection the Czech republic, Hungary and Poland would invest additional US$2.5, 3.2 and 7 billion for about *eight* years.

The investment rate would rise by 0.1 for Hungary and the Czech Republic and by 0.15 in Poland under the first scenario, and obviously by 0.05 in each of the three countries in the second one, if we posit that all structural funds are devoted to investment. In turn, if we follow the 'robust' regression of Levine and Renelt (1992), this means that the growth rates in the three countries would approximately rise according to the following relationship:

Delta (per capita growth rate) = (17.5) x ('Convergence funds'/GDP)

which amounts to an increase of 1.75 percentage points for Hungary and the Czech Republic and of 2.6 points for Poland for four years under the first scenario, and of 0.87 percentage points for each of the three countries for eight years under the second scenario. Therefore, if we take the 'high growth policies' forecast of the IMF as a baseline, the growth rates in the three countries would *temporarily* rise as shown in Table 9.4.

Clearly, the second scenario is dominated by the debt-relief plan, as the growth rates after the allocation of structural funds do not ever reach in any country the threshold value of 6%, which is the growth rate implicit in the stock-of-debt operation (see column 3 in Table 9.4); recall that this scenario is considered *more realistic* by Baldwin *et al.* (1997).

As far as the first scenario is concerned, we have four years of growth rates beyond 6% (see column 2 in Table 9.4) followed by a return to the 'baseline' IMF forecast; in order to compare this pattern with the one stemming from the debt-relief operation, we look at the reduction in the number of years required to obtain convergence with current industrial countries' income levels. Under an allocation of a per capita amount of ECU 400 for four years, convergence with current industrial countries' income levels is achieved in 13.5 years in the Czech Republic, 16.6 years in Hungary and 16.9 years in Poland: with respect to the results obtained with the debt-relief operation

Table 9.4 The impact of structural funds on growth in three CEECs

	IMF high-growth policies simulated annual growth rates (%) [a]	Growth rates achievable for four years with a per capita allocation of ECU 400 [b]	Growth rates achievable for eight years with an aggregate allocation of 5% of GDP [b]
Czech Republic	4.4	6.2	5.3
Hungary	5.0	6.8	5.9
Poland	4.8	7.4	5.6

Notes:
[a] IMF (1996).
[b] Obtained adding IMF growth rate predictions of column 1 and our estimates of the impact of structural funds; see text.

(column 3 in Table 9.3) there is a further reduction of, respectively, 0.5, 1.9 and 1.3 years. Overall, it seems that the allocation of structural funds under the first scenario dominates the stock-of-debt operation; however, one should not forget that while the benefits of the former are confined to a given horizon, the latter has potentially unlimited advantages in terms of inflows of financial resources and, presumably, growth.

Finally, we have checked that our estimates of the contribution of the structural funds to the rise of per capita income in CEECs are broadly consistent with the *upper range* of values obtained by de la Fuente and Vives (1995) in their study of the impact of infrastructures and EU Regional Development Fund in the Spanish regions (see in particular their table 6 and the attached comments). Hence, our approach has by no means understated the contribution of structural funds to the income convergence of Eastern European countries.

CONCLUDING REMARKS

In this chapter we discuss alternative uses of the excess reserves which are likely to be available to EU policy-makers after the introduction of the euro. Given the wide range of estimates of ER, we consider a middle-range value of $100 billion. While a number of alternative uses of ER have been suggested in the literature we focus on two options, both related to the issue of EU enlargement to CEECs: debt-relief operations and the financing of a 'convergence fund'. Our calculations, based on quantitative relationships between foreign debt, investment rates and growth performance in the three major CEECs, point to significant positive effects on the convergence path of these economies towards higher per capita income levels. The two policy options discussed in detail offer different trade-offs with respect to the length of the transition process, the level of obtainable growth rates, the degree of involvement of the EU bureaucracy, and the monitoring of possible moral-hazard problems arising in receiving economies. Our final remark is of a different nature: whatever option for the use of ER is chosen – if any – the availability of ER, as an important by-product of the creation of the single currency, offers a unique opportunity to the European Union to proceed more rapidly and possibly with fewer political obstacles towards its next major target, enlargement. This suggests another important link between the different components of a 'new model for Europe' that the establishment of the single currency requires.

NOTES

1. This section owes much to the discussion in Henning (1997a).
2. In our estimates we assume for simplicity that all EU members join EMU. Different scenarios, explored *inter alia* by Goldman Sachs (1996) lead to significant differences in the value of ER only when an EU core of six members is considered.
3. Lehay (1996) discusses some of the most relevant contributions in this area.
4. Top ECB officials have always dismissed the possibility that 'excess reserves' even exist.
5. See e.g. Benassy, Italianer and Pisani-Ferry (1994), Goldman Sachs (1996), JP Morgan (1996)
6. The Slovak Republic is included among the Visegrad countries.

APPENDIX: THE DETERMINANTS OF NET FINANCIAL INFLOWS IN CEECS

Our estimates[1] of the impact of foreign debt on financial inflows are conducted on a panel of data for ten CEECs. More specifically, we have constructed an 'unbalanced' panel for ten CEECs (the countries with 'Europe Agreements' with the EU) over 1990 through 1995: there are six annual observations on Bulgaria, the Czech Republic (until 1993, we use data referring to Czechoslovakia), Hungary, Poland, Romania and Slovenia, while only three observations (1993–95) are available on the Slovak Republic, Estonia, Latvia and Lithuania. The dependent empirical variable is a *proxy* for net foreign borrowing over GDP and is obtained by subtracting the series of net foreign direct investment (FDI), exceptional financing and IMF lending from net capital flows; the reason why exceptional financing is excluded is that this item often records cancellations and restructuring of foreign debt arrears, which do not necessarily reflect saving-investment imbalances or the capacity to attract new funds. As far as IMF lending is concerned, although it can be conditional on the progress in liberalisation and macroeconomic reform, it also depends on a different set of considerations.[2]

Our set of explanatory variables is meant to capture *two kinds* of potential effects on net foreign borrowing, that could be synthetically defined as 'demand-' and 'supply-side' effects. On the one hand, we have looked for some proxies of the imbalance between national saving and domestic investment. Unfortunately, reliable and comparable measures of the saving–investment imbalance in the *private* sector are difficult to find for all CEECs; as far as the *public* sector is concerned the ratio of fiscal surplus to GDP, on which there exist broadly comparable data, is a proxy for the contribution of the government to the overall saving–investment imbalance.[3] Furthermore, the ratio of FDI to GDP has been included in the regressions to check whether FDI has acted as a substitute of net foreign borrowing in filling the and saving–investment gap in Central and Eastern Europe.[4]

On the other hand, we have selected some variables that are in principle related to the *incentive to lend* to CEECs. We have considered here two distinct kinds of proxies for the incentive to lend: the first one is intended to capture the extent and probability of capital losses on national currency-denominated assets: the higher the (probability of) capital losses, the lower the incentive to lend. The rates of inflation or, alternatively, of *nominal* exchange rate depreciation are used to evaluate this effect, under the hypothesis that the investors believe these phenomena are persistent.[5] Begg (1996, p. 75) argues that the behaviour of the *real* exchange rate also matters for the pattern of capital flows in transition economies, as it affects the current account and thus investors' expectations on the future level of the nominal exchange rate: an overvalued real rate can lead to the deterioration of the trade balance and eventually to a depreciation of the nominal rate.[6]

A second type of variable reflects the (macroeconomic) sustainability of external debt and the solvency prospects of CEECs. Drawing on some basic measures of the foreign debt burden, such as the net debt/GDP and net debt/exports ratios,[7] and adjusting them for the growth rates of output or exports, one can argue that the incentive to lend is *negatively* related to the current debt ratios (unless involuntary or 'defensive' lending prevails, i.e. lending to prevent liquidity or solvency crises); and it is *positively* related to the growth rates of GDP and export (higher growth rates, if maintained in the future, signal a potential decline in the debt burden over time).[8]

The empirical model we estimate is a so-called 'fixed effects model' (for a description, see for instance Greene, 1993, pp. 466–9). The reason why we use fixed, instead of random, effects is that our cross-sectional units are the entire set of CEECs we are interested in (and not a sample drawn from a larger population), and that we do not consider the individual effects to be uncorrelated with other regressors.[9] In brief, our 'eclectic' model of net foreign borrowing can be written in a single equation format as (9A.1):

$$(\text{net borrowing/GDP})_{it} = \beta X_{it} + \mu_t + u_{it} \qquad (9A.1)$$
$$i = 1, \ldots, 10;$$
$$t = 1990, \ldots, 1995$$

where X is a matrix of explanatory variables, i is the country index, t is the time index, μ_t is the country-specific effect and u_{it} is an n.i.i.d. residual term.

The estimated correlation matrix of the explanatory variables (available from the authors) shows a strong positive correlation, as one might expect, between the rates of inflation and nominal depreciation, and between the debt/GDP and debt/export ratios (Table 9A.1). Therefore, we will use the rates of inflation *or* of nominal exchange rate change as alternative proxies for the expected capital losses to be incurred by investors, and the net debt/GDP ratio as a measure of the sustainability of a country's stock of foreign liabilities.

The estimation techniques adopted are the OLS (in the case of fixed effects, usually referred to as 'within estimator'), and the instrumental variables estimator (IV-2SLS) to account for a possible simultaneity bias. The results of the regressions are summarised in Table 9A.2. The regression in column 1 shows that, as expected, net foreign borrowing over GDP is positively (and significantly) related to the rates of growth of GDP and export, while the fiscal balance (as a proportion of GDP) is negatively related to net foreign borrowing, but with a non-significant parameter. Finally the

Table 9A.1 Correlation matrix of exogenous variables

Growth rate	1.00							
Fiscal balance/GDP	0.10	1.00						
Inflation	−0.50	0.07	1.00					
Nominal exchange rate depreciation	−0.38	0.00	0.82	1.00				
Export growth rate	−0.13	0.31	0.18	−0.20	1.00			
Foreign debt/exports	−0.01	−0.64	0.07	0.21	−0.39	1.00		
Foreign debt/GDP	−0.11	−0.74	0.12	0.28	−0.38	0.90	1.00	
FDI/GDP	0.05	0.04	−0.25	−0.33	0.29	−0.26	−0.25	1.00

coefficient of the inflation rate is not significant (and has the wrong sign, if we assume that a more stable price level enhances the incentive to lend to CEECs). However column 1 also shows that, in contrast to what is expected, the stock of foreign debt is *positively* (but insignificantly) correlated with net foreign borrowing.

The regression of column 1 is plagued by an outlier problem which is signalled by the non-normal distribution of the residuals; the outlier is the observation on Bulgaria in 1990.[10] We thus run a new regression on the same explanatory variables, but excluding the outlying observation (column 2). The overall fit of the regression is substantially improved, and the statistical significance of some coefficients is altered: the rate of growth of GDP is now insignificant, while the parameter of the fiscal balance to GDP ratio is now significant at the 5% level and that of net foreign debt has the correct sign (although its standard error is still high). The response of the dependent variable to inflation and export growth is almost unaffected. Most important, the exclusion of the outlier resolves the normality problem (as the Bera–Jarque test shows).

If we replace the rate of inflation with the rate of devaluation of the nominal exchange rate (column 3), we obtain the expected negative sign of the coefficient (more devaluation implies less incentives to lend hence a lower incentive to lend), but the parameter is not significant yet; moreover, there is no relevant impact on the coefficients of the other variables (or on their standard errors).[11]

A problem with the correlation between the rate of growth of GDP and net foreign borrowing is that causation may go both ways: more growth might enhance solvency and creditworthiness (or it might increase the current account deficit) therefore leading to larger borrowing; alternatively, higher

Table 9A.2 *Determinants of net foreign borrowing in CEECs (dependent variable: net foreign borrowing over GDP)* [a]

Estimation method	OLS with fixed effects		OLS with fixed effects		OLS with fixed effects		Instrumental variable 2SLS		OLS with fixed effects		OLS with fixed effects	
Growth rate	0.003	(2.2)	0.0017	(1.43)	0.0015	(1.33)	-0.13E-4	(-0.07)	—		—	
Fiscal balance/GDP	-0.41	(-1.12)	-0.7	(-2.45)	-0.66	(-2.24)	-0.66	(-2.21)	-0.66	(-2.26)	-0.74	(-2.65)
Inflation	0.15E-4	(0.15)	0.24E-4	(0.03)	—		—		—		—	
Nominal exchange rate devaluation	—		—		-0.32E-4	(-0.37)	—		—		—	
Rate of growth of export	0.12	(3.03)	0.09	(3.06)	0.09	(3.11)	0.08	(2.47)	0.08	(2.77)	0.08	(2.8)
Foreign debt/GDP	0.033	(0.37)	-0.1	(-1.42)	-0.089	(-1.19)	-0.14	(-1.77)	-0.13	(-2.18)	-0.15	(-2.49)
FDI/GDP	—		—		—		0.44	(0.89)	0.44	(0.91)	—	
Adjusted R squared	0.29		0.48		0.48		0.45		0.47		0.47	
Ramsey's RESET	0.49	[0.48]	0.3	[0.58]	0.25	[0.61]	1.3	[0.25]	1.16	[0.28]	1.34	[0.25]
Bera–Jarque test of normality of the residuals	21.32	[0.00]	0.76	[0.68]	0.71	[0.7]	0.29	[0.86]	0.34	[0.84]	0.04	[0.98]
F-test of homoscedasticity	0.18	[0.75]	0.33	[0.57]	0.06	[0.8]	0.18	[0.66][b]	0.2	[0.65]	0.016	[0.9]
F-test for the fixed-effects specification	2.73	[0.017]	3.72	[0.00]	4.83	[0.00]	—		5.24	[0.00]	5.2	[0.00]
Wald-test for the fixed effects specification	—		—		—		42.7	[0.00]	—		—	
Number of observations	48.00		47.00		47.00		47.00		47.00		47.00	

Notes:
[a] T-statistics in round brackets. Probability levels in square brackets (the values refer to the probability of falsely rejecting the null hypothesis of, respectively, linearity normality, homoscedasticity and joint zero-restrictions on the individual countries' fixed effects).
[b] Chi-square test.

levels of foreign lending could relax the liquidity and foreign exchange constraints in a transition economy, and thus have a positive impact on the growth rate. A solution to this simultaneity problem is to run an instrumental variables regression (column 4). The results show that the growth rate has no longer the expected sign, and its coefficient is not significant; there is an improvement in the statistical performance of the foreign debt/GDP ratio, while no impact is detected on the coefficients of fiscal balance and the growth rate of exports. The ratio of FDI to GDP has been also tested as a regressor in column 4, to check whether foreign direct investment and net borrowing have been substitutes or complements in transition economies over 1990–95: the sign of the coefficient indicates that complementarity is likely to occur in the CEECs, but the t-statistic is too low to draw any sound conclusion.

Finally, in columns 5 and 6 we have excluded the rate of growth of GDP from the regression. In this case, the coefficients of the fiscal balance, the growth rate of exports and the foreign debt/GDP ratio all have the expected signs and are statistically significant (while that of foreign direct investment is positive, but insignificant).

Notes

1. The estimation procedure and analysis is taken from Manzocchi (1997), where a full description of the empirical model is provided.
2. This can also be true of other kinds of bilateral or multilateral assistance for which, however, it is more difficult to distinguish between concessional and non-concessional flows.
3. Debelle and Faruqee (1996, pp. 18–21) find that the fiscal surplus has a considerable (positive) impact on the current account.
4. Other types of non-debt inflows (equity) were rather marginal in CEECs until 1995, and are neglected here.
5. Of course, this argument does not apply to foreign currency-denominated debt, which represents the largest share of foreign debt in CEECs.
6. The recent experience of the Czech Republic could provide an example of this pattern; another possibility is that an appreciation (depreciation) of the real exchange rate leads to a lower (higher) *real* cost of servicing the external debt if this is denominated in foreign currency.
7. Throughout the chapter, we use data on net foreign debt stocks (gross debt less foreign exchange reserves).
8. The sources of the variables are the *Transition Report* of the EBRD, the *Economic Survey of Europe* of the UN Economic Commission for Europe and the *International Financial Statistics* of the IMF. For further details, see Manzocchi (1997).
9. See Nerlove and Balestra (1992). Notice also that no lagged dependent variable is present on the right-hand-side of our regressions, so that a potential source of inconsistency of the fixed-effects OLS estimator is absent (Debelle-Faruqee, 1996, p. 11).
10. It should be mentioned that, given the still unsatisfactory quality of the statistics on transition economies, measurement errors may affect the estimates.
11. Following Begg (1996) we have tested whether the rate of change of the *real* exchange rate matters for net foreign borrowing in CEECs. The parameter is never significant at the 10% level.

10. Conclusions and policy options for EMU

Pier Carlo Padoan

INTRODUCTION

The introduction of the euro has been marked by mixed signals. On the one hand several monetary authorities as well as market operators have welcomed the single currency as an interesting opportunity for diversification of their portfolios. On the other hand, after a fast start the new currency depreciated against the dollar by about 10% in less than three months, to recover slightly in the second part of 1999. Notwithstanding the fact that the euro represents a major change in the international monetary scene, it is definitely too soon to tell whether the euro project will be a success or a failure. This will be a function of two major factors: the robustness of the structural elements underlying the potential of the euro as a global currency and the capacity of the European Union (or at least Euro-11) to exploit the new currency so as to exit from its long-lasting situation of slow growth and persistent unemployment

MACROECONOMIC ASPECTS

The macroeconomic policy implications of the analysis carried out in this book may be summarised as follows: in the long run, it is in the EU's interest to maximise the size of the 'currency region' of the euro, i.e., of its international use; in the medium run, it is in the EU's interest to pursue a policy oriented towards the stabilisation of the euro's exchange rate.

The euro's introduction highlights a twofold problem. On the one hand, EU policy-makers face the issue of which 'exchange rate policy' to follow vis-à-vis other currencies, especially the dollar; on the other hand, both the EU and the USA have to face the issue of the management of the new international monetary system in a manner quite unlike that of the past.

In the long run, the relevant question is whether the euro will be capable of attaining, as international currency, a weight proportional to that of the EU in world trade and production. In this respect and from this point of view, the crucial issue is the management of a bipolar (or tripolar) monetary system where it is no longer evident which currency assumes the 'residual' role.

As mentioned in chapter 1, we must thus ask whether, and to what degree, the international system provides incentives for co-operation between the USA and the EU. A definitive answer to this question appears complex to say the least, considering the post-war relations in monetary issues between the USA and Europe. What does allow a moderate degree of optimism regarding the future of these relations is the growing interdependence between the two largest economies of the international system; this interdependence raises the costs of a macroeconomic conflict which, based on historical experience, could quickly spread from monetary to trade relations.

The 'medium run' aspects are, to some extent, less problematic. They are dominated by path-dependency phenomena owing to the presence of multiple equilibria in the relations between key currencies. This implies that it is the medium-run evolution of the euro's external dimension that will, most probably, determine the long-term configuration of monetary relations, i.e., whether the euro succeeds in taking on a global dimension or whether it will be relegated to a regional role.

As discussed in chapter 1, in the medium run it is in the EU's interest to pursue a policy aiming at the stability of its currency's exchange rate. This is a desirable objective not only because it would stabilizse European interest rates, but also because an 'activist' policy, targeted to support the EU's export competitiveness, would most probably be counterproductive.

We discussed in chapter 1 how the ongoing adjustment of the EU's public finances underlines dramatically the lack of private investment with respect to savings. A stable external value of the euro in a framework of contained or negligible inflation would allow interest rates to be maintained at low levels, supporting a monetary environment favouring investment, and growth; quite the opposite of what occurred during the 1980s and part of the 1990s, when tight monetary policies targeted at containing inflation, in the face of growing public finance deficits and sluggish – if declining – price dynamics, had caused a sharp rise in real interest rates. The new macroeconomic environment would thus be completed by a stable exchange rate for the euro as a necessary condition for a stable interest-rate policy.

It can, of course, be argued that the euro's exchange rate – against the dollar – would depend in part on the behaviour of Europe, and in part on that of the USA. This brings us back to the question of the role of monetary co-operation between the two economies. A preliminary point in this respect is that a policy of stable exchange rates – understood as a 'non-aggressive' EU policy – is an important initial condition for a strengthened transatlantic co-operation. Second, it remains to be seen whether forms of managed exchange rates – like target zones – would improve the operation of the international monetary system.[1]

Notwithstanding a 'more managed' international monetary system, nonetheless, the introduction of the euro does raise the options for EMU's external monetary policies. The analysis in chapter 2 supports the idea that the expansion of the European money market following the introduction of the euro could weaken the impact of US monetary policy on European interest rates. Assuming Germany's monetary policy as a reference for the ECB's policy stance, the analysis reaches the following conclusions: Germany's monetary policy has been able to maintain a certain degree of independence from US monetary policy, especially during the period following the introduction of the EMS; emphasising the control of inflation and stabilising the fluctuations of the mark/dollar rate, while there appears not to be a significant relation between the *levels* of the interest rate and the exchange rate. These findings offer additional support to the idea that a monetary policy for the euro focused on stability – along a German 'model' but with the benefit of a larger market – will lead to greater independence for the EU. This will leave open the more desirable option of closer co-operation with the USA or – if such co-operation is not immediately feasible – that of 'decoupling' European monetary policy and its orientation towards the 'internal' goal of a stable and low interest rate.

On the other hand, a stable exchange rate does not – as is sometimes argued – clash with the need to sustain the EU's growth through exports. This aspect has been discussed in chapter 6, which comes to the following conclusions. In the first place, the inclusion in EMU of the 'peripheral' countries – Italy, Portugal and Spain – does not result in any greater pressure towards real devaluation. On the contrary, Germany is the country where the exchange rate has the greatest impact given the high exchange rate elasticity of German exports and the export-led features of its economic model.

In the second place, it is the large intra-EU market, rather than exchange rate competitiveness in extra-EU markets, that supports EU countries' exports. This result confirms the intra-industry nature of intra-EU trade and highlights the non-price factors in competitiveness. It follows that intra-EU trade will benefit from the growing integration of European markets as a result of the completion of the single market, of its enlargement and of the introduction of the euro itself.

The independence of European monetary policy will be increasingly strengthened by the process of integration of the euro's financial markets. As is discussed in chapter 3, the introduction of a single currency favours the development of extensive and thick financial markets, even if the (initial) non-participation of the UK were to slow the process down. The expanded financial market will lead to greater diversification of financial instruments and greater competitive pressure on the banks from other intermediaries as well as within the banking system.

This, in turn, will lead to greater efficiency of the banking system, lower cost of financing and greater effectiveness of the transmission of monetary policy, even though there will continue to be differences among the EMU's member countries owing to differences among national financial structures.

A summary of the macroeconomic issues discussed in this book could lead to a relatively optimistic conclusion. To the extent that a stability oriented macroeconomic policy favours investment and output growth it also favours employment creation. A 'simple' macroeconomic approach, however, leaves out many of the elements needed to identify the appropriate policy options for the euro, especially in relation to the issue of unemployment. It remains to be seen to what extent such a policy is feasible given the underlying structural characteristics of EMU. To address the point let us recall the framework, discussed in chapter 1, of the identification of costs and benefits of a monetary union.

Benefits from a monetary union increase with the extension of the union, as expressed in terms of either the number of participating countries or of economic size. Costs increase with an increasing diversity of the preferences of the area's policy-makers regarding stabilisation policies. In other words, the costs of Union membership for a country with a high preference for containing inflation increase if other union members share the same preference for output stabilisation oriented monetary policies. In general, the higher the convergence of the member countries' preference for low inflation and stability-oriented monetary policy, the lower the costs. From this point of view, EMU's composition becomes crucial, but it is equally evident that the process of financial convergence suggests that the costs of the EMU will be quite moderate as even the least disciplined among the Union's members have implemented rigorous anti-inflationary and fiscal reform policies and to the extent that the stability pact will be in force.

This approach suggests that the success of a monetary union depends on two variables: the intensity of integration and convergence of policy preferences towards stability. In other words net benefits will be a function of both the structural and microeconomic features of the Euroland economy as well as of the definition of common or at least mutually consistent economic policies. It is precisely in this respect that critics of EMU raise their voice, especially when considering the relationship between monetary union and labour markets.

IS EMU ENDOGENOUS?

The most serious doubts on the sustainability of a common monetary policy in Europe are based on the traditional approach to optimum currency areas according to which the changeover to a single currency delivers net benefits only if the countries involved are not subject to asymmetric shocks. Whenever such a condition does not apply, the optimal choice is to keep independent monetary policies that can offset country specific shocks.

The conclusions drawn on the basis of the theory of optimum currency areas may, nevertheless, be questioned regarding (a) the correctness of the methodologies and (b) the practical relevance of the issues raised. With respect to the first point, Frankel and Rose (1997) emphasise that trade integration and synchronisation of business cycles will most likely increase with monetary integration, so that (at least some of) the criteria suggested by the literature on optimum currency areas would be met *ex post* by the countries joining EMU. This approach seems the more appropriate if we consider that the single currency requires a wholesale redefinition of the European economic policy model (Allsop and Vines, 1996).

With reference to the real costs associated with the adoption of a common exchange rate policy, Gros (1996) observes that possible asymmetric shocks on exports – which bear most of the cost from loss of the exchange rate – would have limited impact on growth and employment creation in European countries.

The literature on 'endogenous currency areas' is barely in its infancy yet it represents a useful approach to assess the perspectives of EMU. Indeed some of the issues discussed in the previous chapters can be usefully reconsidered as evidence of EMU's endogeneity. These points can be quickly recalled with respect to convergence of economic cycles and regional catching-up.

One of the preconditions for sustainability of a monetary union is convergence of national economic cycles. Different cyclical patterns would point to differences in sensitivity to exogenous shocks, which would produce asymmetrical consequences.[2] The endogenous currency area approach suggests that monetary integration deepens trade integration and leads to converging cyclical profiles. Evidence discussed in chapter 5 provides clear evidence of cyclical convergence along with increasing monetary integration in Europe.

Additional evidence, discussed in chapter 8, relates to regional catching-up where we report[3] tests of the hypothesis that monetary convergence has a positive effect on regional catching-up in Europe. Over the 1980–87 period, which was marked by a regime of fixed, yet adjustable exchange rates, there is no evidence of income convergence among the European regions.

Conversely, there appears to have been regional convergence during the period of the 'hard EMS', 1987–92, featuring strict nominal exchange rigidity. In the following period, 1992–95, which was marked by a more flexible exchange regime and by several devaluations of currencies participating in the European exchange agreements, the opposite case seems to have occurred, i.e. divergence among the European regions' growth rates.

Evidence discussed in chapter 8 also shows that between the mid 1980s and the early 1990s regional specialisation and geographical concentration of production at the regional level both increased. This is only partially related with the endogeneity of currency areas. This evidence confirms that production specialisation increases as a consequence of integration but it does so on a regional scale. We know that increasing specialisation increases the risk of asymmetric shocks. This, however, increases the costs of monetary union only to the extent that specialization between countries increases, but not in the case of increasing regional specialisation. From this point of view evidence reported in chapter 8 points to a stronger, not weaker, EMU, as only the benefits of specialisation are delivered by increasing monetary integration. Evidence reported in chapter 7, on the other hand, shows that, for some sectors at least, a country factor dominates, hinting at the possible negative consequences of asymmetric shock in EMU.

To conclude, while there is some evidence that deeper monetary integration may increase the adaptability of EMU countries to the new monetary regime, results are not conclusive. Above all the 'endogenous currency area approach' has to be tested against the most relevant factor: labour markets.

EMU'S PRESSURE ON LABOUR MARKETS

The analysis of the impact of monetary integration on labour markets is still quite limited and, at the same time, offers different and possibly conflicting views. They are briefly reviewed here.

Jimeno[4] examines the consequences of the introduction of a single monetary policy with several labour markets (i.e., the markets of the EMU member countries). In this context, the consequences for employment of a monetary policy targeted at price stability will be the more negative the greater the rate of structural unemployment (defined as the average of national unemployment rates). The natural rate of unemployment – as we have seen in chapter 4 – is the greater the higher the degree of institutional rigidity, the lower the degree of adaptability of wages to labour market conditions and the weaker the competitive pressure in the product markets.

In this context a centralised monetary policy will produce different effects for national labour markets, but it is precisely this that could lead to greater flexibility. Jimeno suggests that monetary policy – by way of greater competition among 'national systems' – will bring about (a) greater flexibility in the labour market, (b) institutional changes in the labour market, (c) greater competition in the product markets as a result of greater integration[5] which reduces the market power of the firms. The three effects improve employment opportunities as they lower the inflationary bias of EMU by lowering the average rate of structural unemployment as well as its dispersion.

Jimeno, however, considers a fourth effect, i.e., wage catching-up. As a result of the introduction of the single currency and of greater transparency and comparability of prices and wages, workers in the lower-wage regions could align their demands to the levels of the higher-wage regions. If alignments do not reflect productivity trends – i.e., if productivity in the backward regions is lower – the average cost of labour in Europe rises, inducing higher inflationary pressures and structural unemployment. We might add that these effects would interact with high capital mobility, heighten the geographic concentration of investment, the differentiation of regional production structures and the disparities in productivity.

A different approach looks at the interaction between the supranational central bank and labour market organisation. One of the main pillars of EMU is the independence of the central bank, according to the widely held view that central bank independence is a necessary and sufficient condition for price stability.[6] This principle has been (partially) challenged in recent contributions[7] on the ground that the correlation between central bank independence and inflation has to be assessed taking into account the characteristics of industrial relations and of the wage bargaining process in particular. More precisely, one result of these analyses is that the higher the level of wage bargaining co-ordination the more efficient and less costly in terms of unemployment is (independent) monetary policy in curbing inflation.

Wage co-ordination refers to a complex set of institutional arrangements, involving both trade unions and employer organisations that differ from country to country.[8] These include five set of interactions: (a) the interaction, in each firm/sector (dyad), between workers' organisations and employers' organisations; (b) the interaction between the leaders of the bargaining organisation and the rank-and-file members; (c) the interaction between the bargainers in each dyad and their counterparts in other dyads; (d) the interaction between the wage bargainers as a group and the policy authorities; (e) the interaction between monetary and fiscal policy authorities (which determines the actual degree of monetary policy independence).

It can be seen at a glance that all of these interactions are directly (the last) or indirectly (the first four) affected by the establishment of EMU. This point will be taken up later. Let us now concentrate on the reasons why, for a given level of central bank independence, the structure of wage bargaining matters. To see the point, following Hall and Franzese (1998) consider the case where wage bargaining is not co-ordinated. In such a case each bargaining unit (a dyad of employer and union) has to reach an agreement while being uncertain about the results of agreements in other units. Three consequences follow. First, the union in each dyad will try to obtain an additional inflation increment in each wage settlement in order to protect itself from real wage losses resulting from other settlements that are more inflationary than its own. Second, as each bargaining unit is usually too small to have a substantial impact on the aggregate inflation rate, negotiators in each bargaining unit will not take into account aggregate considerations in their bargaining (free riding). Third, bargainers know that policy authorities will respond by adopting restrictive measures to *aggregate* inflationary wage behaviour, the result of which might be unemployment; however they will not take into consideration this information in their behaviour as they know that policy action will be taken in response to an outcome (aggregate wage inflation) which is out of their control. In sum, in unco-ordinated settings wage bargainers, both unions and employers, will be less responsive to threats of restrictive monetary policy even if central bank independence makes these threats credible.

Let us now look at the case of co-ordination where typically a 'lead bargain' sets the tune for the entire bargaining process. In such a case the lead bargain has a great influence over the level of economy-wide wage settlements. This leads to the following implications. First, as the members of each bargaining unit are aware of the results of other wage settlements, they do not need to ask for extra inflationary concessions to protect themselves from unanticipated relative wage losses. Second, the lead bargainer is aware of the consequences of its actions over the whole economy both in terms of overall inflation and employment and, in particular, it will take into account in its bargaining the likely policy response. This makes the centralised bargainers highly sensitive in their settlements to signals coming from the central bank, especially if the latter enjoys a high degree of independence, which increases the credibility of monetary policy signals.

The implications of the above can be summarised as follows. If wage bargaining is co-ordinated the central bank is able to influence the level of settlements, and hence of inflation, simply by signalling its policy intentions, so that monetary policy will not need to raise the level of unemployment. If wage bargaining is not co-ordinated small bargaining units do not expect a

Table 10.1 Monetary policy and wage bargaining regimes and results

	High unemployment	Low unemployment
High inflation	CBI low	CBI low
	CWB low	CWB high
Low inflation	CBI high	CBI high
	CWB low	CWB high

Notes:
CBI = Central bank independence.
CWB = co-ordinated wage bargaining.

Source: Hall and Franzese (1998).

direct response to their settlements and will not follow a self-restraint policy. In such a case the central bank will have to apply a stricter monetary policy stance, and hence produce higher unemployment, to reach its targets.

Following the above considerations Hall and Franzese advance, and successfully test, the following three hypotheses: (a) there is a negative relationship between inflation and central bank independence (the traditional view about central bank independence and monetary stability); (b) the level of wage bargaining co-ordination has a direct effect on inflation irrespective of the role of central bank independence; (c) in cases where the level of wage co-ordination is low central bank independence lowers the rate of inflation only at the costs of higher rates of unemployment. Taken together these three hypotheses determine a structure of monetary independence and wage bargaining structures leading to different macroeconomic performance patterns summarized in Table 10.1 and based on evidence, reported by Hall and Franzese, on the average performance of the OECD countries over the period 1955–90.

These results are, to some extent and as far as the rate of unemployment is concerned, confirmed by estimation results carried out by Nickell (1997)[9] – who also takes into account a wide range of institutional characteristics of national labour markets – and that are discussed in chapter 3. At first sight the implications are a source of concern. The establishment of EMU introduces no incentive to increase the degree of wage bargaining centralisation to match the degree of centralisation and independence of monetary policy. As a matter of fact the establishment of EMU and of the European Central Bank *decreases* the centralisation of wage bargaining centralisation as it leaves it, in the best case, at the national level. The straightforward implication is that EMU will keep price stability at a higher cost in terms of unemployment with respect to cases where there is more wage bargaining centralization. In addition, according to this view, such higher costs would be unevenly distributed among different countries according to their levels of wage bargaining centralisation, while facing the same degree of central bank independence; countries where this level is lower will suffer from higher unemployment.

The view just presented may be challenged, however. Another view [10] holds that the amount of unemployment, for a given level of monetary policy independence, is inversely correlated with the degree of labour market flexibility, itself dependent on the characteristics of the institutions regulating labour markets. In addition, with a supranational central bank, unemployment costs of monetary stabilisation will be a function of the level of structural unemployment (i.e. the rate of unemployment not dependent on cyclical factors) which is the average of national levels of structural unemployment. In such a case what improves the smooth operation of monetary union is an increase in the level of labour market flexibility, itself dependent on national institutional characteristics.

The role of rigidities has been discussed in chapter 4. Here we can recall the main conclusions and implications for the current discussion. While some labour market institutions may affect unemployment more than others it is their interaction that plays a relevant role. Conclusions reached in the previous section are to some extent reinforced (with respect to the role of wage setting institutions) but they also shed only partial light on the issue as it is clear that the level of employment depends on labour market institutions other than those regulating wage setting procedures. Increased 'flexibility', understood as the appropriate combination of different labour market institutions, may increase employment perspectives for a given degree of monetary policy independence.

INSTITUTIONAL COMPETITION OR SOCIAL DUMPING?

What are the implications for the endogenous approach to EMU? The two elements we have been discussing above, the priority of a national as opposed to a European dimension in labour market policies and the relevance of the labour market institutions in affecting employment perspectives, have led many analysts and policy-makers to describe the scenario that will prevail under EMU as one of 'institutional competition' or, even worse, of 'social dumping'. The point is easily clarified. Deeper international integration and 'globalisation' as well as the elimination of exchange rate movements increase competition between products and factor (especially labour) markets. To the extent that labour market regulations affect labour costs and hence competitiveness, in the absence of supranational labour market regulation, national (and subnational) regulatory bodies, often with the agreement of or under the pressure of workers' and employers' organisations, will tend to loosen labour market regulations in order to increase competitiveness. Better competitive positions, and hence better employment opportunities could be the result of both lower domestic production costs and/or increased foreign capital inflows attracted by more favourable labour market conditions. As a consequence a 'race to the bottom' might result in labour regulations. This concern has been raised especially with respect to the EU's future enlargement to Central and Eastern European countries, which typically have much lower labour costs compared with current EU members.[11]

How real is this possibility? Some empirical evidence might provide further insight. A first set of evidence [12] looks at the competition effect produced on the 'cohesion countries' of the EU (Greece, Ireland, Portugal and Spain) and the core EU countries by the recent steps of European integration (the launching of the Single Market, the accession of Portugal, Spain and Greece, the Europe Agreements). Such evidence may provide some information about similar effects presumably generated by future enlargement waves. The changing environment in European integration over the 1980s has led to relevant changes in the trade specialisation pattern of the European Union. In particular: (a) the peripheral ('cohesion') countries have gone through an intense process of restructuring in trade specialisation (as we have seen in chapter 7); (b) sectors where most changes have taken place have been the labour intensive and the labour and capital intensive ones (i.e. those sectors where three out of four peripheral countries – Greece, Portugal and Spain – have their strongest competitive positions); (c) an important process of geographical and sectoral trade restructuring has taken place over the period considered, and the peripheral countries have reacted positively to the changing trade environment; (d) the core EU countries have benefited from increased trade integration with Central and Eastern European countries in the period following the fall of the communist regimes.

Integration deepening in Europe has also led to an increase in the cross-border activity of firms, both EU and non-EU, in terms of mergers and acquisitions as well as foreign direct investment (FDI). This process, however, has followed different patterns across sectors and countries. Knowledge intensive sectors have been characterised by stronger transnational activities, which have led to polarisation of production specialisation in core countries. Evidence [13] shows that FDI and trade specialisation patterns in core European countries lead to polarisation effects (i.e. concentration in the centre economies); nonetheless, diffusion of investment towards the peripheral EU countries is present and, in some cases, substantial. Some diffusion of production activities takes place in knowledge intensive and, especially, in more traditional sectors. However, national (more than sectoral) differences emerge. Countries such as Spain and Ireland are successful in attracting FDI, which result in strengthening trade comparative advantages, while others, such as Greece, much less so, with Portugal taking an intermediate position.

A second set of evidence [14] is related to the effects of international competition on employment and wage levels in manufacturing sectors in the core EU countries and it is useful in assessing the degree of exposure of these economies to competition from low wage countries. As we have seen in chapter 7, estimation results show that labour markets in continental European countries, irrespective of the manufacturing sector considered, react to international competition more through changes (decreases) in employment levels than through wage cuts, contrary to the case of the UK and of the smaller Nordic countries. This can be taken as evidence of a generalised 'labour market rigidity' in continental Europe. Second, international competition exerts a stronger (negative) pressure on both wages and employment levels in sectors where the country exhibits a trade comparative *disadvantage*, while such a pressure is much weaker or absent in sectors where the country enjoys a comparative *advantage*. This implies that the assertion that international competition, which may be increased by forms of social dumping, will hurt especially unskilled labour intensive sectors must be qualified. One implication for the issue under discussion is the following. The role of labour market institutions which do affect performance of both wage and employment levels cannot be separated from the role of other factors (most notably, cumulated learning, scale effects and specific knowledge) which determine the overall trade performance of a sector.[15] However, as the availability of such other factors crucially depends on capital accumulation (human, technological and physical), to the extent that monetary convergence depresses investment activity, it does not facilitate labour and product market adjustment to the new environment.

INCENTIVES TO POLICY ACTIONS

In the previous sections we have discussed the changes generated by monetary integration to the performance of the EU economy. The basic message is that, while monetary integration does produce some convergence towards a structure that is closer to the requirements of optimum currency areas, this implies a cost in terms of lower growth, and especially lower investment growth. Convergence in labour market behaviour and regulation is much less advanced. In this area the coexistence of several national institutional models might lead to forms of institutional competition. On the other hand, more labour market flexibility may be a necessary yet not sufficient condition for adjustment to the new competitive environment if the appropriate policy actions are not taken in a number of areas, both at the macro and at the micro (structural) level. In other words, in order for an endogenous monetary union to materialise, the appropriate policy actions must be implemented, and hence the appropriate incentives for policy must be available, i.e. centralisation of monetary policy is not enough to assure sustainability of a monetary union.

This is a very general issue that can be only superficially addressed here. To do this let us briefly consider the evolution of the policy-making regime in Europe in the run up to monetary union. Table 10.2 offers a summary of the evolution of the EU macro-monetary regime since the introduction of the EMS. While the matter is undoubtedly complex a possible reading is the following. Over a 20-year period the EU macroeconomic regime has shifted from a 'weak hegemonic' regime (where the role of hegemon has been carried out by Germany) to a co-operative (club)[16] regime. This has been made possible by a shift in the policy incentive set from an 'individualistic' (resisting discipline) to a co-operative behaviour (based on the exclusion threat). Such an institutional setup has provided the policy framework for the 'endogenous' monetary integration process we have discussed above. The evolution of the macro policy regime has also shifted the distribution of benefits from the sheltered (rentiers) to the exposed, more competitive sectors within national economies. This process has not been linear however. The 1992 crisis of the European exchange rate mechanism can be interpreted as the consequence of both policy conflicts – which cumulated over the previous period (increasing discipline in the 'hegemony' setup) – and of distributional conflicts between the sheltered and the exposed sectors. To some extent the crisis was welcome as it, eventually, led to an acceleration of the integration/adjustment process.

With the introduction of the euro the scene has changed again. While the new environment favours the more dynamic exposed sectors, incentives for policy actions come more from the competition than from the co-operation side. This is the real challenge EMU has to face and has to assess taking into account that policy competition/co-operation issues are related to a number of policy areas which can be summarised – in a non-exhaustive listing – as follows: (a) the relationship between monetary and budget policy; (b) relationships between national budget policies; (c) tax policy; (d) labour market policies.

Table 10.2 Policy regimes in Europe

	1979–87 Soft EMS	1987–92 Hard EMS	1992–96 Small EMS	1996–98 Run up to EMU	1999– Emu
Macro environment	Less than full cap mob. Partial mon. policy autonomy	Conflicting policy mix Costly convergence	New equilibrium Slight divergence	Disinflation Fiscal adjustment	Monetary stability High unemployment
Role of macro EU institutions (consensus)	Weak external constraint (weak)	Strong external constraint (weak)	Absent/partial (multi-speed EMU (disillusion)	Strong (strong)	Strong? (unstable)
Incentives for national policy action	Resisting discipline	Importing discipline Weak co-operation	Domestic goals	Non-exclusion (building common institutions)	Competitive adjustment
Favoured / unfavoured groups	Sheltered / exposed	Sheltered / exposed	Exposed (devaluing economies)	Exposed / rentiers	Dynamic exposed / uncompetitive
Regime	Weak hegemony	Regional hegemony	Anarchy	Co-operative (club)	Co-operative / competitive

INTERACTIONS BETWEEN POLICY AREAS

To look only superficially at the issue, let us consider the following approach. Given that there are spillovers between the policy areas listed above, let us consider to what extent co-operation/conflict outcomes in one area influence outcome in other areas.

Level 1 Co-operation between the single monetary policy and national budget policies increases benefits in terms of improved performance. Spillovers between monetary and fiscal policy support the idea that co-ordination is beneficial. OECD (1999) simulations show that switching to a common monetary policy increases the effectiveness of monetary stabilisation with respect to national monetary policy stabilisation to the extent that common monetary policy is geared to average and not country specific inflation rates.

Level 2 OECD (1999) also shows that losses in stabilisation power of budget policies decrease when the number of countries allowing automatic stabilisers to operate increases. This number, in turn, is increased to the extent that budget flexibility is restored. The issue here is the following: the extent to wich budget co-operation in EU-11 increases the speed of convergence towards a 'stable budget regime' (understood as a situation in which requirements of the Stability and Growth Pact are fulfilled). In a low growth situation in some of the core EU-11 countries (notably Germany, Italy) fiscal stabilisation measures are harder to obtain. Budget co-ordination increases, if marginally, the overall growth rate making it easier to converge to the 'stable budget regime'. Incentives for co-ordination increase if externalities can be exploited. Within the EU-11 incentives for a co-ordinated if limited policy action are larger in the core countries. Peripheral countries (Ireland, Portugal, Spain) experiencing higher growth would rather see a restrictive policy stance. However, since co-ordination *does not* imply the same policy stance in all countries, full co-ordination would really aim at a redistribution of budget policy stances within EU-11 in the respect of the Stability and Growth Pact.[17] Increasing co-operation at this level could further increase the scope for co-ordination at level 1.

Level 3 One common view is that monetary union requires tax harmonisation to operate effectively under a regime of full capital mobility. An alternative view is that tax competition is beneficial as it stimulates policies to attract mobile capital and the efficiency of financial markets. To the extent that tax competition produces effects on national budgets it may interfere with level 2 co-ordination. It is not clear to what extent an 'optimal' tax regime can be designed in a monetary union. Different views and incentives are present. Core EU-11 countries seem to favour some form of tax harmonisation (one of the problems is the definition of 'unfair tax competition'). The key issue here is the attitude of the UK and, presumably, the debate on crucial aspect of this policy area (the 'Monti package') will be affected by the attitude of the UK government regarding EMU membership.

Level 4 It has been argued that tax competition has led to excessive labour tax loads, which in turn may explain a large part of European unemployment (Daveri and Tabellini, 1997). So it may be that lack of co-operation in level 3 may lead, as discussed above, to less co-operation and more competition in labour market regulations and adjustment. It is also unclear to what extent co-operation in level 2 may accelerate or slow down labour market adjustment. It is sometimes argued that higher growth (which could be obtained from closer macroeconomic co-operation) would lower incentives to – badly needed – labour market adjustments. In addition, persistent labour market rigidities might negatively feed back on level 1 policy by requiring tighter monetary policy responses. The real issue is whether increased labour market flexibility may be obtained through more or less co-ordination of labour market policies. Policy preferences in the EU-11 group are largely differentiated, suggesting that we will see more institutional competition and to some extent 'social dumping' on the part of the 'peripheral countries'. This issue has been discussed above.

CONCLUSIONS

EMU is, to some extent, endogenous. However, endogeneity must be obtained from two, complementary viewpoints. As suggested by Collignon (1997) approach to currency areas, benefits from monetary union increase with the degree of economic integration for a given distribution of policy preferences among countries, but, given the degree of integration, convergence in the distribution of policy preferences is necessary for net benefits to be generated by monetary unification. Pre-EMU monetary convergence has led to deeper integration thus increasing net benefits. This has been obtained because the process of monetary integration in Europe has produced (or rather 'forced') convergence in 'revealed' policy preferences. However, while convergence relates to preferences for financial stability the same is not yet clear for preferences for more flexible product and labour market policies. To the extent that 'macroeconomic' and 'policy preference' convergence are self reinforcing, EMU is indeed endogenous, i.e. it is a self-fulfilling mechanism. However, macroeconomic convergence – see chapter 5 – has been obtained at the cost of lower investment, and this trend, if not reversed, might lead to undesirable negative consequences for the sustainability of monetary union. More investment in Europe is necessary both for macroeconomic reasons – i.e. to fill the investment gap in a more balanced public finance environment – and for microeconomic reasons – so that the necessary adjustment in labour markets is complemented by a larger availability of human, technological and physical capital. The extent to which such a strategy is successful and the growth process in Europe is restored will draw the line between a 'strong' and a 'weak' euro.

NOTES

1. For an assessment see e.g. Bergsten and Henning (1996).
2. Bayoumi and Eichengreen (1998).
3. Results are discussed in CER (1999)
4. Jimeno (1998).
5. Also as a result of full implementation of the Single Market.
6. For a recent reassessment of the issue see Eijffinger and De Haan (1996).
7. Iversen (1998); Hall and Franzese (1998).
8. See Hall and Franzese (1998) for a detailed analysis of these issues.
9. See Nickell (1997), and discussion in chapter 3.
10. See for instance Center for Economic Policy Research (1995); Nickell (1997).
11. Central and Eastern European countries have hourly labour costs which are from one third to one tenth of EU average. See CEPR (1998), Table 4.4.
12. Discussed in Padoan (1997), see also CEPR (1998).
13. See Padoan (1997a) and CEPR (1998), chapter 4.
14. Discussed in chapter 7.
15. For a formal treatment see De Benedictis and Padoan (1999).
16. For an assessment of European integration in terms of club theory see Padoan (1997b).
17. This is a complex issue considered in a stimulating paper by Casella (1999).

References

Aizenman, J. (1991), 'Trade dependency, bargaining and external debt', *Journal of International Economies*, 31, 101–120.

Allen, F. and D. Gale (1994), 'A welfare comparison of the German and US financial systems', LSE Financial Markets Group, *Discussion Paper*, 191.

Allsop, C. and D. Vines (1996), 'Fiscal policy and EMU', *National Institute Economic Review*, 4, October.

Alogoskoufis, G. and R. Portes (1997), 'European Monetary Union and international currencies in a tripolar world', in Canzoneri J., V. Grilli and P. Masson (eds), *Establishing a Central Bank: Issues in Europe and Lessons from the US,* Cambridge: Cambridge University Press.

Alogoskoufis, G., R. Portes and H. Rey (1997) 'The emergence of the euro as an international currency', *CEPR Discussion Paper,* 1741.

Andrews, D. (1997) *Bargaining Power and Policy Interdependence: Monetary Diplomacy in the Postwar International System*, presented at the 93rd annual meeting of the American Political Science Association, Washington D.C., August 28–31.

Antonelli, V.C. (1995), 'Cambiamento tecnologico localizzato e disoccupazione in un'economia aperta: un approccio schumpeteriano', in Messori, M. (ed.), *La Disoccupazione in Italia. Diagnosi e Linee di Intervento*, CESPE materiali, 4, Rome.

Artis, M. and W. Zhang (1995), 'International business cycles and the ERM: is there a European business cycle?', *CEPR Discussion Paper* 1191, August.

– (1997), 'On identifying the core of EMU: an exploration of some empirical criteria', *CEPR Discussion Paper* 1689, August.

Audet, D. (1996), 'Globalisation in the clothing industry', in OECD, *Globalisation of Industry*, Paris.

Axelrod, R. (1984), *The Evolution of Cooperation*, New York: Basic Books.

Baldwin, R., J. Francois and R. Portes (1997), 'The costs and benefits of eastern enlargement: the impact on the EU and Central Europe', *Economic Policy*, 24, April.

Banca d'Italia (1998), Base Informativa Pubblica, December.

Barro, R.J. and X. Sala-i-Martin (1991), 'Convergence across states and regions', *Brookings Papers on Economic Activity*, 1, 107–182.

– (1992), *Economic Growth*, Cambridge MA: The MIT Press.

Baumol, W.L. (1967), 'Macroeconomics of unbalanced growth: the anatomy of the urban crisis', *American Economic Review*, 57.

Baumol, W.L., S.A. Blackman and E.N. Wolff (1991), *Productivity and American leadership: the long view*, Cambridge, MA: MIT Press.

Bayoumi, T. and B. Eichengreen (1992), 'Shocking aspects of monetary unification', in Torres, F. and F. Giavazzi (eds), *Adjustment and Growth in the European Monetary Union*, Cambridge: Cambridge University Press.

– (1998), 'Operationalising the theory of optimum currency areas', *CEPR Discussion Paper* 1484.

Begg, D.K.H. (1996), 'Monetary policy in Central and Eastern Europe: lessons after half a decade of transition', *IMF Working Paper* 96, 108, Washington, D.C.

Belke, A. and D. Gros (1997), 'Estimating the costs and benefits of EMU: the impact of external shocks on labour markets', *CEPS Discussion Paper* 9795.

Benassy, A., A. Italianer and J. Pisani-Ferry (1994), 'The external implications of the single currency', Institute for Statistics and Economic Studies, Special Issue: *Economic and Monetary Union*, 262, 63.

Benassy, A., M. Benoit and J. Pisani-Ferry (1997), 'The Euro and exchange rate stability', presented at the Fondation Camille Gutt, IMF Seminar on EMU and the International Monetary System, Washington, March 17–18.

Benassy, A. and A. Quere (1996), 'Potentialities and opportunities of the euro as an international currency', *Economic Paper*, European Commission, 115.

Bergsten, C.F. (1996), *Dilemmas of the Dollar: The Economics and Politics of United States International Monetary Policy*, New York: M.E. Sharpe.

– (1997), 'The impact of the euro on exchange rates and international policy cooperation', presented at the Fondation Camille Gutt, IMF Seminar on EMU and the International Monetary System, Washington, March 17–18.

Bergsten, C.F. and R. Henning (1996), *Global Leadership and the Group of Seven*, Washington D.C: Institute for International Economics.

Bernanke, B.S. and M. Gertler (1995), 'Inside the black box: the credit channel of monetary policy transmission', *Journal of Economic Perspectives*, 9, 3.

Bernanke, B.S. and I. Mihov (1996), 'Measuring monetary policy', mimeo, Princeton University, June.

Bini Smaghi, L. and S. Vona (1986), 'Le tensioni commerciali nello SME: il ruolo delle politiche di cambio e della convergenza economica', *Contributi all'analisi economica*, Banca d'Italia, 2, December.

Blanchard O.J. and L. Katz (1997), 'What we know and do not know about the natural rate of unemployment', *Journal of Economic Perspectives*, 11, 3.

Boitani, A. and G. Pellegrini (1997), 'Lo sviluppo di nuove attività produttive: i servizi', in P. Ciocca (ed.), *Disoccupazione di fine secolo*, Turin: Bollati Boringhieri.

Bongini, P., M. Di Battista, P. Morelli and G.B. Pittaluga (1997), *Il controllo dei costi e degli organici nelle banche italiane: il contesto attuale e le prospettive*, research by Sintel.

Bonvicini, G., F. Cecchini, P.C. Padoan and N. Ronzitti (eds) (1997), *L'Italia senza Europa: il costo della non partecipazione alle politiche dell'Unione*, Milan: F. Angeli.

Carrè, H. (1997), 'Exchange agreements with Eastern Europe, Mediterranean and African countries', presented at the Fondation Camille Gutt, IMF Seminar on EMU and the International Monetary System, Washington, March 17–18.

Casella, A. (1999), 'Tradable deficit permits: efficient implementation of the Stability Pact in the European Monetary Union', prepared for the Economic Policy Panel, April.

CEPR (1995), *Unemployment, a choice for Europe*, Monitoring European Integration 5, London: CEPR.

– (1998), *Social Europe: One for All?*, Monitoring European Integration 8, London: CEPR.

CER (1995), Europa: convergenze e divergenze, *Rapporto,* 5

– (1996), Nebbia sull'Europa?, *Rapporto,* 5.

– (1997), *Le esportazioni italiane nel 1996*, in 'Ancora un passo', *Rapporto,* 1.

– (1997), 'Passaggio in Europa', *Rapporto,* 5.

– (1997), 'Una politica monetaria per l'euro', *Rapporto,* 6.

– (1998), 'Il lavoro negli anni dell'euro', *Rapporto,* 3.

– (1999), *Occupazione e crescita nell'Europa della moneta unica*, Quaderni, April.

CER-SVIMEZ (1998), *Rapporto sull'industria e sulle politiche di industrializzazione nel Mezzogiorno*, Bologna: Il Mulino.

Ciocca, P. (ed.) (1997), *Disoccupazione di fine secolo*, Turin: Bollati Boringhieri.

Clarida, R. and M. Gertler (1996), 'How the Bundesbank conducts monetary Policy', *NBER Working Paper* 5581, May.

Cohen, B. (1997), 'The political economy of currency regions', in Mansfield, E. and H. Milner (eds), *The Political Economy of Regionalism*, New York: Columbia University Press.

Cohen, D. (1991), 'The solvency of Eastern Europe', *European Economy*, Special Edition, 2, 263–303.

– (1997), 'How will the Euro Behave?', presented at the Fondation Camille Gutt, IMF Seminar on EMU and the International Monetary System, Washington, March 17–18.

Collignon, S. (1996), 'Bloc floating and exchange rate volatility: the causes and consequences of currency blocs', mimeo, Association pour l'Union Monetaire en Europe.

– (1997), 'European Monetary Union, convergence and sustainability', mimeo, Association pour l'Union Monetaire en Europe.

– (1998), 'Sustaining monetary stability', mimeo, Association pour l'Union Monetaire en Europe.

Cottarelli, C. and A. Kourelis (1994), 'Financial structure, bank lending rates, and the transmission mechanism of monetary policy', *IMF Staff Papers*, December.

Crouhy Veyrac, L. and M. Saint Marc (1997), 'L'euro face au dollar: quel taux de change?', paper presented at 'Les Journées Internationales d'Economie Monetaire et Financière', Orleans, June 5–6.

Daveri, C. and G. Tabellini (1997), 'Unemployment, growth and taxation in industrial countries', *CEPR Discussion Paper* 1615.

Davies, S. and B. Lyons (1996), *Industrial Organisation in the European Union*, Oxford: Oxford University Press.

Debelle, G. and H. Faruqee (1996), 'What determines the current account? A cross-section and panel approach', *IMF Working Paper* 96, 58, Washington, D.C.

De Benedictis, M. and P.C. Padoan (1999), 'Dynamic scale economies, specialisation, and the cost of the single currency', *Journal of International Development Planning Literature*, 14, 4, October–December.

De Grauwe, P. (1992), *The Economics of Monetary Integration*, Oxford: Oxford University Press.

de la Fuente, A. and X. Vives (1995), 'Infrastructure and education as instruments of regional policy: evidence from Spain', *Economic Policy*, 2, April.

De Melo, M., C. Denizer and A. Gelb (1995), '*F*rom plan to market: patterns of transition', mimeo, Washington, D.C.: World Bank

De Nardis, S. and M. Malgarini (1998), 'Cambiamento, stabilità, rafforzamento. I vantaggi comparati dei paesi europei nell'era della globalizzazione', mimeo, Rome.

De Nardis, S. and F. Traù (1998), 'Specializzazione settoriale e qualità dei prodotti: misure della pressione competitiva sull'industria italiana', *CSC Working Paper* 17, Rome: Confindustria.

Deutsche Bundesbank (1997a), 'Exchange rate and foreign trade', *Monthly Report*, January.

– (1997b), 'The role of the Deutsche Mark as an international investment and reserve currency', *Deutsche Bundesbank Monthly Report*, April.

De Vincenti C. and A. Montebugnoli (eds) (1997), *L'economia delle relazioni*, Bari: Laterza.

Di Battista, M., P. Morelli, G.B. Pittaluga and A. Resti (1997), 'La sfida tecnologica per l'industria bancaria e i riflessi occupazionali', in *Più tecnologia, più concorrenza*, Ottavo Rapporto CER-IRS, Bologna: Il Mulino.

Dignan R. (1995), 'Regional disparities and regional policy in the EU', *Oxford Review of Economic Policy*, 11.

Durlauf, S. and D. Quah (1998), 'The new empirics of economic growth', *NBER Working Paper* 6422.

Eaton, J., E. Gutierrez and S. Kortum (1998), 'European technology policy', *Economic Policy*, 27.

Eijffinger, S. and J. De Haan (1996) 'The political economy of central bank independence', Special paper in *International Economy*, 19.

Elmeskow I. (1993), 'High and persistent unemployment: assessment of the problem and its causes', *OECD Working Paper* 132.

Engel C. and J.D. Hamilton (1989), 'Long swings in the exchange rate: are they in the data and do markets know it?', *NBER Working Paper* 3165, November.

Ernst, D. and P. Guerrieri (1997), 'International production networks and changing trade patterns in East Asia: the case of the electronics industry', *DRUID Working Paper* 97, 7.

European Bank for Reconstruction and Development (1996), *Transition Report 1996*, London.

European Commission (1990), 'One market, one money', *European Economy*, 44, October.

– (1996) *First Report on Economic and Social Cohesion*, Brussels.

– (1997a), *Agenda 2000*, Brussels.

– (1997b), 'Indicators of price and cost competitiveness', *European Economy*, Supplement A, 3/4, March/April.

– (1998), 'European competitiveness in the Triad', *European Economy*, Supplement A, 7, July.

European Monetary Institute (1997), *The Monetary Policy in Stage Three*, Frankfurt am Main, January.

Fantacone, S. (1997), 'L'Unione monetaria europea: aspetti macroeconomici', in Bonvicini, G., F. Cecchini, P.C. Padoan and N. Ronzitti (eds), *L'Italia senza Europa: il costo della non partecipazione alle politiche dell'Unione*, Milan: F. Angeli.

Fatas, A. (1997), 'EMU: counties or regions? Lessons from the EMS experience', *CEPR Discussion Paper* 1558.

Feldstein, M. (1997), 'EMU and international conflict', *Foreign Affairs,* 76, November/December.

Fernandez-Arias, E. (1996), 'The new wave in private capital inflows: push or pull?', *Journal of Development Economics*, 48, 389–418.

Fernandez-Arias E. and P. Montiel (1996), 'The surge in capital inflows to developing countries: an analytical overview', *World Bank Economic Review,* 10, 1, 51–77.

Ferri, G., P. Morelli and G.B. Pittaluga (1997), 'Banche e mercati: sostituibilità e complementarietà nella diversificazione del rischio', paper presented at Consob Seminar, *Ricerche sull'industria dei servizi mobiliari in Italia*, Milan, January 22–23.

Ferri, G. and G.B. Pittaluga (1996), 'Finanziamento delle imprese nelle fasi di restrizione monetaria: il caso del Credito Cooperativo', *Cooperazione e Credito*.

Fitoussi, J.P (1997), *Il Dibattito Proibito*, Bologna: Il Mulino.

Fontagnè, L., M. Freudenberg and N. Péridy (1998), 'Intra-industry trade and the Single Market: quality matters', *CEPR Discussion Paper* 1959.

Foster, E. (1978), 'The variability of inflation', *Review of Economics and Statistics*.

Frankel, J.A. and A.K. Rose (1997), 'The endogenity of the optimum currency area criteria', *NBER Working Paper* 5700, August.

Friedman, M. (1997), 'Ma all'Europa l'Uem non serve', *Il Sole-24 Ore*, September 2.

Funabashi, Y. (1988), *Managing the Dollar: From the Plaza to the Louvre*, Washington, D.C.: Institute for International Economics.

Gandolfo, G. (1986), *Economia Internazionale*, Turin: UTET.

Gandolfo, G., P.C. Padoan and G. Paladino (1990), 'Exchange rate determination: single equation or economy-wide models? A test against the random walk', *Journal of Banking and Finance*.

Goldman Sachs (1996), *EMU's Excess Foreign Exchange Reserves*, London, September, www.gs.com.

Gordon, R.J. (1995), 'Is there a trade-off between productivity and growth?', *NBER Working Paper* 5081, April.

Greene, W.H. (1993), *Econometric Analysis*, Englewood Cliffs, N.J.: Prentice Hall.

Gros, D. (1996), 'A reconsideration of the optimum currency area approach: the role of external shocks and labour mobility', *National Institute Economic Review*, 4, October.

Gros, D. and N. Thygesen (1992), *European Monetary Integration from the European Monetary System to the European Monetary Union*, London: Longman.

Guerrieri, P. and S. Manzocchi (1996), 'Patterns of trade and foreign direct investment in European manufacturing: convergence or polarisation?', *Rivista Italiana degli Economisti*, 2, 1.

Hall, P. and R. Franzese (1998), 'Mixed signals: central bank independence, co-ordinated wage bargaining, and european monetary union', International Organization 52, Summer. 505–535

Hallet, M. (1997), 'National and regional development in Central and Eastern Europe: implications for EU structural assistance', *Economic Papers of the European Commission* 120, March.

Hartmann, P. (1996), 'The future of the euro as an international currency', mimeo, Washington, D.C.: Institute for International Economics.

Helg, R., P. Manasse, T. Monacelli and R. Rovelli (1995), 'How much (a)symmetry in Europe? Evidence from industrial sectors'. *European Economic Review*, 39.

Henning, R. (1997a), 'Cooperating with Europe's Monetary Union', *Policy Analyses in International Economics*, 49, Institute of International Economics, Washington D.C.

– (1997b), 'International sources of european monetary integration', mimeo, Washington, D.C.: Institute of International Economics.

Honohan, P. (1997), 'Miniblocs and fringe currencies of the EMU', presented at CEPR Seminar *Options for the Future Exchange Rate Policy of the EMU*, Brussels, February 6–7.

Hubbard, R.G. (1995), 'Is there a "credit" channel for monetary policy?', *Federal Reserve Bank of St. Louis Review*, May–June.

IMF (International Monetary Fund) (1996), *World Economic Outlook*, Washington, D.C.

– (1997a), 'globalisation: opportunities and challenges', *World Economic Outlook*, May, Washington, D.C.

– (1997b), 'EMU and the world economy', *World Economic Outlook*, October, Washington, D.C.

Iversen, T (1998), 'Wage bargaining, central bank independence, and the real effects of money', *International Organization*, 52, Summer, 469–504.

J.P. Morgan (1996), *The Euro, FX Reserves and Vehicle Currencies: Some Unusual Findings*, September, www.jpmorgan.com.

Jimeno, J. (1998) 'EMU and the labour market: the Initial conditions', paper presented to the Tenth Villa Mondragone International Economic Seminar, Rome, July 6–7.

Juselius, K. (1996), 'An empirical analysis of the changing role of the German Bundesbank after 1983', *Oxford Bulletin of Economics and Statistics*, 58, 4, 791–819.

Kashyap, K. and J.C. Stein (1997), 'The role of banks in monetary policy: a survey with implications for the European Monetary Union', *Economic Perspectives*, September–October, Federal Reserve Bank of Chicago.

Krugman, P. (1991), *Geography and Trade*, Cambridge, MA: MIT Press.

– (1992), 'The international role of the dollar: theory and prospects', in *Currencies and Crises*, Cambridge, MA.: MIT Press.

– (1993), 'Lessons of Massachusetts for EMU', in Torre F. and F. Giavazzi (eds), *Adjustment and Growth in the European Monetary Union*, Cambridge: Cambridge University Press.

Lall, S. (1998), 'Exports of manufactures by developing countries: emerging patterns of trade and location', *Oxford Review of Economic Policy*, 14, 2.

Lehay, M. (1996), 'The dollar as an official reserve currency under EMU', *Open Economies Review*, 7, 4, 371–390.

Levine, R. and D. Renelt (1992) 'A sensitivity analysis of cross-country growth regressions', *American Economic Review*, 82, 4, 943–963.

Logue, D. and T. Willett (1976), 'A note on the relationship between the rate and variability of inflation', *Economic Notes*.

Machlup, F. (1966), 'The demand for monetary reserves', *Quarterly Review*, 78, Banca Nazionale del Lavoro.

Mankiw, G., D. Romer and D. Weil, (1992) 'A contribution to the empirics of economic growth', *Quarterly Journal of Economics*, 107.

Manzocchi, S. (1997), 'External finance and foreign debt in Central and Eastern European countries', *IMF Working Paper* 97, 134, Washington, D.C.

Masson, P. and B. Turtelboom (1997), 'Characteristics of the euro: the demand for reserves and policy coordination under EMU', presented at Fondation Camille Gutt, IMF Seminar on EMU and the International Monetary System, Washington, March 17–18.

McCallum, B. (1992), 'Specification of policy rules and performance measures in multi-country simulation studies', *NBER Working Paper* 4233.

McMorrow, T. (1996), 'The wage formation process and labour market flexibility in the Community, the US and Japan', *Economic Papers*, 118, October.

Milesi-Ferretti, G.M. and A. Razin (1992) 'Persistent current account deficits: a warning signal?', *International Journal of Finance and Economics*, 1, 3, 161–182.

– (1996b), 'Current account sustainability: selected East Asian and Latin American experiences', *NBER Working Paper* 5791, Cambridge, MA.

Modigliani, F. (1997), 'The shameful rate of unemployment in the EMS: causes and cures', in Collignon, S. (ed.), *European Monetary Policy*, London: Pinter.

Muet, P.A. (1997), *Deficit de croissance et chomage: le cout de la non-cooperation*, Etude n. 1, Paris, Centre d'Etudes Notre Europe.

Nerlove, M. and P. Balestra (1992), 'Formulation and estimation of econometric models for panel data', in Mathias L. and P. Sevestre (eds.), *The Econometrics of Panel Data*, Dordrecht: Kluwer Academic Press, 3–18.

Neven, D. and C. Wyplosz (1996), 'Relative prices, trade and restructuring in European industry', *CEPR Discussion Paper* 1451.

Nickell, S. (1997), 'Unemployment and labor market rigidities: Europe versus North America', *Journal of Economic Perspectives*, 11, 3.

NIESR (1997), *National Institute Economic Review*, 4, 97, October.

OECD (1996), *Globalisation of Industry*, Paris.

– (1998), *The OECD Stan Database for Industrial Analysis*, Paris.

– (1999), *EMU: Facts, Challenges and Policies*, Paris.

Okun, A. (1971), 'The mirage of steady inflation', *Brookings Papers on Economic Analysis*, 2.

Paci, R. and R. Rovelli (1997), 'Do trade and technology reduce asymmetries? Evidence from manufacturing industries in the EU', *Collana di economia applicata*, 17, Università di Bologna.

Padoan, P.C. (1989), *Instabilità e cooperazione*, Rome: La Nuova Italia Scientifica.

– (1995), 'The international system and the diversity of states and markets', in Benjamin R., C.R. Neu, D. Quigley (eds), *Balancing State Intervention*, New York: St. Martin's.

– (1996), *Dal Mercato Interno alla Crisi dello SME*, Rome: La Nuova Italia Scientifica.

– (1997), 'Waiting for EMU. Europe's (not so strong) competitive advantage and (limited) technological integration', presented at the International Seminar of Villa Mondragone, June 23–24.

– (1997a), 'Globalization and European regional integration', *Economia Internazionale*, November.

– (1997b) 'Regional agreements as clubs: the European case', in Mansfield, E. and H. Milner (eds), *The Political Economy of Regionalism*, New York: Columbia University Press.

– (1998), 'Technology and trade: a sectoral perspective', *Structural Change and Economic Dynamics*, September.

– (1999) 'The role of the euro in the international system: a European view', paper prepared for the ECSA-TEPSA Project on Transatlantic Relations.

Pasinetti, L. (1993), *Economic Structural Dynamics*, Bologna: Il Mulino.

Persson, T. and G. Tabellini. (1996), 'Monetary cohabitation in Europe', *American Economic Review, Papers and Proceedings*, May.

Pritchett, L. (1997) 'Divergence: big time', *Journal of Economic Perspectives*, 11.

Proudman J. and S. Redding (1998) 'Persistence and mobility in international trade', *CEPR Discussion Paper* 1802.

Prowse, S. (1997), 'Il sistema di gestione aziendale nel settore bancario: qual'è lo stato attuale delle nostre conoscenze in merito?', in *Proprietà, controllo e governo delle banche*, Quaderno di Moneta e Credito, March.

Rifkin, J. (1995), *The End of Work*, New York: Putnam.

Rodrik, D. (1997), *Has globalization Gone Too Far?*, Washington, D.C.: Institute for International Economics.

Schinasi, G. and A. Prati (1997), 'European Monetary Union and international capital markets: structural implications and transitional risks', paper presented at Fondation Camille Gutt, IMF Seminar on EMU and the International Monetary System, Washington, March 17–18.

Shorrocks, A.F. (1978) 'The measurement of mobility', *Econometrica*, 5.

Solow, R.M. (1956), 'A contribution to the theory of economic growth', *Quarterly Journal of Economics*, LXX, 65–94.

– (1985), 'Lessons on the theory of endogenous growth', in Inman, R.P. (ed.), *Managing the Service Economy*, Cambridge: Cambridge University Press.

Spinelli, F. (1997), 'Il Silenzio degli Economisti sull'Europa degli Accordi', *Il Sole-24 Ore*, July 19.

Taylor, J. (1993), 'Discretion versus policy rules in practice', *Carnegie Rochester Conference Series on Public Policy*, 39, December, 195–214.

The Economist (1998), 'The strange life of low-tech America', *The Economist*, October 17.

Thygesen, N. (1997), 'Relations among the IMF, the ECB and Fund/EMU members', paper presented at Fondation Camille Gutt, IMF Seminar on EMU and the International Monetary System, Washington, March 17–18.

Tobin, J. (1969), 'A general equilibrium approach to monetary theory', *Journal of Money, Credit and Banking*, March.

UN-ECE (1996), *Econometric Survey of Europe in 1995–1996*, Geneva: UN Economic Commission for Europe.

Vinals, J. and J.F. Jimeno (1996), 'European unemployment and EMU', *CEPR Discussion Paper* 1485.

White, W.R. (1997), 'The euro and European financial markets', paper presented at Fondation Camille Gutt, IMF Seminar on EMU and International Monetary System, March 17–18, Washington D.C.

Williamson, J. (1994), *Estimating Equilibrium Exchange Rates*, Washington D.C.: Institute for International Economics, September.

Index